LOCATING THEOLOGY

NCQ TITLES

Legal Fictions	Time Pieces
Politics & Letters	Critical Paranoia
On Yeats: Upon a House	On Joyce: 3 easy essays
Drama & Democracy	On Eliot
Locating Theology	Literary Conversions

Film-texts

A Trip to Rome	A Week in Venice
A Short Break in Budapest	Four Days in Athens
Magic in Prague	The Last Priest of Horus
WWW: the weekend that warped the world	

Play-texts

Darwin: an evolutionary entertainment
Strange Meetings & Shorts

Eliotics

Forthcoming

Rubbishing Hockney & other reviews
On Collecting Walter Benjamin
Autobiography & Class Consciousness
Considering Canterbury Cathedral

*Though each can be read independently,
these NCQ publications, taken together,
comprise a single hyper-text collection.*

LOCATING THEOLOGY

Bernard Sharratt

New Crisis Quarterly
2015

NEW CRISIS QUARTERLY

ncq@newcrisisquarterly.myzen.co.uk

First published 2015

ISBN : 978-1-910956-09-0

in memoriam

Herbert McCabe O.P.
1926-2001
who prompted the theology
&
Xavier Gorostiaga S.J.
1937-2003
who also exemplified it

CONTENTS

FOREWORD

This short book mainly brings together some essays which were originally published in a small number of journals which in the 1960s and early 1970s tried to explore the relations between christian theology and political commitment. It may seem perverse, and certainly futile, to re-publish them now—but to a large extent it seemed so at the time anyway. By now, at least, they may have a certain historical interest, since *Slant* has attracted some recent attention while the journal itself remains hard to find. Making them available as a tiny footnote to a historical ripple is perhaps only on a par with putting one's old photos up on the net: they may find someone still interested and at least they act as a kind of record of past moments.

That the predominantly Roman Catholic groups around *Slant*, *New Blackfriars*, and *The Newman* tended to argue that christian believers should as a consequence of their faith find themselves committed to bringing about a socialist society may indeed come as a considerable surprise to many today, who regard the active associations between self-declared christians and virulent right-wing causes as axiomatic, especially in the USA. But this was most often the case anyway among many Roman Catholics in the 1930s, and long afterwards, in Spain, Portugal, Italy, France and certainly for much of the Cold War among the Catholic hierarchy in Central and South America.

That things can change is, of course, clear. Now, the most obvious and wide-spread connections between religious belief and political action would seem to take the form of various kinds of ultra-fundamentalists systematically endeavouring by violence and terror to impose their own warped versions of religious allegiance upon those who don't concur with them. It is not clear that any rational or even theological argument has much place in their world-views, still less a humanist socialism.

So perhaps, after all, a certain counter-case should still be put. Terry Eagleton, one of the original editors of *Slant*, has been doing so ever since, and I can only admire his prolific persistence. The dedication records my debt to a Dominican theologian who helped shape a generation's way of thinking intelligibly about theological matters, and to a Jesuit who was Director of the Economic and Social Planning Commission for the Sandinista goverment of Nicaragua in 1979-1982 and who endeavoured, amid vicious external attacks and desperate internal failings, to maintain his life-long commitment to redressing injustice.

I could never fully share the religious faith of any of these friends, and I have myself retained more of a belief in the moral necessity of a future socialist form of society than I have any continuing or coherent religious beliefs. What strikes me most when re-reading, sometimes with gritted teeth, these old arguments is that they rehearse, in the small world of a specifically christian debate, many of the issues of theory and practice which still confront any current attempts at radical change, whatever the character of the group or movement endeavouring to implement such change. However, the particular flavour of these debates remains intriguing: as the one-time revisionist marxist Leszek Kolakowski remarked, and as Walter Benjamin also recognised, in some areas of thought 'theology' still seems to provide almost the only language we have for adequately thinking through the full range of issues involved in any commitment to bringing about a just society.

The volume opens with an attempt to situate these particular efforts within an overview of what was happening in and to English Roman Catholicism more generally in the 1960s, and ends with a personal set of responses to inquiries by Jay Corrin, whose *Catholic Progressives in England After Vatican II*, University of Notre Dame Press (2013) offers a recent assessment of that now-historical moment. I am grateful to him for his book and for allowing me to make use of this exchange. Between these pieces, I include some attempts at a kind of atheist theology, some reflections on strategy, and some indications of how these local and even parochial debates were part of wider European and even global developments.

The imprint 'New Crisis Quarterly' appositely revives the title of another journal, that of an exceedingly short-lived periodical: its first, only, and farewell issue appeared in 1984, under the guise of my *The Literary Labyrinth*. Its editorial programme was to publish reviews of imagined books I didn't feel I had the time actually to write, so its readers were invited, if inclined, to write the reviewed books themselves.

That overall invitation to readers remains the same, to complete this work if they so wish: in this case, the partly failed and partly defeated attempts of a number of groups to try to make the relations between theology and politics a viable and effective contribution to the kind of just and humane society which if anything seems even more remote than before.

B.S.
Feast of Fools
January 6th 2015

Acknowledgements

I am grateful to various editors and publishers for making possible the following:

'English Roman Catholicism in the 1960s': published in *Bishops & Writers*, edited Adrian Hastings, Anthony Clarke, 1977.

'Revolutionary Intersections', *The Newman*, 5 : 3, July 1970, the final issue of the journal, edited by Laurence Bright O.P.

'Locating Theology', *Slant*, 22, August-September 1968.

'Absent Centre I', *Slant* 24, March 1969.

'Absent Centre II', *Slant* 25, May/June 1969.

'Towards a Political Theology of Marriage', *New Blackfriars*, February 1971.

'Metaphor and Metaphysics', *New Blackfriars*, October 1976.

Kolakowski review, *New Blackfriars*, September 1969.

Foucault review, *New Blackfriars*, June 1972

ENGLISH ROMAN CATHOLICISM IN THE 1960s

> Roman Catholicism has a power of elimination that
> many living organisms might envy. Once a position has
> been abandoned, surprisingly little time is needed for
> the belief to develop that it was never occupied, and we
> do need to remind ourselves occasionally that we have
> come a long way.[1]

In 1958 Eugene Langdale wrote, concerning historians of
English Catholicism, that 'for them, the history of Catholicism in the 19th Century seems to be summed up by the
struggle alongside O'Connell for Catholic Emancipation, the
Oxford Movement, the Earl of Shrewsbury's foundations
and Pugin's architecture, Newman's intellectual brilliance,
and the great dynasty of Archbishops of Westminster, which
began so majestically with Wiseman and Manning' and he
noted, correctly, that of the few works concerned with the
post-1850 period perhaps the most accessible did not
contain even a chapter on the RC church among the
working class.[2] It is a mark of one small shift since 1958
that in 1975 there finally appeared a major scholarly study of

---

[1] G. Egner, 'Contraception: Tradition Revisited', *New Blackfriars*,
March 1966. I have mainly relied on periodical articles and press
material published during the decade itself. This has necessitated a
fairly large, though still obviously selective, number of references.
I am generally indebted to *Herder Correspondence* which, as a
monthly journal of report, was able to offer perceptively
compressed accounts of contemporary developments. Place of
publication is London unless otherwise indicated.
[2] Cf. E. Langdale, 'Les milieux ouvriers', in D. Mathew, ed.
Catholicisme Anglaise, Paris 1958, pp. 82-96, esp. p. 83. His target
was clearly G. A. Beck, ed. *English Catholicism 1850-1950,* 1950.
The omission has been partly but unsatisfactorily remedied by e.g.
K. S. Inglis, *Churches and the Working Classes in Victorian England,*
1963; S. Mayor, *The Churches and the Labour Movement,* 1967; and J.
Hickey, *Urban Catholics,* 1967.

English Catholicism which at least acknowledged that a more complex kind of social history is required.[3]

But the problem of historical method remains acute for the study of Catholicism. Various models might be proposed. At a relatively preliminary sociological level, it has been suggested that English Catholicism is best seen in terms of tension and overlap between the 'Hiberno-Catholic' and 'Pure English Catholic' strains or the interaction between 'old Catholic gentry', immigrant-derived working-class and aristocratic and upper-class-convert elements.[4] Another approach might be developed by elaborating historically the distinction between the governmental-episcopal, the intellectual-prophetic and the devotional-'mystical' structures of the RC church generally.[5] More secular models might be adapted, drawn perhaps from the study of sub-cultural formations (such as recent work in labour history) or from anthropological perspectives. A brief essay, particularly one focussed on the 1960s, can only be drastically selective, but the chosen angle of presentation is offered with at least an awareness of these historiographical difficulties.

My point of entry is education, since it is possible to employ the concept of 'education' at a variety of levels: to grasp a religious body as primarily an arena of ideas, defined not by economic power or institutional organisation but centrally by beliefs and ideological cohesion; to recognise Catholicism in the 1960s, the decade of Vatican II, as predominantly characterised by a process of complex re-education, including the articulation and assimilation of a body of influential texts, the constitutions and decrees of the Council; and, thirdly, to pinpoint the catholic schools system

[3] J. Bossy, *The English Catholic Community, 1500-1850*, 1975.
[4] Cf. e.g. B. Bergonzi, 'The English Catholics', *Encounter* Jan 1965; G. Scott, *The RCs*, 1967; D. Fisher, 'The Changing attitude towards the Irish in Britain', *Hibernia*, March 1965; O.R. Sweeney, 'The Emigrant', *The Furrow*, June 1964.
[5] See J. H. Newman, preface to third edition of *Lectures on the Prophetical Office of the Church*, 1877; F. von Hügel, *The Mystical Element of Religion*, 1909.

as the sociologically central component of specifically English Catholicism, the major mechanism by which the RC community both maintains its group-identity and aligns itself to the norms of the wider society.[6]

The first part of this essay interweaves these three emphases in a schematic reading of the history of 1960s English Catholicism; the second part attempts a further re-patterning to suggest a more specifically theological fourth dimension to the notion of education.

1. *Education, Laity and Theology*

In the mid-1960s the number of baptised Roman Catholics in Great Britain was estimated at about 5 million, or nearly 10% of the population; those 'practising' in England and Wales was reckoned at 2.2 million. In 1964 a Catholic Teachers' Conference claimed a total of 741,000 pupils in Catholic maintained and independent schools; by 1972 that total was given as 900,000, of whom about 750,000 were in the 2,500 maintained schools, and the Catholic school population was said to have increased by 25 % during the decade. Clearly the capital outlay on schools was large, an estimated £150M from 1945 to 1970, of which the Catholic community was directly responsible for approximately £50M, most of it borrowed, with interest payments running at £2.5M to £3M each year. Archbishop Beck, the hierarchy's spokesman on education, estimated in 1965 that the overall debt would take 20 or 30 years to erase. At diocesan level, the financial centrality of Catholic schools is clear: between 1952 and 1970 the Archdiocese of Birmingham Building Fund spent £21M, of which 99.7 % was devoted to schools (buildings, interest, fees, administration); in 1969/70 the Arundel and Brighton Diocese Development Fund spent well over 60% of its total budget on school buildings and interest payments.

In the light of this degree of investment, both of personnel and of money, one can speculate that in a

---

[6] See Adrian Cunningham, 'Notes on Strategy', *Slant* 30, 1970.

situation where, suddenly, there were no Catholic schools to maintain, 'Not only would the church find itself with thousands of activists and vast sums of money with no obvious purpose, it would have to find some other collective identity capable of holding its members together.' The crisis of identity and of priorities hypothetically indicated here is a useful preliminary measure of the actual crises and preoccupations of the 1960s.[7]

Whatever the sociological function of the RC schools system, the consistently declared policy of providing a place for every Catholic child in a Catholic school derived, officially and legally, from Canon 1374 which simply stipulated that policy; but attitudes in this area were also tinged by the tone of Canon 2319 which prescribed ex-communication for a Catholic who entered a 'mixed marriage' with the intention of educating the children outside the Catholic faith. The link between these two constitutive moments — education and marriage — suggested a deliberately self-perpetuating process of social enclosure and also focussed some delicate problems for ecumenism during the decade.[8]

---

[7] A. Cunningham, *art cit.* For population figures in this paragraph, cf. *Herder Correspondence*, III, 4, 1966 and III, 7, 1966, Statistical Supplements; E. K. Taylor, 'Ecumenism and Conversion', *Dublin Review*, Spring 1965. For slightly different figures and a detailed breakdown cf. A.E.C.W. Spencer, 'The Demography and Sociography of the Roman Catholic Community of England and Wales', in *The Committed Church*, ed. L. Bright and S. Clements, 1966. For expenditure on schools cf. M. P. Hornsby-Smith, 'A Sociological case for Catholic schools', *The Month*, Oct. 1972. For Beck's estimate, cf. *Tablet*, 15 Jan. 1965.

[8] For opposed views on the linked issues of mixed marriages and education, cf. e.g. articles by L. Kovacs and J. McKee in *Clergy Review*, March and July 1964, and L. Orsy in *Gregorianum* 1964, iv. On 18th March 1966 an *Instruction* from Rome made minimal modifications to mixed marriage regulations; five days later Pope Paul and Archbishop Ramsey of Canterbury had their first official meeting; the *Instruction* gravely disappointed Archbishop Ramsey, cf. *Church Times* 20 May 1966; for Archbishop Heenan's possible role in this rather gauchely-handled timing cf. D. Fisher, 'Catholics

Yet, despite this impressive expenditure, by the mid-60s only 60% of English RC children actually had Catholic school-places to go to, and the effectiveness of those schools was often challenged. In 1966 Cardinal Heenan stated: 'I am not sure how, sociologically, it could be proved that Catholic education is not justified; that must be left to personal opinion.'[9] Various efforts were made to transform personal opinion into research-based knowledge: a psychology-based survey of current pupils revealed considerable internalization of views and values taught at school, mainly of an other-worldly and privatized devotional kind, but various sociological investigations seemed to reveal that, on leaving school, the level of religious practice, even by the minimal criterion of Sunday mass-attendance, was hardly affected by previous education at a Catholic as opposed to a non-Catholic school. Other studies showed a distinction in attitudes to the parish as a social organization — that those who remained at a parochial secondary school till 18 often recognised the parish as a social unit (providing a youth-club, dances, social contact, etc.) while the religious activities of the church became secondary, merely habitual or non-existent for them, whereas those who attended a non-parochial grammar school often showed higher awareness of the parish as a religious focus but were ignorant of or uninterested in its social functions.[10]

---

still coasting', *New Christian* 24 Feb. 1966. Ecumenical developments have been largely omitted from this essay, as its focus lies elsewhere, though ecumenism might be analysed as one facet of the problems broached in Part II; cf. e.g. M. Miegge, 'Ecumenism and neocapitalism', *Slant* 30, 1970.

[9] Cited in *The Case for Catholic Schools*, published by the Union of Catholic Students, 1966, from a teach-in at University College, London, in Feb. 1966. Cf. also A. E. C. W. Spencer, 'How effective are catholic schools?', *Slant* 4, 1965; *Religious Education*, ed. P. Jebb, 1968; *Catholic Education in a Secular Society*, ed. B. Tucker, 1968.

[10] Cf. M. Lawlor, *Out of this World: a study of Catholic values*, 1965; L. de Saint Moulin, 'Social Class and Religious Behaviour', *Clergy Review*, Jan 1968; J. Brothers, 'Two Views of the Parish', *The Furrow*, Aug. 1965 and *Church and School*, 1964. For the debate in

Such findings both provoked and indicated complex consequences. The increasing awareness that in Catholic schools 'religion' might be meaning little more than private feelings, both devotional and sexual-moral, and 'doctrine' sometimes only a pattern of propositions, akin to geometry, stimulated a movement to assimilate at the pedagogical level many of the emphases also being incorporated, in the early 60s, into the debates and documents of the Vatican Council. A 'catechetical' awareness began to develop: in 1964 the first lecture-tour in England of Johannes Hofinger, director of the Manila Pastoral Institute, helped to publicize the then comparatively little-known work of the National Catechetical Centre, established in London in 1959. In 1965 only about 30 graduates of the Lumen Vitae centre in Brussels (established 1946, open to international students since 1957) were at work in England. That same year the London Centre became a College of Catechetics and by 1967, as 'Corpus Christi College', it was widely-known, with about 45 graduates a year and able in addition to provide weekly lectures to 1,000 people, a summer school, and short courses at each of 13 Catholic Colleges of Education.[11]

A range of new textbooks and periodicals began to appear, supplementing the once-lonely *Sower*: an English edition of the *On Our Way* series was undertaken, the American *Bible Today* became popular, the *Clergy Review* ran a regular feature on 'Teaching the Faith'. The two main

---

the 1960s on the role of the parish, cf. e.g. C. K. Ward, *Priests and People*, Liverpool 1961; C. Davis ed. *The Parish in the Modern World*, 1964; C. Boxer, 'The Church as a community in the world: 1: the parish experience' and '2: an interpretation'. *Slant*, 13, and 14, 1967; L. Pyle, 'Vatican II and the parish' in *Directions*, ed. T. Eagleton, 1968; cf. also the debate between Eagleton and M. Dummett in *New Blackfriars*, Aug., Oct. and Dec. 1965, and the pamphlet series entitled *The Living Parish*.

[11] For developments in catechetics see, e.g., the reports in *Herder Correspondence*, II, 5, May 1965; III, 6, June 1966; IV, 3, March 1967.

groups involved in this upsurge were lay teachers and nuns, other aspects of whose lives were also slowly changing.[12]

One characteristic series of the mid-6os marks a number of shifts: *Where We Stand* was the collective title of a sequence of cheap 60-page books, which can be compared with the late 1950s *Faith and Fact* books. Both series were planned systematically, but whereas the earlier series rested on an encyclopaedic arrangement combining semi-apologetics with an emphasis on 'knowledge' (church history, other faiths, etc.), the later series was structured round a biblical and trinitarian theology. The collective titles indicate the change of mood, the later having a provisional overtone, a sense of viewpoint rather than fact; moreover the later series was almost entirely produced by English writers, unlike the earlier which was largely composed of translations from the French *Je sais; Je crois* library; and among those English contributors were a few lay Catholics writing theology.

The lay theologian was a fairly important aspect of English Catholic life in the 1960s. Whereas Chesterton and Belloc might provide apologetics, polemic or spiritual reflections and Frank Sheed produce popularizations of neo-Thomism, the 60s lay writers were possibly a new breed. Before the war perhaps only a few hundred Catholics graduated from universities each year; by the mid-60s some 5,000 Catholics were graduating and another 4,000 qualifying at colleges of education every year, so that by the end of the decade at least a considerable body of educated laypeople was present in the Catholic community.[13]

Their opinions and attitudes, expressed organizationally in such groups as the Newman Association (with about 3,000

---

[12] Cf. e.g. *The New Nuns*, ed. Sr. C. Borromeo, 1968; for the wider problem cf. e.g. Sr. Mary Cuthbert, 'Women in the church', letter to *Ampleforth Journal*, Feb. 1966, and Dympna Pyle, 'Glory, jest and riddle: woman in a man's world', *Slant* 15, 1967.

[13] Cf. A. E. C. W. Spencer, 'The Crisis of Priestly Vocations in England', Presidential Address to 9th International Conference on Sociology of Religion, Montreal, Summer 1967, printed in *Herder Correspondence* IV, 12, Dec. 1967.

members in mid-decade) or the more diffuse Catholic Renewal Movement, and in letters to the Catholic or national press, in articles and books, and at the local parish level, were one focus of the re-education process of the period. An early sign of this lay theological presence was the semi-private newsletter of Michael de la Bedoyere, *Search*, which in the early 60s raised many of the issues later to become publicly contentious; another was the role played by Neil Middleton and Martin Redfern at Sheed and Ward, in making available English translations in paperback form of such continental theologians as Rahner, Schillebeeckx and Küng, and in providing an outlet not only for English professional theologians (Charles Davis, Herbert McCabe, Nicholas Lash, *et al.*) but also for laymen writing theology from a professional background in other disciplines (Brian Wicker, Terry Eagleton, Adrian Cunningham, Walter Stein, Hugo Meynell, *et al.*).[14]

Other lay-controlled periodicals appeared: *Herder Correspondence* (January 1964 to June 1970) described by Cardinal Heenan as 'the poor man's ecclesiastical *Private*

---

[14] The dates may be worth recording of the English translations of: Rahner, *Free Speech in the Church*, 1959, *Nature and Grace*, 1963, *Mission and Grace I*, 1963, *II*, 1964, *Theological Investigations I* 1961, *II* 1963, etc.; Schillebeeckx, *Christ the Sacrament*, 1963, *Marriage, Secular Reality and Saving Mystery*, 1965, *Mary, Mother of the Redemption*, 1964. *Vatican II: the real achievement*, 1967, *Revelation and Theology*, 1967, *Concept of Truth and Theological Renewal*, 1968; Hans Küng, *Council and Reunion*, 1961, *Justification*,1964, *The Church*, 1967, *Infallibility*, 1971. The English school produced, e.g.: Davis, *Liturgy and Doctrine*, 1960, *The Study of Theology*, 1962, *The Making of a Christian*, 1964; McCabe, *The New Creation*, 1964, *Law, Love and Language*, 1968; Lash, *His Presence in the World*, 1968; Wicker, *Culture and Liturgy*, 1963, *Culture and Theology*, 1966; Eagleton, *The New Left Church*, 1966, *The Body as Language*, 1970; Cunningham, *Adam*, 1968; Stein, ed. *Nuclear Weapons and Christian Conscience*, 1961, *Peace on Earth*, 1966; Meynell, *Sense, Nonsense and Christianity*, 1964, *Nature versus Grace*, 1965; Rosemary Haughton, *Christian Responsibility*, 1964, *On Trying to be Human*, 1966, *The Transformation of Man*, 1967.

Eye,[15] provided detailed investigative journalism on the Council and international Catholic developments; *The Newman*, particularly in its new format from 1968 to 1970, acted as a forum for its members and others; *Slant* (Spring 1964 to January 1970), originally an undergraduate venture which tried to argue for a marriage of marxism and Christianity, went on to develop an idiosyncratic style of theological thinking;[16] *New Christian* (Sept 1965 to mid-1970) offered a fortnightly comment on more current affairs from an ecumenical and often radical stance.

The lay, and clerical, personnel involved in these efforts overlapped considerably and also tended to be active in other influential areas, as in the Downside Symposia, which met frequently from 1952 onwards and produced a series of books on issues that both anticipated and developed conciliar themes, or the December Group, annual from 1958, which gradually became a gathering-point for 'radicals' of a *Slant* or *New Blackfriars* tendency; and a wider circle of lay people became active in parish councils, diocesan and national commissions. These groups of lay activists were distinguished from older — and continuing — forms of lay organization (the Legion of Mary, Catholic Womens Guilds, YCW,) by their sense and assertion of relative independence from clerical or hierarchical control and perhaps by an increasing and sometimes frustrated awareness that they had assimilated and responded to Vatican II more rapidly and enthusiastically than had many of the clergy and episcopacy. Behind that awareness was the accessibility of information

---

[15] Cf. *Sunday Telegraph* 6 Feb. 1966. For *Herder Correspondence*'s assessment of Cardinal Heenan, cf. *HC* II, 11, Nov. 1965.

[16] For a sympathetic account of *Slant* cf. B. Wicker, *First the Political Kingdom*, 1967; for unsympathetic accounts cf. *Herder Correspondence*, V, 1, Jan. 1968; Peter Hebblethwaite, 'Ambivalence in the Catholic Left', *The Tablet* 9 Aug. 1969, and correspondence 23 Aug. 6, 13, 20 Sept. 1969; cf. also the critiques by Donald Nicholl, 'A Layman's Journal', *Clergy Review*, August 1966; B. Sharratt, 'Locating Theology', *Slant* 22, 1968; A Wall, '*Slant* and the Language of Revolution', *New Blackfriars*, Nov. 1975.

about the Council and of the Council's own declarations.[17] As Abbott's *Documents of Vatican II* (1966) became almost a best-seller, there was a new, authoritative and easily-available norm against which to judge the actions and decisions of those who previously could claim to speak authoritatively without declaring the specific reference-point for that authority.

Given the availability of those texts, which seemed both to be easily intelligible and to have displaced much previous thinking and teaching, and given the presence of an articulate and educated laity, the question of clerical education became — if for no other reasons — a pressing one. Articles multiplied on 'the vocations crisis' and on 'seminary reform', and some reforms were actually made.[18] The traditional major seminary course consisted of two years

---

[17] The reporting on the Council by Desmond Fisher, editor of the *Catholic Herald* from March 1962 to early 1966, was of crucial importance here. The circulation figures of the Catholic press in 1966 were: *Universe*, 300,000; *Catholic Herald* 100,000; *Catholic Pictorial* 38,000; *The Tablet* and *New Christian* had about 14,000, *Clergy Review* 5,500 and *New Blackfriars* 2,200; cf. *Herder Correspondence* III, 5, May 1966 and letters in III, 7. Add to these the coverage by the national press and the various journalistic books about the Council by Xavier Rynne, Bernard Wall, and many others.

[18] On vocations cf. e.g. Spencer *art. cit.* note 13 above; the special issue of *Christus Rex*, no. 2, 1967, and articles by J. F. McGrath, 'Where have all the young men gone?', *Clergy Review* June, July, August 1965. In 1965 there were about 5,000 secular priests in England and Wales, or 1 to every 500 practising Catholics, cf. *Catholic Directory 1965*. On seminaries cf. e.g. C. Davis, 'Theology in a seminary confinement'. *Downside Review* Oct. 1963, J. F. Randall, 'Seminary community' *Clergy Review* March 1965; C. Ernst, 'Philosophy in the seminary', *New Blackfriars* March 1965; M. de la Bedo-yere, 'Freedom for the seminarian', *Search* April 1965; A. Cunningham 'Seminaries' and F. McDonagh 'Education for the priesthood', *Slant* 4 1965; S. Moore, 'Training in the junior seminary' *Clergy Review* Oct. 1965; A seminarian, 'Intellectual freedom in the seminary' *Slant* 8, 1966; D. Hickey, 'Philosophy: the old or the new?' *Clergy Review*, Aug. 1966.

mainly neo-scholastic philosophy followed by four years of theological study, again largely based on neo-scholastic premises, with Church History, Scripture and Canon Law accompanying these. From about 1963 a small element of 'pastoral work' was introduced — deacons began venturing outside the enclosed seminary and visiting local hospitals or helping in neighbouring parishes — and soon changes in curricula followed. From September 1965 Ushaw re-arranged its courses to inter-weave philosophy and theology through the six years and made increased use of seminars rather than lectures, while students were allowed some flexibility in arranging their own timetables. At the Westminster diocesan seminary at Ware, the teaching trio of Charles Davis, Hubert Richards and Peter de Rosa made more considerable changes in the content of courses, aligning them with the biblical and liturgical emphases dominant at the Council. In 1965 Richards and de Rosa were transferred to Corpus Christi College and Davis to the Jesuit seminary at Heythrop, which was formally elevated the same year into a Pontifical Athenaeum.

Heythrop, sixteen miles from Oxford, was symptomatic of two issues of the time: since all seminaries but especially those of religious orders tended both to be generous in staff-student ratios and to have difficulty in ensuring suitably qualified staff, it was intended that Heythrop should gather under its wing the less viable Religious seminaries; and it was also hoped that its 'proximity' to Oxford would encourage some relationship with the university. A concern for accreditation by ordinary academic bodies was also apparent in the negotiations of Ushaw with the University of Durham in 1967 and of Upholland with Liverpool and Manchester universities. Eventually in 1970 Heythrop moved to London and became a constituent college of the University of London.

More widely, dissatisfaction was sometimes voiced with the quality of Catholic theology in England, and the need for contact with and training in university theology faculties was urged. In 1968 one writer could declare that 'as a result of recent deaths and other forms of departure from the ranks, the age group of the forties contains no-one with an established, or even promising, theological reputation' and that in the last century the seminaries 'between them have not produced a single theologian with a nation-wide reputation'. Judged by international and non-Catholic standards both statements were, and remain, true.[19]

The reference to 'departures from the ranks' indicates some related problems. By the end of the decade, the director of 'Bearings', an organization for helping ex-priests, could suggest that 'perhaps 100 or so priests and religious are leaving the ministry each year'; many of those would have difficulty in finding employment due to lack of acknowledged qualifications, despite full-time education up to their mid-twenties.[20] Some of those departures — which included a number of theologians and scholars[21] — were due to ecclesiastical conflict or frustration, others to specific and personal issues and some at least seemed to be based on the decision that their Christian vocation could be more fruitfully followed precisely as laymen.

It was also argued that the possibility of an active, and relatively independent, lay involvement within a large grouping of concerned laity was a factor in the decline in numbers of seminarians.[22] Moreover, in contrast to the absence of major theologians, the English catholic community in the 1960s included a number of laypeople eminent in their secular and academic professions. In 1966 John M. Todd could claim: 'Sociology, demography, medicine, psychiatry, delinquency, family and

---

[19] M. Winter, 'Catholic Theology in England', *Clergy Review*, June 1968. Compare Nicholas Lash, 'English Catholic Theology', *The Month*, Oct. 1975.

[20] D. Gibson, 'Don't Answer back. Children', *New Christian* 19 March 1970. It is difficult to judge the accuracy of his estimate but no official figures seem to be available.

[21] By the mid-1970s the list of English theologians who had ceased to practise an ordained ministry included such well-known names as Charles Davis, Hubert Richards, Peter de Rosa, Peter Harris, Nicholas Lash, Peter Hebblethwaite, Joseph Blenkinsopp. A list of 25 prominent figures is given in A. Hastings, 'The Priesthood Today: II', *Tablet*, 15 May 1976.

[22] Spencer, art cit., note 14.

neighbourhood problems, public relations, mass media — in these and many other spheres I could name Catholics near the head of their professions and highly respected. Yet the whole of this world is held at arm's length by our bishops.'[23]

That final sentence indicates a felt gulf, but a second and different gap could also be claimed to exist. John Todd spoke as one of the minority of educated laity which Geoffrey Moorhouse, in a 1964 *Guardian* article, saw as enjoying the tacit support of some Regulars but as mainly in latent conflict with the majority of the episcopacy and diocesan clergy; 'somewhere in between', he added, 'are the mass of the laity, unaccustomed to anything but dutiful response to orders from above, ill-equipped intellectually to reconcile faith with the other gifts that God has given them, and tragically bewildered by the imminent rift in their church.'[24] It is a journalist's comment, but it directs attention back to that elusive category, 'the mass of the laity', and to the wider process of re-education that involved, in a different sense, 'the mass of the laity'.

2. *Language, Liturgy and Marriage*

On March 20th 1960 Archbishop Heenan of Liverpool received a reply from the Sacred Congregation of Rites establishing, in answer to his query, that section 12 of the Congregation's *Instruction* of 1958 did indeed exclude the

---

[23] J. M. Todd, 'Making the Council work in England', talk on German radio, printed in *Herder Correspondence* III, it, Nov. 1966. In other fields he could have added the significant number of philosophers, often Wittgensteinians, who were from a Catholic background: Anscombe, Geach, Kenny, Dummett, Smiley, Cameron, Barrett, etc. Catholics were also prominent in such diverse fields as anthropology and the trade unions. An example of the hierarchy's suspicion of sociology and related disciplines was the continued refusal, throughout the decade, to finance an adequate study of Catholic educational assumptions; the plea was still being made in 1972, cf. Hornsby-Smith, art. cit.

[24] G. Moorhouse, 'Catholics at the Crossroads', *Guardian*, 29th Oct. 1964.

public recitation of the rosary during Mass in October. 'We have come a long way. . . '

The 1958 *Instruction* was concerned with 'encouraging the active participation of the faithful' in the Mass. It was one of a series of instructions and permissions which had included allowing the Easter Vigil to be held at midnight on Holy Saturday, experimentally for one year, in 1951, a permission renewed for three years in 1952 and then made permanent. In 1953 evening Masses were cautiously allowed for the whole church, with the eucharistic fast reduced, and in 1957 both regulations were extended and clarified. By 1959, when Vatican II was announced, these were almost the only changes to have impinged upon the English laity *en masse*. In the early 60s those who advocated the use of the vernacular in the Mass were, in England, a smallish minority, though 'Dialogue Masses' in Latin were becoming acceptable.

There was, in other words, very little preparation before the promulgation, in December 1963, of the *Constitution on the Liturgy*. The catechetical movement and changes in seminary theology had barely begun, while the laity depended more upon press-reports than on parish instruction or episcopal pastorals for an awareness of the coming changes. When the hierarchy issued the new 'Rite of Low Mass for use from November 29th 1964', the response in some lay quarters was immediate and fearful: Douglas Woodruff, veteran editor of *The Tablet,* wrote to the *Daily Telegraph* (17th Nov 1964): 'in *The Tablet* ... we have not left our readers in doubt how much we regret what is happening, seeing it as a regression into nationalism, and a widely unpopular one'. Another correspondent wrote (*Telegraph,* 7th Nov 1964): 'There are many Roman Catholics who do not express their views outwardly, who are filled with sorrow at the passing of Latin in the liturgy and look forward to the coming changes with dismay. The laity as a whole were not clamouring for the vernacular until the idea was driven into them by clever propaganda.' On 30th November 1964 a personal 'ad' in *The Times* announced: 'Will anyone wishing to preserve the ancient Latin liturgy in England, and who wishes to join me in an appeal write Box . . . ' A petition against the vernacular, signed by perhaps 3,000, was sent to the hierarchy. The later Latin Mass Society was to build upon such responses.

When English for some parts of the Mass (*Epistle, Gospel, Gloria, Credo, 'Domine non sum dignus'*, 'prayers at the foot of the altar') was finally introduced in Advent 1964, a fully Latin Mass was not excluded; a majority of the dioceses made the vernacular obligatory at all Low Masses on Sundays and at weekday evening Masses, and in many dioceses the parish priest could decide to use English also at weekday morning Masses; some dioceses, at least, allowed some Masses entirely in Latin each Sunday. At that stage, only a few dioceses, such as Westminster and Portsmouth, were readily willing to grant permission for Mass to be said facing the people. At a press conference on 12th February 1965 Bishop Dwyer of Leeds was reported as saying that 'eventually' the Mass would be divided into distinct blocs of English and Latin. On 2nd May 1967 an *Instruction* from Rome finally allowed the whole of the Mass, including the Canon, to be said in English.[25]

Clearly, a detailed chronology of the liturgical and other changes cannot be given here, but the selective account offered above highlights, first, the speed both of the changes and in the expectations about coming changes, and, secondly, the fact that some Catholics saw the introduction of the vernacular as the abandonment of a fundamental position. Certainly by 1970 it would be unthinkable to enter a normal parish on a Sunday and find the congregation engaged in the public recitation of the rosary while a priest and server murmured a Mass, including Epistle and Gospel, in Latin.[26]

---

[25] Cf. *Herder Correspondence* II, 4, April 1965, to which I am indebted for the quotations in this paragraph.

[26] By the mid-1970s indeed such practices were being severely criticized and even proscribed by a papacy and episcopacy insistent upon a new uniformity; cf. the cases of Fr. Baker of Downham Market in 1975 and of Archbishop Lefebvre in 1977. In 'The reform of the Roman church', *Sunday Times*, 12 Dec. 1965, Hans Küng had expressed the fear that post-Vatican II Catholicism would soon assume the same rigidity as post-Tridentine

Yet given that the major liturgical changes were compressed into about four years and that, far from there having been 'clever propaganda' for the changes, the dominant religious education of English Catholics had previously produced an non-liturgical, privatized, inner-devotional spiritual attitude, it is possible to see that there was indeed a fundamental 'danger' in the change from Latin to English. For insofar as contemporary English 'ordinary' language has tended to suffer from a historically recent inflection that provides no adequate common vocabulary for acutely personal experiences, in anguish and in love, or for the complexity of social experience, it has also been disabled in developing an appropriate language for changing modes of spiritual and liturgical experience. Indeed, the split between 'the personal' and 'the social' embedded and articulated in everyday language is an aspect of that deep legacy and also chimes with certain central problems in ecclesiology. The Anglican tradition, with the richer resources of an earlier linguistic heritage still resonant in its liturgy and hymns, has perhaps retained a fullness of religious language which — whatever its own current disadvantages — was never available to the same degree within the English Catholic community.[27]

The 'danger' of a change from Latin to an English marked by the distinct vocabularies of contemporary discourse and of biblical-liturgical research, perhaps lay most dramatically in the fact that, previously, it was not just the language *of* the Mass that was in Latin but also, to a crucial extent, the language *about* the Mass. While the Mass was a mystery in which one took no active part and the Gospel and Epistle were inaudible and unintelligible runes, and while, most importantly, 'transubstantiation' was something that occurred while you bowed your head and a bell tinkled, it was possible for the language of private devotion or the use

---

Catholicism and urged as a priority the fundamental reform of the Curia.
[27] For aspects of the argument in this paragraph, cf. e.g. Raymond Williams, *Culture and Society*, 1958, and *Keywords*, 1976; and Ian Robinson, *The Survival of English*, 1973.

of a prayerbook to substitute itself for the language of theology; but when the Mass became the 'Eucharist', the 'Lessons' or 'Readings' suddenly said unfamiliar things in English (Paul's letters and the Old Testament do not make easy reading, let alone listening), and the language about the Eucharist (in 'homilies' rather than 'sermons') became talk not about private devotion or a neo-scholastic conundrum but about apparently familiar experiences like a meal, a meeting or a community, it was suddenly easier and perhaps unavoidable to ask whether one really *understood* what it all *meant.*

And since meaning and language cannot be finally separated, the absence of an adequate language would lead to an awareness of unintelligibility of a different order from the unintelligibility of unknown Latin. In theological circles one facet of this problem had emerged, even in England, in the debate about 'remythologization' in the early 1960s, an issue that also haunted the catechetical movement.[28] Another aspect was indicated by the brief popularity of various books of prayers and meditations in 'modern' or 'urban-style' language, such as Michel Quoist's *Prayers of Life.*[29]

In 1964-5 this problem touched on more controversial ground: the Eucharist itself. Throughout 1964 considerable press coverage was given to the debates in Holland on the

---

[28] Cf. e.g. E. Hill, 'Remythologizing: the key to the Scriptures', *Scripture*, Jan. 1964. On 21 April 1964 the Pontifical Biblical Commission issued an 'Instruction on the Historical Truth of the Gospels'. *The English Jerusalem Bible*, 1966, provoked further debate; its general editor, Alex Jones, had earlier raised the issue of language and theology in his *God's Living Word*, 1963; later treatments revealed the influence of Leavis's literary criticism and of Wittgenstein's philosophy, e.g. McCabe, *Law, Love and Language*, 1968, Eagleton, *Body as Language*, 1970, S. Moore, *God is a New Language*, 1967.

[29] English translation 1963; cf. his *The Christian Response* 1968, and e.g. D. Rhymes, *Prayer in the Secular City*, 1967, C. Burke, *Treat Me Cool, Lord*, 1968. Compare these with the spiritual reading fare briefly examined in E. O'Brien, 'English Culture and Spirituality', *Concilium* IX, 2, Nov. 1966: Marmion, Vonier, Goodier, Leen etc.

meaning of 'transubstantiation'; the debate came nearer home with the response, at least among clergy, to an article on 'The Real Presence' in the *Clergy Review;* and finally on 3rd September 1965 a papal encyclical, entitled *Mysterium Fidei,* reaffirmed a traditionalist interpretation. On 1st December Cardinal Heenan invited Francis Clark S.J. to lecture the English Bishops, assembled in Rome for the Fourth Session, on 'The Real Presence: an appraisal of the recent controversy'. Both the encyclical and Fr. Clark's version of the doctrine caused ripples of relatively muted discontent among some theologians in England and, more specifically, among ecumenically-minded non-Catholics.[30] But neither the controversy nor the encyclical provided a language accessible and intelligible to the non-theologically educated lay-person.

Its immediate effects in England, perhaps, were to encourage some heresy-hunting by the conservative Catholic Priests' Association, an avoidance of the real difficulties in pulpits, and a self-censorship in pursuing the necessary theological reformulation; but its most long-term effect was almost certainly to re-encourage the kind of attitude articulated, somewhat later, in a historical comment meant to have a contemporary application: 'Within the Church, it [Liberalism] led to excesses far from the reasoned modification of doctrine that it claimed, and to a refusal to understand the beliefs and feelings of a large mass of Catholics, let alone to explain things to them in their own terms.'[31]

As a formula for the 1960s this would presume that the 'large mass' had 'their own terms' in which it was possible to 'explain' or 'understand' their 'beliefs', but the fact that much new theological writing in the 1960s was regarded, by ordinary laity and by some clergy, as 'above the heads' of the 'large mass' not only led to misunderstandings and eventually to a hostile, uncomfortable or simply indifferent

---

[30] Cf. H. McCabe 'The Real Presence', *Clergy Review*, Dec. 1964, and F. Clark, 'The Real Presence', *Unitas* (Rome) summer 1966.

[31] R. Griffiths, 'The Catholic Revival: Reaction then and now', *Clergy Review*, Oct. 1972.

atmosphere for serious theological thought, but also revealed retrospectively just how inadequate Catholic education in England had proved to be. Whatever its success in maintaining a Catholic identity sociologically, the massive investment in education seemed still to have left many Catholics 'ill-equipped intellectually to reconcile faith' with some post-conciliar expressions and explorations of that faith.

But if some of the liberals or radicals were guilty of a failure to understand the 'beliefs' of Catholics, others seemed capable of not understanding the 'feelings' of large numbers of Catholics. Since the second major effect of a Catholic education seems to be an unusual emphasis on sexual morality, it was not surprising that for many Catholics the most contentious issue of the 1960s involved a matter of sexual morals.

The initial debate on contraception was relatively temperate in tone. When Archbishop Heenan on 7th May 1964 issued a statement on behalf of the English hierarchy maintaining that 'We cannot change God's law' in the matter of birth-control, one typically-restrained reaction was voiced by M. de la Bedoyere: 'The very negative statement of Archbishop Heenan about birth control will cause dismay among the more progressive and informed Catholics'; an Anglican scholar wrote to the *Times* pointing out that the statement misquoted St. Augustine in a 'special pleading' way to allow the changes that were already accepted; there was a slight flurry over an interview with Bernard Häring in the *Guardian* and a survey claimed that 40 % of Catholic couples in Britain were using 'outlawed' methods.[32] The same year the special papal commission was established and when lay

---

[32] Cf. *Herder Correspondence* I, 7, July 1964, *Evening Standard* 7th May 1964, *Times* 11th May and *Guardian* 9th May 1964. The hierarchy's statement was probably prompted by an article in *Search*, April 1964, by Archbishop Roberts, in which he rejected the 'rational grounds' for the Roman position as unconvincing. For the official treatment of Roberts, cf. Charles Davis, 'The Case of Archbishop Roberts', *Clergy Review*, April 1966 — a perhaps significant article for Davis himself.

experts became the majority of the reconstituted commission in early 1965 it seemed possible that the Pope's request for public silence on the issue might be a straw in the wind of change.

In October 1965 a survey of the private opinions of Newman Association members indicated a probable majority opposed to the traditional teaching.[33] In 1966 the strains became more visible: a detailed demolition of traditionalist arguments was refused an *imprimatur* and had to be published under a pseudonym; even a 'liberal' position like Häring's came under attack for a fundamental inability to speak the language of 'experience' when dealing with the actualities of marriage; but at the same time Cardinal Heenan, in his June Pastoral, could speak significantly of changes in moral teaching.[34] Early in 1967 reports filtered through that perhaps 90% of the Commission were in favour of change, and in April the secret report, supporting change, was published; yet as the final decision was delayed and delayed it became increasingly apparent that the issue might produce a crisis based on claims of authority rather than the merit of arguments.[35]

When, finally, on 29th June, 1968, *Humanae Vitae* was published, the reaction of many prominent laity and even clergy was openly critical. Though delayed till after an official statement from the hierarchy, a dissenting letter signed by 55 priests, many of them nationally known,

---

[33] M. Lawlor, 'Birth Control: report on members' attitudes', *The Newman*, Oct. 1965; a 'probable' majority because only 984 (c. 30%) of the membership responded and because some Newman Circles tended to be suspicious of the London-based leadership; cf. *Catholic Herald*, March 24th 1967 for later tensions in the Association.

[34] 'G. Egner', *Birth Regulation and Catholic Belief*, 1966; cf. Neil Middleton, 'Roman Censorship', *New Christian* 17 Nov. 1966; R. Haughton, 'The Renovation of the Old Jerusalem', *New Blackfriars*, Sept. 1966, reviewing Häring.

[35] Cf. Archbishop Roberts interview, *New Christian*, 9th March 1967; Robert Nowell, 'An Agonizing Choice', *New Christian* 4th May 1967. For the *Report* itself see *National Catholic Reporter* (U.S.A.) 19 April 1967 and *Tablet* 22, 29, April, 6 May 1967.

appeared in the *Times* on October 2nd 1968; the same week the *Tablet* published a dissenting statement signed by 75 laypeople, most of whom were not only eminent as doctors, lawyers and academics but were also leading members of Catholic organizations and National and Diocesan Commissions.[36]

The more immediate reactions of diocesan bishops, during August and September, had significantly varied. Two days after the encyclical Fr. Paul Weir, of the Southwark diocese, was quoted in the *Evening Standard* (1st Aug 1968) as saying: 'I have in the past told people that they are entitled to freedom of conscience because the teaching of the church was in doubt. I don't see how I can continue to do that. At the moment I would say that it was also impossible to accept the Pope's decision or to urge it upon others. What the solution is for me I don't yet know.' His Vicar-General immediately suspended him from preaching and hearing confessions and on 12th August his bishop, Archbishop Cowderoy, suspended him from all priestly functions.

A pastoral letter on 11th August from the same Archbishop said, in part: 'Some of our poor, simple people have been misled by disobedient priests, who did not heed the command of the Holy Father that the traditional rules be followed until and unless he made a change. They, like other priests, were told not to confuse their people with the specious argument that the law was in doubt, when the Pope said it was not in doubt.' In similar vein. Archbishop Murphy of Cardiff said in his pastoral — presumably without intending any irony — 'If this encyclical has proved anything, it has proved in these matters of interpreting the natural law that all honesty, all compassion, all erudition, all theological acumen is of little account.' In Nottingham Bishop Ellis followed Southwark's example in suspending critical priests.

Cardinal Heenan's pastoral of 4th August anticipated the more compassionate tone and attitude of the later joint statement, in emphasising that those married couples unable

---

[36] *Tablet* 5th Oct. 1968. Between them they held some 55 senior posts in Catholic organizations of a voluntary and official kind.

to cease practising 'unlawful' contraception 'must not abstain from the sacraments'; such a proviso marked the distance travelled since the much-publicized case of Dr. Anne Biezanek in the early 60s.[37]

But perhaps the most significant statement came from Archbishop Beck of Liverpool in an interview in the *Catholic Herald* (23rd Aug 1968): 'In a moral crisis of this kind I think the only thing one can tell people is that they must do what they think is right . . I think everybody has the duty to form his conscience and it is part of my responsibility, and part of the responsibility of the teaching church, to help people to form their own consciences.' In the same interview Archbishop Beck remarked: 'I think we have gone away from the concept of the Church teaching and the Church taught to a realization that these two are organically so closely connected that they must form one — the whole people of God.' The second comment speaks the language of Vatican II, but it is clearly in tension with the narrower concept of 'the teaching church' in the first comment.

A similar tension is apparent in the agreed formulations of the letters *ad clerum* sent to each priest by their diocesan bishops in late October 1968, concerning dissent over *Humanae Vitae:* 'The Bishops of England and Wales have no wish to inhibit reasonable discussion . . Priests are required in preaching, teaching, writing in the press, speaking on radio, television or public platforms, to refrain from opposing the teaching of the Pope in all matters of faith and morals. If a priest is unwilling to give this undertaking the bishop will decide whether he can be allowed without scandal to continue to act in the name of the church.'[38] It is

---

[37] Cf. A. Biezanek, *All Things New*, 1964.

[38] Letter *ad clerum* of Thomas Holland, Bishop of Salford, 22nd Oct. 1968; almost identical phrasing occurs in e.g. the *ad clerum* of Charles Grant, Bishop of Northampton, 23rd Oct. 1968. Behind the formulae lies the curious notion of 'keeping quarrels in the family' of the church — a plea emitted by Cardinal Heenan e.g. at a reception for the Newman Association in 1965 and by the Apostolic Delegate during the 'McCabe affair' in 1967; the notion is curious because no way of generally communicating within that 'family' is immune to the attention of the national press.

difficult to see how these conditions could not 'inhibit reasonable discussion', but the strain indicated here was deeply symptomatic: the problem of who spoke and acted 'in the name of the church' and the question of the relationship between 'our poor simple people' and other elements in the church's composition underlay both a number of other issues and the formal changes in the institutional structure of English Catholicism during the decade.

3. *Institution, Authority and Conscience*

'In him the Church looks at itself from the outside, and understands from that perspective the depth of its own corruption.' Herbert McCabe quoted these words, from a *Guardian* article (5th January 1967) concerning Charles Davis's decision to leave the Catholic church, in his editorial comment in *New Blackfriars* for February 1967, and also quoted some of the reasons given by Davis in an *Observer* article (1st January 1967): 'The official church is racked by fear, insecurity and anxiety, with a consequent intolerance and lack of love . . There is a concern for authority at the expense of truth, and I am constantly saddened by the workings of an impersonal and unfree system.'

But after citing some of the more objectionable or foolish actions and statements of ecclesiastical authorities, McCabe argued that: 'It is because we believe that the hierarchical institutions of the Roman Catholic Church, with all their decadence, their corruption and their sheer silliness, do in fact link us to areas of Christian truth beyond our own particular experience and ultimately to truths beyond any experience, that we remain and see our Christian lives in terms of remaining, members of this church.'[39] Fr. McCabe

---

[39] H. McCabe, 'Comment', *New Blackfriars*, Feb. 1967, reprinted in *The McCabe Affair: Evidence and Comment*, ed. S. Clements and M. Lawlor, 1967, which documents the whole incident, and in *Purification of the Church*, S.C.M. Press 1967, which also reprints Michael Dummett's 'How Corrupt is the Church?' from *New Blackfriars* Aug. 1965. The reference to 'experience' also had local

was immediately removed from his editorship, on orders from a Roman authority that seemed incapable of understanding either the English language or English sensibilities, and was further, if briefly, suspended from his priestly functions.

The resulting movement of protest on the part of many who knew McCabe, read *New Blackfriars* or simply valued the claims of open justice, and the somewhat obscure story of the source of the dismissal itself, highlighted one point which the editorial had made. Charles Davis had written of those who 'remain Roman Catholics only because they live their Christian lives on the fringe of the institutional church and largely ignore it'. Disputing this use of 'institutional', McCabe had argued:

> Consider a few institutions: Spode House, the Newman Theology Groups, the Union of Catholic Students, the Young Christian Workers, University Chaplaincies, the Catholic press including even *New Blackfriars*. None of these are exclusively for Catholics but no sociologist would hesitate to describe them as Roman Catholic institutions. It is within institutions such as these that a great many Catholics nourish their Christian lives.

It was largely through the personal contacts and informal connections fostered by such institutions that the protest over McCabe's dismissal was organized, but, more importantly, the relationship between such groupings and 'the overall and relatively impersonal structure of the

---

overtones, cf. the two symposia. *The Experience of Marriage*, 1965, and *The Experience of Priesthood*. For other reactions to Charles Davis's decision, cf. *New Christian* editorial, 29th Dec. 1966, B. C. Butler in *Sunday Telegraph* 29th Jan. 1967, N. Middleton in *New Christian* 23rd Feb. 1967, J. Wilkins in *Frontier* Spring 1967, and the later reviews of Davis's *A Question of Conscience*, 1967, by P. Harris, *Tablet*, 18th Nov. 1967, G. Baum, *Frontier* Spring 1968, B. C. Butler, *Clergy Review*, Feb. 1968. Perhaps the most considered response came in the Spode House conference, September 1967, which produced *Authority in a Changing Church*, ed. N. Lash, 1968; cf. *Herder Correspondence* V, 4, April 1968.

hierarchy', visible in this incident, not only poses a general problem for the social historian of Catholicism but also, during the 1960s, constituted a practical — and ultimately theological — problem for the Catholic community in trying to implement some of the teachings of Vatican II.

Three aspects of this problem can be briefly noted. The Vatican Council had encouraged the setting-up, at parish, diocesan and national levels, of various commissions, on ecumenism, liturgy, education, among others. Given the concentration of expenditure on more traditional priorities, the financing of these commissions posed a problem: thus in 1967, at a time when one diocese was committed to a debt of £4M for a new cathedral and was planning nine new churches for a small new town of 80,000 population, the annual budget of the National Council for the Lay Apostolate was reckoned to be £100.[40] In 1967 it was estimated that £200,000 needed to be raised to ensure the efficient existence of the new commissions. On 7th March, at the hierarchy's request, a small committee, of three laymen, Bishop Worlock and Mgr. Norris, met to plan a fund-raising campaign. The idea emerged of an appeal to be made in each church by lay-people, both for money and for the offer of skills and talents to be put 'at the service of the church'. The scheme was entitled 'The New Pentecost' and was announced at a press conference by Cardinal Heenan on 9th May, the appeal itself to be made on June 2nd, Whit Sunday; adverts in the press also announced the scheme — at an estimated cost of £10,000.

Given the very compressed schedule, it was no surprise that the appeal was not very successful. But more importantly, it was presented — both in the Cardinal's press conferences and in letters *ad clerum* — as the initiative of 'the laity'. Yet only three laymen were at all responsible; even those making the local appeals were to be 'chosen' by the parish priest and the text of what they were to say was

---

[40] The building figures were given at the 13th Spode House Visual Arts Week, April, 1966, the budget figure by Spencer, *art cit.*, note 13.

stipulated beforehand.[41] As an exercise in 'consultation' and in the description of a fund-raising campaign as 'The New Pentecost' the episode indicated that, still, 'the bishops have not really begun to grasp that Vatican II implies a different type of attitude to their lay people'[42] and that the hierarchy had not yet even learned to speak the language of the Council, or the New Testament, in appropriate ways.

The actual establishment of some diocesan commissions and councils revealed more of a shift in attitude: for example, the Portsmouth Pastoral Council, which met for the first time in March 1968, had a total membership of 144, of whom all but 19 were elected by deaneries, religious orders and existing organizations, and the majority overall was lay; Liverpool's Pastoral Council was composed of 20 priests, 10 religious and 30 lay-people, elected by a process of nomination from diocesan-wide recommendations.

If the principles of consultation and election were increasingly operative in these areas, in the matter of episcopal appointments themselves such principles were clearly more difficult to establish.[43] It is a comment on the historical amnesia even of 'progressives' that whereas in the 1780s it seemed most likely that an English hierarchy, if formally established, would be chosen by a committee of laymen, in the mid-1960s the most 'liberal' suggestion seemed to be that the laity might be 'consulted' on the choice of their bishops — and even that suggestion had no visible practical effect.[44] At least by the end of the decade, in

---

[41] Cf. e.g. the *ad clerum* of the Bishop of Leeds, 7th May 1968. For a general account cf. *Herder Correspondence* V, 8, Aug. 1968.

[42] Todd, *art. cit.*

[43] See the series 'How Not to Appoint a Bishop', in *Herder Correspondence* VI, 3, March, 6, June, 1969, VII, I, Jan., 2 Feb., 5, May 1970. For Pastoral Councils cf. *Herder Correspondence* V, 5th May 1968.

[44] Cf. Todd, *art. cit.* D. Fisher, 'In the Long Run', *Frontier*, Winter 1966; compare: Bossy, *op. cit.*, ch. 14 and Eamonn Duffy, 'Ecclesiastical Democracy Detected: i: 1779-87; ii: 1787-96', *Recusant History*, X, 1970; cf. also G. D. Sweeney, 'The "wound in the right foot": unhealed?', *Clergy Review*, Sept. 1975 and in *Bishops & Writers*, ed A Hastings, 1977, pp. 207-34.

1969, Cardinal Heenan could register, in a curious conflation of rhetorics, a new official attitude: 'It is certain that it is no longer possible for central authority to hand down decisions affecting the whole church without full consultation with representatives of all sections of the church. The growth of education has altered the attitude of both clergy and laity. They still want to belong to the one fold of the one Shepherd but they do not want to be treated like sheep . . . Citizens of the City of God, no less than citizens of modern nations, are prepared to submit to authority only if it is seen to be reasonable and responsible.'[45]

Four months later, however, the Cardinal forbade any discussion of celibacy at the nationally-elected Conference of Priests at Wood Hall, thereby revealing that a tradition of authority changes most slowly. In 1958, for example, his predecessor Cardinal Godfrey had forbidden the discussion of war and peace at a meeting of the Catholic Nuclear Disarmament Group![46] What had, perhaps, weakened somewhat was a corresponding tradition of deference to such authority; but even where a selective repudiation of clerical-episcopal control was hesitantly evident, the line tended, crucially, to be drawn — despite popular talk of 'the priesthood of all believers' — at the doors of the liturgical gathering itself: that source of extra-liturgical hegemony remained, in practice, the almost unquestioned province of the ordained priest.

Some did, indeed, go further, in different ways. If the issues of controlled liturgical reform, ecclesiastical reorganization, lay participation and consultation, episcopal appointments, celibacy and birth-control, seemed to many the dominant concerns, there was also a current that increasingly saw such matters as peripheral, as 'the detailed

---

[45]   *Tablet*, 25th Oct. 1969, reporting a press conference of 18th Oct. 1969.
[46]   *Tablet* 28th February1970; in June 1967 Pope Paul had published his encyclical, *Sacerdotalis Caelibatus*. For Godfrey's ban, see A. Downing, 'The Thought Barrier', *Slant* 2, 1964.

eccentricities of ecclesiastical ant-heaps.'[47] From occupying a central position within the ecclesiastical institutions, as ordained priest, Council *peritus*, professor of theology at Ware seminary and Heythrop, editor of the *Clergy Review*, and veteran of many official committees, Charles Davis moved, in December 1966, with public suddenness, to being a Christian without formal membership of any ecclesiastical organization, a stance of 'creative disaffiliation'. By the early 1970s he could look back and find the internal affairs of the Roman church quaintly irrelevant.[48]

Something of that attitude found expression among Catholics and other Christians during the decade. From an apparently traditional position, the liturgical reforms of the Council could be seen as a 'preoccupation with questions of cultus' and the issue of the vernacular as fundamentally irrelevant except to bishops and priests professionally concerned with outward forms, while what really mattered, as always, was only the inner spiritual rebirth of the individual.[49] From a more fashionable standpoint, models of the early church or the image of a future 'church of the diaspora' could be evoked, in which the church had no property, no schools or seminaries, no complex organization and few full-time priests.[50]

In various modes and mixtures both these attitudes were intermittently embodied, in *agapés*, in home-made liturgies, in unofficial ecumenical communions, in explorations of old and new forms of meditation and mysticism, among loosely-knit networks of Christians who deliberately did 'live their Christian lives on the fringes of the institutional church and largely ignore it.' And, characteristically of the times, some

---

[47] Timothy Beaumont, announcing the launch of *New Christian* in the last issue of *Prism*, Sep. 1965.

[48] Cf. interview with Davis, *The Month*, Jan. 1971.

[49] Aelred Graham, 'The Pathos of Vatican II', *Encounter*, Dec. 1965.

[50] See e.g. J. O'Connell, 'Purification as Decay: the church and the process of modernization', *Clergy Review*, July 1966; E. Hill, 'The post-conciliar Papacy', *New Blackfriars*, Aug. 1966. Cf. also D. Fisher, 'Sjaloom', *Frontier*, Spring 1967.

of those of whom the hierarchy was most wary on other issues offered trenchantly effective critiques of such positions.[51]

In another sense, however, there were more fundamental issues than those which concerned Vatican II. Beneath all the preoccupations of church reform, the basic questions of theology loomed again. Particularly after Bishop Robinson's *Honest to God* in 1963, it became clearer to many Christians that 'heated conviction and reforming zeal born of impatience with the ecclesiastical set-up are no substitute for concrete beliefs about God and man when one is face to face with those who do not share one's assumptions.'[52] That recognition was perhaps especially present in the slow growth of dialogue between Christians and marxists during the decade, and in the assimilation by some theological thinkers of the fundamental challenge inherited from the 19th century, not the apparent clash of 'science' and 'religion' but the undercutting of 'belief' by the sociology of knowledge, the awareness that all forms of understanding are socially determined and therefore historically relative.[53] In that perspective, issues not only of biblical interpretation and development of doctrine became newly problematical, but also the very possibility of theology itself, of any talk about God. By 1973 one theologian could formulate the basic problem the 1960s left unresolved: 'The flight to biblical studies and patrology, or to sociology and poetry, so typical of the opposing wings in the new generation . . must lead to an impasse in the long run unless we face up to the

---

[51] E.g. Rosemary Haughton, 'The Christian Dilemma', *New Christian* 30th Nov. 1967, Terry Eagleton, 'Why we are still in the Church', *Slant* 14, 1967.

[52] R. Hughes, 'Arguments and Experience', *Prism*, Sept. 1965. Perhaps the most effectively critical review of *Honest to God* was that by H. McCabe, *New Blackfriars*, July/August 1963.

[53] See for example G. Vass, 'Last April in Marienbad', *Slant* 18, 19, 20, 1968, and A. Cunningham, 'Cultural Change and the Nature of the Church' in *The Christian Priesthood*, ed. N. Lash and J. Rhymer, 1970. And e.g. B. C. Butler, 'Belief in Science and Reason in Religion', *Downside Review*, Jan. 1966.

philosophical problems that all these various disciplines ignore.'[54]

A minor incident in early 1970 drew together many of the threads of the previous turbulent decade. David Konstant, the highly-respected chief adviser on religious education to the Archdiocese of Westminster, and John Cumming, a member of the editorial board of the notorious *Slant*, published a jointly-written school textbook which attractively and intelligently presented the results of much of the new catechetical and theological thinking. It was refused an *imprimatur* for the Dublin Archdiocese; aware of that refusal, the censor for the Westminster Archdiocese nevertheless granted an *imprimatur*. Among the passages to which the Dublin censor objected was a sentence which stated that 'conscience' should be seen more as 'a faculty dependent on formation by society and individual inquiry.' The book was called *Beginnings*.[55]

II

> Roman Catholicism has a power of elimination that many living organisms might envy . . . However helpful this negative capability may be for promoting peace in the Church, the theologian must face the historical facts of change without attempting to palliate them.

The question of the relation between history and theology was a characteristic concern of Catholic thinkers in the 1960s, variously posed in terms of 'salvation history', 'development of doctrine', a 'theology of history', or

---

[54] Fergus Kerr, O.P., 'The "Essence of Christianity": Notes after de Certeau', *New Blackfriars*, Dec. 1973. The new English translation of Aquinas, *Summa Theologiae*, 1963-76, emphasised this point.
[55] Appropriately, the final report in the last issue of *Herder Correspondence*, VII, 6, June 1970, was concerned with this episode.

apparent in an interest in Teilhard de Chardin, the process theology derived from Whitehead, or even the 'death of God' school of Altizer and Hamilton. But perhaps only in the fields of biblical study and liturgical research did the precise details of actual history seem to impinge upon more strictly theological writing, since the more overarching question tended to be formulated largely with an emphasis on abstract possibilities or in terms of epochal generalizations and the history of 'ideas'.

By the end of the decade, however, the accepted academic practice of a relatively autonomous 'history of ideas' was itself experiencing a crisis of method: new models of the history of scientific theories were proposed, in terms of 'paradigm shifts'; a post-structuralist notion of 'epistemic shifts' in the deep structure of a period's fundamental intellectual assumptions became briefly fashionable; and the influence of a newly 'anti-humanist' marxism suggested both that changes in ideology were logically structured within an interdependence of concepts (the notion of 'problematic') and that such changes were dependent upon changed social relations within the fundamental economic and secondary institutional (educational, legal, familial, political) apparatuses of a society.[56] By way of conclusion, it may be worth briefly sketching a wider context and possible interpretation of 1960s Catholicism in the light of these accounts of change.

For some purposes, it remains possible broadly to divide the history of English Catholicism into periods. The pre-1850 tenor of Catholicism is only just being re-examined, as is the brief complex moment of Modernism; the 1960s concentrated more on the 'rediscovery of Newman' as in tension with his own period, from 1850 to Vatican I, and then as patron figure for the ending of the restrictive phase

---

[56] See T. S. Kuhn, *The Structure of Scientific Revolutions*, 1962; *Criticism and the Growth of Knowledge*, ed. I. Lakatos and A. Musgrave, 1970; M. Foucault, *The Order of Things*, 1970; L. Althusser, *For Marx*, 1969, and 'Ideology and Ideological State Apparatuses' in his *Lenin and Philosophy*, 1971.

between Vatican I and Vatican II.[57] More specific parallels were drawn: the abandonment in 1966 of a Roman allegiance by Charles Davis, the leading English Catholic theologian, was sometimes compared in significance to Newman's conversion to Roman Catholicism in 1845, as the issues involved in Herbert McCabe's dismissal from *New Blackfriars* might be seen to reproduce those in the turmoil over *The Rambler*.[58] Newman's process of conversion produced his *Essay on the Development of Doctrine*, while the publication in the July 1859 *Rambler* of his *On Consulting the Faithful in Matters of Doctrine* led to his secret delation to Rome.

The two texts are linked in their theological concern with the relation between the '*consensus fidelium*' and episcopal or papal functions, a problem that first came to critical prominence for Newman in his historical study, *The Arians of the Fourth Century* (1833). But that concern is also linked to two other central texts of Newman, *The Idea of A University* (1852) and *Grammar of Assent* (1870); one is concerned with the place of theology as a science among others and with the need for an educated laity, in the context of establishing a Catholic university in Dublin, the other with the complex convergence of considerations that lead not so much to scientific proof as to a commitment in belief and conscience — an inquiry conducted in the shadow of Vatican I's definition of infallibility. At the centre of the links between these texts and issues is the problem of the 'knowledge' that the 'simple faithful' have of their Christianity.

The 1960s saw perhaps the emergence of a different, though related, pattern of links, a re-working of that

---

[57] John Coulson's work was influential here: J. H. Newman, *On Consulting the Faithful*, ed. J. Coulson 1960; *Newman: A Portrait Restored*, ed. Coulson, 1965; *The Rediscovery of Newman*, ed. Coulson and A. M. Allchin, 1967; Coulson, *Newman and the Common Tradition*, 1970.

[58] E.g. J. M. Cameron, 'Problems of the editors of religious journals', *Times*, Feb. 25th 1967; cf. J. Derek Holmes, 'Newman's attitude to ultramontanism and liberal Catholicism on the eve of the first Vatican Council', *Bishops & Writers*, ed. A. Hastings, 1977, pp. 15-33.

'problematic'. Again, at the centre were the relations between belief, lay education, and theological understanding. The impact of Vatican II in England could be experienced by many of 'the faithful' as an extraordinarily compressed period of 'development of doctrine', at the practical heart of which was the rediscovery of the role of the laity itself, the *laos* or whole people of God. In that respect Newman's insistence on the function of the laity received partial endorsement. But the policy of 'consulting the faithful' was actually implemented only at various levels of administration and then only hesitantly and minimally. In this process it was, inevitably, the minority of highly-educated laity which played a predominant role; that minority was, on the whole, university-trained but not in 'theology' as an academic discipline of knowledge; they therefore only incompletely fulfilled Newman's hopes of the 1850s.

Yet in taking their new-found place within the ecclesial community, many insisted upon retaining the values of a secular academic community even in areas more theological than administrative: freedom of research and debate, autonomous organization, forceful articulation of the viewpoints of opposing schools of thought, an awareness of the complexity of language appropriate for adequate thought and sensibility, a recognition of the rigorous standards involved in any appeal to 'reason'. And some tried in various ways to probe beyond the shifts of Vatican II towards a further development of theological thought, from a basis not in the familiar pattern of clerical-scholastic training but from the locus of their own experience and from the resources of their own disciplines, often with significantly different criteria of argument and of method. In particular, Catholic literary critics, working from a sense of literature as the 'centre' of a humane education, evolved a distinctively English mode of theological writing during the 1960s, at the core of which was, again, a concern with theological reflection upon the relations of language, experience and thought.

But at the same time two features of the wider intellectual life of the decade impinged upon the task of theological re-education: a developing critique, within the universities themselves, of both the academic assumptions and internal practices of higher education, and a fundamental erosion of the claim of any 'science' to be objectively rational. In the student movement of the late 60s, in England as elsewhere, these issues were linked to wider concerns with the political and economic structure of the society.[59]

Political and even economic issues figured intermittently in specifically Catholic pre-occupations during the decade, with the publication of papal encyclicals such as *Pacem in Terris* and *Populorum Progressio*, Pope Paul's visit to the UN in 1965, and parish-organized petitions against abortion reform; and in many respects the structural tensions and changes within the church reproduced those both in the larger society and within the radical political currents of the time — a questioning of authoritarian or only shallowly democratic modes of organization and a serious challenging of congealed traditions of thought, behaviour and attitude.

Yet the major intersection between Catholics and politics was of a quite different order. The decade began with a mildly-interested national press discovering the news-value of Pope John, the Council and ecumenism; it ended with daily coverage of a bitter civil war in Northern Ireland, with armed Catholics and armed Protestants killing one another in the name of a cross-tangle of religious loyalties, political allegiances and economic interests. The brutal fact of Ulster again posed, in yet another way, the problem of the relation that actually obtains between the 'belief of the faithful' and a commitment to Christianity. In the cruellest fashion 'ecumenism' was a visible part of that problem, but so also, in a more profound and disturbing manner, was the

---

[59] See, for example, *Student Power*, ed. R. Blackburn and A. Cockburn, 1969, in particular Perry Anderson, 'Components of the national culture', which helps situate both English marxist thought and the centrality of F.R. Leavis; cf. also M. Horkheimer, *The Eclipse of Reason*, New York 1947 and compare the urge to 'encyclopaedic' knowledge in the *Faith and Fact* series discussed above.

question of the social and ideological determinants of religious 'faith'.[60]

The conflict in Ireland seemed to make clear the final message, and warning, of the decade. If theological thought is intimately linked to and has to reflect upon the complexities of historical change and conflict — as Newman's own study of Arianism had once indicated — and if Christian belief is only fully incarnated in the actual life of the 'whole people of God', then Northern Ireland may eventually demand and stimulate, even in English Catholics, a more searching theological and practical response to the problem of being a serious Christian believer than Vatican II did. If that response does not occur, the difficult renewal of the 1960s may finally be seen to have remained largely an instance of the 'detailed eccentricities of ecclesiastical ant-heaps'. Newman put the basic point well enough in 1859, in words that now have a sadly ambiguous application:

> I think certainly that the *Ecclesia docens* is more happy when she has such enthusiastic partisans about her as are here represented than when she cuts off the faithful from the study of her divine doctrines . . and requires from them a *fides implicita* in her word which in the educated classes will terminate in indifference and in the poorer in superstition.

*

---

[60] Cf. e.g. P. Gibbon, 'The Dialectic of Religion and Class in Ulster', *New Left Review*, 55, 1969; R. Rose, *Governing without Consensus*, 1971; R. Rose and D. Unwin, 'Social cohesion, political parties and strains in regimes' *Comparative Political Studies*, 2, i, 1970; E. McCann, *War and an Irish Town*, 1974; M. Farrell, *Northern Ireland: The Orange State*, 1976.

REVOLUTIONARY INTERSECTIONS?

I was asked[1] to consider '*de facto* revolutions going on at present, as well as some necessary revolutions within the Christian community'. It seems to me that there is another element I will have to look at to talk seriously about those two areas, so I want to give a three-part paper: first, a look at some of the *de facto* revolutions; second, an attempt to see what strategic analysis of the church this allows or prompts us to make; third, to consider some problems for English catholic radicals which seem to result from that stage of the analysis.

De facto revolutions : Spain and Portugal

I will concentrate on two particularly interesting and linked areas for church-revolution relations: Spain and Portugal, then Latin America. One could, starting from the same metropolitan 'catholic' european powers, go instead to Africa—to Mozambique and Guiné, where revolution is a military reality—or even to India, to ex-Portuguese Goa. The fact that one can go in such trans-continental directions already illustrates one fact about the church to which I shall return. But first, Portugal.

It is a commonplace that state-enthroned Roman Catholicism and poverty go together. An English Catholic bishop on a visit to southern Portugal allegedly offered the complacent remark: "Ah, a donkey! Whenever I see a donkey, I know I'm in a Catholic country." Some of the facts are these: in Portugal 40% are illiterate, with only 1.4% of the GNP spent on education; average income is about £100 per annum; censorship is openly accepted by the

---

[1] This article was originally a paper for a small group in October 1969. I leave it in that form partly to make the point that it is perhaps more in such limited situations than in print that theological inquiry actually develops at present.

government: in 1963 Salazar wrote: '. . the Government only suppresses writings that criticise the President, Prime Minister and other members of the Executive, Members of the Chamber, Judiciary, officers of the Armed Forces, Heads of Civil Service, irresponsibly or insolently—i.e. without factual substantiation or the politely worded reference due to the authorities as such'. Though 77%, of the population are 'working class', no strikes are allowed and the only trade unions are vocational (industrial), the compulsory Corporative Syndicates; one major company, CUF, has a monopoly control on almost every consumer product; at present about 40°% of the budget is spent on the wars against FRELIMO in Mozambique and PAIGC in Guiné. Portugal, in other words, looks highly unlikely as a revolutionary possibility.[2]

Yet Portugal is, at the level of such facts, not much better or worse than Spain. But there, even without the impetus of an armed anti-colonial struggle abroad, a revolutionary movement is a faint possibility, and the church, given its formally powerful position in the country, is obviously a crucial factor in whether or not that develops, or at least in what form it develops. Events in the last year or so indicate the tensions.

In August-September 1968 a 'state of emergency' was declared in the Basque province— Euzkadi, a region with a long history of asserted independence—after the assassination of a police inspector in San Sebastian, presumably by ETA members (the Basque NLF). Sixty priests immediately organised a sit-in to protest. The Bishop of Bilbao suspended them, but died within a fortnight. The new bishop lifted their suspension and supported them. The sit-in lasted 24 days and was followed by another involving more priests and the wives of political prisoners. These sit-ins took place in churches and the government authorities

---

[2] [And yet: in April 1975 the semi-socialist Revolução dos Cravos led by the Armed Forces Movement toppled the long-standing fascist regime in Portugal. A later version of this talk compared Nicaragua and Poland. And then..?]

could not intervene. On January 24 1969 the 'state of emergency', on the pretext of student demonstrations in Madrid, was extended to the whole of Spain. In Barcelona 300 priests demonstrated against it; 40 professors and 300 students from the Theology Faculty issued a statement opposing the emergency measures and a further 300 priests appealed to the pope, U Thant, etc., for condemnation of Franco; in Euzkadi 500 priests signed a statement criticising their bishops for remaining silent; 96 chaplains to Spaniards in Europe did the same; out of 81 bishops about a dozen issued pastorals criticising the state of exception. All this was, of course, in conditions of total press censorship (probably the original motive behind the measures).

There was thus fairly wide-spread and open criticism by priests, relatively little public criticism by ordinary citizens (the channels were simply not open to them, except in a theology faculty), while few bishops joined the protest—and the standing committee of the episcopate supported the government measures. The general stance of the hierarchy is complex: while, for example, 700 priests now refuse the state wage paid under the Concordat, some bishops seek a strengthening of the Concordat while others, perhaps with papal backing, want it repudiated. As part of this issue, there has been a lengthy tussle over appointments to nine vacant dioceses, with younger bishops eventually introduced; despite this, the 1969 episcopal conference remained, by a few votes, in the hands of the right, its head for the next three years being the Archbishop of Madrid, until March a member of the Cortes, the Regency Council and the Council of the Realm.

Nevertheless the same conference issued a statement setting out the following:

> Among the fundamental rights of man is that of freely founding associations which authentically represent the worker . . .
> One of the fundamental principles of the church's social doctrine is trade union freedom.

It then went on to criticise, in broad terms, the syndicalist unions but not to support the use of strikes. Minimal, by non-Spanish criteria; but enough to rock Franco: it is still one of the fundamental principles of the Spanish constitution that the state is bound to implement the church's teaching.

So far I am simply giving facts—another fact being that no other group in Spain could have said such things so publicly. There are other facts—the involvement of priests in the underground trades unions (Workers' Commissions) or the collaboration of some priests in the Basque independence movement (of the eight Basques reported to be on trial at time of writing, four are priests). From certain viewpoints, which I partly share, theirs is the more revolutionary direction. But they are not in any relevant sociological sense in such movements as 'church' and I am restricting myself fairly drastically to that perspective.

Other brief points should also be made, for later comment, before moving from the Iberian peninsula. The passive acceptance or active support by large sections of clergy in the face of fascist regimes is given a precedent by the failure of the German church. The ideology underlying this support, and most clearly expressed by the old Opus Dei in Spain—a dynamic mediaevalism advancing ever onwards into the tenth century—derives basically from French catholic spirituality, particularly as developed after the condemnation of Action Française in the twenties (Maritain's *Primacy of the Spiritual* is a source-book here). The latent influence of such spirituality, emphasising moral or attitudinal change, rather than structural revolution, helped vitiate the efforts of the Spanish revolutionary anarchists even in the thirties. The role of the church as a crucial ideological factor in Spain is clear from the catechism taught to most present adults in their childhood:

Q. Is it a sin for a Catholic to read a Liberal newspaper?
A. He may read the *Stock Exchange Gazette*.
Q. What kind of sin is committed by him who votes for a Liberal candidate?

A. Generally a mortal sin.

On the other hand, the influence of committed Spanish and especially Basque priests on developments in European political theology is beginning to be apparent: Prêtres Solidaires draws its political concerns from its Basque members, though its theology still comes from German and Dutch sources.

Latin America

In moving from Spain and Portugal to their ex-colonies in Latin America, one preliminary point needs to be made. Just as colonialism has given way to formal independence within a neo-colonialism, under the same or different imperialist powers, so the church in Latin America is still in a position of 'ecclesiastical neo-colonialism', which one might define as territorial and administrative ecclesiastical jurisdiction canonically granted to foreign clergymen within a state whose hierarchy is formally national. Bishops may now be mainly indigenous, but the echelons of administrative posts, school headships, seminary professors, provincials of religious orders, and particularly purse-control posts, are often still held by foreign clergy. These are often now German, Belgian, and especially North American rather than Spanish and Portuguese. This further complicates a complex situation.

But again let us look at specific events over the last year or so. On 24 August 1968 Dr Montini gaily opened the Latin American bishops conference at Bogota in Colombia. His stirring counter-revolutionary words there profoundly depressed many Christians throughout Latin America, in particular several hundred Chilean priests who took over their cathedral in protest. But the meeting he opened was more hopeful in its outcome. What has since become known as the *Medellin Statement*, approved and issued by CELAM, gave a reasonably sharp analysis of the present situation. Its conclusion then read, in part:

To sum up: The foregoing analysis reveals a state of under-development which affects the general situation in our continent. Men see the injustice of differing social conditions and realize that they are not fated to live in such a manner for ever; and, if it should be necessary, they will seek violent methods to overcome this state of affairs. It is not surprising that violence is taking root, since the situations mentioned above are already violent—in that they are inconsistent with human dignity and oppress freedom. What is really more surprising is the patience of a people who for many years have borne a condition which would have been less easily tolerated given a greater awareness of the rights of man.

The lack of technical development, blind oligarchical classes, large-scale foreign capitalists, all hinder the necessary transformations, and offer active resistance to everything which might threaten their interests. This consequently creates a situation of violence. But the alternatives are not *status quo* or change, but rather peaceful or violent change.

That's not bad for the whole hierarchy of a continent to state publicly as their position. It's considerably closer to the truth than any statement likely to be issued by a Spanish—or English—hierarchy. But of course it cloaks differences. We can take Brazil as one crucial Latin American country, and the Nordeste as one crucial area in Brazil.

The North-East has a population of 26 million (about one-third of Brazil's total); two-thirds are rural; 62% live on and own 4.1% of the cultiviable land, 1% own 32%; 1m people are favella-dwellers, marginalised; 50% are under 21 years of age, 40% under 14 years—i.e. about 6m out of the 26m are breadwinners. In Brazil as a whole, about 70% of families live on an absolute minimum wage; 180m hectares, out of a total of 400m, are owned by 1% of the population; the top 6% own in all 94% of the acreage. American industrial and economic influence is of course dominant:

one can gauge the scale of the battle for economic independence from the fact that in 1965 General Motors' sales ($20,700m) were ten times Brazil's total budget; the same year GM, Ford, Standard Oil and Chrysler together amassed sales ($55,225m) equal to seven times the budgets of Brazil, Argentina, Mexico, Chile, Venezuela and Colombia combined.

But what is particularly interesting about these, hopefully familiar, facts is that they are taken in this instance from speeches delivered by a Roman catholic archbishop at graduation ceremonies all over Brazil in the last year or so— by Dom Helder Camara of Recife. As such, of course, the figures could be the basis for almost any policy. They can be put in context with a few quotations from Camara's recent speeches:

What is needed is a structural revolution.

Economically speaking, it is common knowledge that the under-developed countries suffer from internal colonialism, i.e. a small group of rich and powerful people in each country maintains its power and wealth at the expense of the misery of millions of the population.

Capitalism, despite its championship of the human individual and freedom, is egotistic, selfish and cruel. It does not hesitate to crush human beings when profit demands it.

National and international trusts are already more powerful than the most powerful states and they manage to shield the gangsters they hire to eliminate certain personalities who are judged too much of a nuisance.

The United States is a living demonstration of the internal contradictions of capitalism . . while under the guise of anticommunism, but in fact driven by a lust for prestige and the expansion of its sphere of influence, it is waging the most shameful war the world has ever seen.

Following from this analysis, Archbishop Camara was arguing in July 1968 that the option he then took for non-violence was based on the gospel, but also on reality:

> If an explosion of violence should occur anywhere in the world, and especially in Latin America, you may be sure that the great powers would be immediately on the spot—even without a declaration of war—the super-powers would arrive and we would have another Viet-Nam. You ask for more realism?

By September, he was saying:

> It will take a great deal of mysticism and skill to prove that it is possible to promote a revolution in peace, without violence, and to change socio-economic and politico-cultural structures by moral pressure alone, with courage and determination, but without bloodshed.

By Christmas the government was trying to ban Camara from speaking even in his own diocese.

I have quoted Camara at some length. But it is important to recognise three things: first, relatively few people in Latin America could say even that much to as many people and still survive the present Brazilian wave of repression.

Secondly, he does not stand alone—about 40% of priests in Brazil have declared support for a non-violent revolution, and perhaps half of those would condone a violent change; nor does he stand farthest to the left: Camilo Torres has been followed by others, still in small numbers, but there, where guerillas are active.

Third, Camara is operating in a rapidly developing church situation in Brazil. Again one can survey the past year or so:

43

Oct. 1968: Camara's residence machine-gunned.

Nov. Four priests arrested for CP activity.

Dec. 10th Institutional Act gives absolute presidential powers.

Jan. Various bishops support Camara against government's silencing attempts.

Jan. Fr Vitte expelled from one state and arrested in another as 'communist'.

March. Dominican house raided by political police.

March. Tibor Sulik, president of the World Movement of Christian Workers and member of the Commission for Justice and Peace arrested at Caritas HQ.

April. machine-gun attacks on Recife curial offices, on regional secretariat of bishops' conference, on Catholic Action HQ, and on the cathedral.

May. Brother Bomfim imprisoned for insulting the armed forces in a sermon.

May. Fr Neto, a colleague of Camara, found hanged and shot.

June. episcopal conference gave formal support to Camara, 5,000 people attended a service for Fr Neto.

8 June. many priests in Rio read a statement from pulpits attacking the 'minority which holds all political and economic power' and a situation in which 'there is no justice and no peace', ending: 'there remains only recourse to struggle in order to transform Brazilian society.'

It would be heartening to end the account there. But at the same time the following could happen: a statement sent by Brazilian priests to the episcopal conference spoke in part of:

> The spectacle offered to the Brazilian people by the enthronement of Archbishop Dom Vicente Zioni at Botucatu on the same day as the oppressors were engaged in action against militant catholics in Sao Paulo who were defending some ill-treated workers against the law. The circumstances of Dom Vicente's enthronement were themselves shocking: the presence of the Minister

for Justice, Senhor Gama e Silva, seated at the side of Dom Vicente in the official car marked the union between the government and the hierarchy of the church. A car armed with machine-guns followed them. On the official dais, right beside the archbishop and the dictatorship's minister were the twelve bishops of Sao Paulo, representatives of the magazine *Flora Presente*, some army officers and numerous policemen. The crowd was protected on all sides by large numbers of police armed with rifles, machine-guns and bombs.

That statement called on the assembled bishops to follow through the implications of the Medellin conference. It was rejected by 135 votes to 60 and the five Brazilian cardinals cordially met President Costa e Silva for coffee.

Strategic analysis

Clearly this summary survey of some events in 1968-69 in three 'catholic' countries is inadequate, and to some extent out-of-date. The purpose it is meant to serve, however, is to indicate the kind of specific analysis that must underlie any talk of the church and revolution. Such analysis is necessarily a continuous task, but the broad outlines of a strategic analysis for this historical moment seem clear enough. Overall, three situations can be distinguished:

1. In Spain and Portugal, the catholic church is formally and massively integrated within the official and political structures; yet a shift of political option within the church is possible; in such a situation, a radicalisation of church members is politically of great importance: the church can become a 'sociologically inaccessible area', even a constitutionally immune zone of opposition, against which normal repressive measures are to some extent impotent.

2. In Brazil, the church is not officially integrated, but is culturally embedded; political radicalisation is even more of a reality than in Spain; such radicalisation is politically important, offering possibilities of 'free zone' activity (the

Brazilian regime was baffled by a recent wave of pray-ins: mass arrests, let alone a machine-gun response, would have been poor public relations) but is not as such a crucial leverage.

3. The third situation is that of Britain: here the catholic church is neither officially integrated nor culturally very significant; political radicalisation can (therefore?) take even extreme left forms; but such radicalisation is then of extremely marginal political importance.

If this general schema holds, it offers the basis for a political analysis of the church generally. The guiding description is that the church is 'oblique' to other structures of society. In terms of any revolutionary strategy, this means that a reformist movement in almost any other sector of society (TU demands in education, for example, as in the recent teachers' strike) eventually intersects, if pushed hard enough, with crucial aspects of the overall social structure (via, for instance, Burnham scale financial awards to schools based on a pupil-points system, to the distorting role of public schools, the control of a ruling elite). Theoretically, however, the church need not so intersect; ecclesial reformist movements (the Renewal Movement, for instance) could therefore transform their demands into extremely 'radical' redefinitions of the church and be successful in doing so (perhaps in an 'underground' direction) —while at no point actually challenging thereby the controlling features of our society.

English intersections?

But if again this schema holds, such an analysis raises acute questions for political radicals in the catholic church in this country. The international nature of the church may give their theoretically radical positions some significance in terms of their mediated effect on catholic radicals in Spain or Brazil—just as earlier theological positions have had their mediated reactionary effect. To influence the inquiries of mainstream European theology towards 'political theology' is still a servicing activity for hard-pressed catholic radicals elsewhere needing theological arguments against their local reactionary hierarchies—for a Spanish workers' group to ask an England-based radical catholic to prepare study-outlines and position-papers is not unusual. But is this all that an English catholic radical can hope for? Is any direct political activity to be entirely 'secular'—involvement in some of the many left groups active in England—with consequently an increasing divorce between experience (secular left) and ideology (christian-marxist)? This may well be the case, but some suggestions might first to be examined.

The British Communist Party seem fondly to believe that the large Irish element in this country's working class can be approached through their Catholicism. This seems dubious; probably only a minority of Irish catholic men in this country are 'practising' and even fewer would be open to a radical transformation of their inherited Irish Catholicism. If one sought an 'Irish-based' intersection, Northern Ireland (schematically somewhere between Brazil and Spain) is an obvious possibility; but in that area, English radical catholics are simply client socialists, since they are dependent on the activities of groups like People's Democracy.

In Europe, an opening to intersection or intervention has been traditionally offered by catholic institutions—CTUs, CD parties, even catholic universities—but these did not develop in England; their diluted equivalents—CSG, YCW, chaplaincies, Newman Society, etc.—are, to put it mildly, rather weak leverages upon our society, even if the suspicious hostility in some of these organisations towards anything even vaguely recalling 'communism' could be overcome. The plethora of other RC organisations—CEG, UCM, SVP, LM, CM, CWL, GSA, YMS, through to the Catholic Needle-work Guild—may be important carriers of a certain traditional catholic ideology and form of life, but any radicalisation of their ideology would logically entail their dissolution. In any case, many such organisations are notable for the minimal membership of under-forties, as the church itself seems increasingly to be.

If one wants to radicalise the generations that seem more likely to be open to revolutionary perspectives, the catholic schools system offers itself, with the catholic teachers' training colleges as the crucial point of entry. After the experience of numerous campaigns on precisely this issue, this too, though perhaps of great political importance in the long run, does not seem an immediate area: only an extremely well-planned campaign with definite political aims could be of use here. The same is probably true of the emerging parish councils—but it is now 150 years since parish politics, centred on control issues, could lead, as it once did, to the formation of a great Radical Association (and even that was middle-class dominated).

One interesting area, both marginal and central, remains: marriage. The point at which traditional catholic ideology, the ordinary experience of most adult members of the church, and certain deeply political socialising mechanisms in our society, all intersect is in the conventional forms and limits of the mass-consumer, pre-packaged, privatised family home. But does this offer a viable point of political-theological leverage for the radical Christian, considering the massive vested interests in this area? After *Humanae Vitae* and with the enforced renewal of celibacy 'vows' on the immediate agenda, this may just possibly offer an interventionist opportunity over the next decade. After all, even the Brazilian guerillas acknowledge the political significance of both contraception and celibacy.

I shall be interested to hear what people think.

*

LOCATING THEOLOGY

Slant's claim to be in some sense concerned with 'theology' has undoubtedly raised eyebrows in 'professional' theological circles. While Bernard Lonergan, for example, has spent half a lifetime preparing a book on the method of theology, *Slant* has pursued its undeniably idiosyncratic theologising with hardly a pause to articulate in public just what it supposes itself to be doing; it is perhaps time the question was put directly in its own pages: what does *Slant* mean by 'theology'?

This article is necessarily a personal answer to the more general question 'what is theology?' but since it begins from a consideration of previous *Slant* articles and since its conclusions seem in line with whatever can be characterised as the '*Slant* approach', perhaps it can also stand as a response to the challenge from *Slant* critics. It is thus critique and recapitulation as well as exploration.

That there is a difference of approach between supposedly theological articles in *Slant* and those in 'professional ' theological journals seems fairly obvious; one pointer might be the noticeable absence in its pages of any response, using the same exegetical tools, to Cornelius Ernst's thoroughly 'professional' and ultimately neutral article on 'Charity and revolution in the gospels' (*Slant* 8).

It would be interesting here to compare typical articles from *Slant* and from, say, *Gregorianum* or *Nouvelle Revue Théologique*; but the problems raised by *Slant*'s theological methodology can be examined more directly. Terry Eagleton's recent article, 'Politics and the Sacred', in *Slant* 20, is a convenient example.

The article is structured round two parallels, that between primitive notions of dirt and of the sacred and the Christian notion of the *anawim Yahweh*, and between these two conceptions and the postulated role of the oppressed in contemporary society. It seems to me that Eagleton is not here constructing an argument in any logical sense, but

49

rather illuminating one set of terms by reference to another. He is clearly justified in setting side by side the theses of Mary Douglas and Mercia Eliade, thereby pointing up the contrast, the 'paradox of the sacred', but he then continues:

> It is this paradox that I want now to examine in terms of Christianity. One could, to begin with, draw a general connection between this ambivalence in the primitive notion of the sacred and the Christian perspective on the relations between any social order and the power of God.

It is the 'in terms of' and the 'general connection' that are puzzling: is the 'connection' anything more than an illuminating parallel, or is it essentially superfluous? Crucially, could not the point about the oppressed proletariat be made directly from the Eliade-Douglas tension without a detour through a Christian framework? (It is significant perhaps that the same article in *Commonweal* had a further parallel drawn from *Macbeth* which can drop out entirely in the *Slant* version.)

One could make the same kind of point about other articles. In 'Politics and Benediction' again by Terry Eagleton, in *Slant* 9, a description of benediction is given in terms drawn from Marx and Sartre; the second part of the article is a parallel description of capitalist society. The link is made as follows:

> The way we have just described benediction is also essentially a way of describing a human society under capitalism. It is not the only language we can use, and perhaps cannot stand by itself as a mode of description, but these are significant terms, and we must now try briefly to translate what they say about benediction into what they say about society.

Later, the terms 'connection' and 'parallel' again relate the second part back to the first, as in, for example: 'Within this system the position of the capitalist or manager parallels that of the priest in benediction.' The interesting link-term here is 'translate'. What Eagleton is basically doing is trying to use one language to describe both phenomena, but there is still felt to be a kind of disparity between the two descriptions, requiring 'translation'.

In an important article in *Slant* 14, 'Why we are still in the church', Eagleton seems to come close to collapsing a double description successfully into one: his language allows him to describe human-being in a way that is simultaneously 'Christian' and 'Marxist', but in this article an interesting substitution for 'connection' or 'parallel' appears. Eagleton writes:

> Man can therefore only truly be himself when he has interiorised his own species-being and thus the life of the community as the ground of his personal identity, and one image for this is a unity of language and body.

'Image' is now the link-term to the more subtly 'Christian' part of the description. 'Image' reappears later in the article where a phrase involving 'parallel' could almost have been used instead:

> . . the image of the dance has been traditionally linked with the Christian liturgy. . . We can find an image for these ideas in Shakespeare's *Macbeth* . . .

This way of conducting a theological discussion obviously has affinities with the Thomist insistence on analogy, but it also seems at times to be more the style of a sermon, a kind of rhetoric relying on metaphors. In brief, this mode of theology often reminds one more of a metaphysical poem than of classical metaphysics.

Put that way, my comments may seem merely dismissive criticism. To show that they are not involves a lengthy argument. We can begin by remarking that the comments apply more widely than to *Slant*. Eagleton's 'Politics and the sacred' appeared also, in fact, in *Commonweal*; it could once have appeared equally well in *New Blackfriars*.[1] A wide range of journals now publish articles that are certainly not 'professional' theology in the mode of, say, *Concilium*. Theology, to put it mildly, is today a problematic discipline for most of its practitioners. Barth, Bultmann, and Tillich all seem in various ways *passé* (or dépassed) to the younger theologians on the continent and in the USA. Even in England, John Robinson, the Bishop of Woolwich (for example) has distinguished between 'deep-mining' and 'open-cast' theology, the one involving all the historico-critical tools of the university divinity school, the other being the kind of temporary and tentative, exploratory work he sees himself as doing (characteristically, his invitation to participate in 'open-cast' theology was issued in *New Christian*—15th June 1967). New 'styles' of theological writing have emerged with, say, William Hamilton, Harry Williams, or, from the Roman catholic side, Sebastian Moore. Hamilton and T. J. J. Altizer in their recent preface to the English edition of their *Radical Theology and the Death of God* have commented:

> . . . theological agendas have varied over the past decades: Niebuhr centred on the doctrine of man; the Barthian influence led us to christology; now, the problem for a while will surely be the doctrine of God. The debate appears to be one between the 'translators' and the 'doers-without'. Radical theology is a doing-without theology.

Their formulation could be applied directly to the *Slant* articles discussed above: are these 'translations' (even two-way translations) or could the Christian element be 'done without'? It is the familiar question put in terms of theological methodology: are *Slant* Christians really *only*

---

[1] [A reference to the then-recent dismissal of Herbert McCabe from the editorship. See Simon Clements and Monica Lawton, *The McCabe Affair*, London 1968.]

marxists or humanists; what place has God and the church in their framework, etc? Perhaps an inquiry directly into the nature of theology can provide some pointers to a reply to that question.

*

We can begin to propose an answer using various summary formulations we will eventually find to be in need of modification. One obvious point is that theology is in some way concerned with the notion of God, even when it is his 'death' that is in question, and that the notion of God is traditionally associated with that of revelation. This second connection can be put in terms of inspiration or of salvation history. The latter is the history of Israel viewed in a particular way and the story of that history is well-trodden: Abraham, the Egyptian captivity, the Exodus, Sinai, the Canaanite campaigns, the monarchy, the prophets, the exile, etc. But the bible is not 'history' in any positivistic sense; it not only recounts the political, economic and cultural facets of the life of a people, but also is itself a reflection in religious terms on the 'significance' of that history. As related, the history of the Israelites is also the history of their changing conception of their god.

Put briefly: for Abraham, his 'god' is to be seen in terms of the blood-brotherhood, the covenant with god as Abraham's *go'el*; the exodus and Sinai experiences result in a naming of that god as 'Yahweh', while in the struggles in Canaan Yahweh becomes the 'Lord of Armies'; as the nation-state is stabilised, Yahweh the Lord of Hosts is seen as the warrior-king, the king of a theocracy; in the proclamations of the prophets other conceptions arise, and in particular the covenant relation is reinterpreted in terms of a marriage relationship; the exile situation brings an awareness of the Israelite god as 'Lord of History', of all history, not just of their own national story.[2]

---

[2] Cf. G.Von Rad, *Theology of the Old Testament*, Edinburgh, 1962, or, very briefly, L.Johnston, *A History of Israel*, London, 1964.

The Judaeo-Christian claim has been that the story of this Israelite nation is not simply the interrelationship of events, interpretations, and the people who experience the events and interpret them, as would be the story of any nation, but that in some way 'the living God' is a further factor in that interrelationship. His relation to the interpretation offered by the community of the events which involve them can be examined in theological terms partly as the problem of 'inspiration'.

Karl Rahner and Dennis McCarthy have offered complementary studies of inspiration, in the Old and New Testaments, that give us one partially adequate way of making sense of 'inspiration'. Rahner's argument can be given briefly in quotations:

> The human author perceives something because God effectively wills him to do so, with a will which is not merely permissive . . . but rather pre-defining—what is called in technical theology, a *praedefinitio formalis* . . . The determining factor in an efficacious (as distinct from a merely sufficient) grace can consist in some external circumstance which God foresees, through his *scientia media*, will be decisive in a man's coming to his choice and is willed by God as such. . . .
>   God wills the church and brings it into being . [because]...his design for the incarnation of the Logos includes within itself the founding of the church. . . . The concrete, fully realised essence of the church includes the scriptures; they are a constitutive element of her. . . . the bible is not merely an externally adopted indifferent instrument of the apostolic church in performing her task; her normative function for the future church was exercised precisely by reducing to writing her *paradosis*, her faith, her self-constitution. . . . the life-situation within which and out of which the scriptures arise is God's astonishing and mighty work of manifesting himself in human history through the prophets and through his Son. The scriptures' (formally

54

predefined) emergence from this vital context is what makes them scriptures.[3]

McCarthy makes basically the same points, here writing (for example) of the Yahwist strand in the composition of the Old Testament:

> In the reaction of the writer to his own historical experience resulting in a new interpretation in the light of Yahwist traditions, we have the same general factors as in the prophets—experience, tradition and personal reaction. However, the experience, instead of being a mystical contact with the divine, *came simply from living through a momentous era of history;* we can find no mark of extra-ordinary divine communication, yet this also is inspired writing.[4]

What has clearly happened in both these theories is that the inspiring action of God has been pushed further back or behind the whole process of writing. No longer, as for example in Pierre Benoit's theory of inspiration, is the divine influence to be felt directly in the 'mind and will' of the individual writer (though Topel in an article in *Scripture*, 1964, has argued that the Rahner- and Benoit-type theories supplement each other, and McCarthy clearly wants to retain a Benoit-type notion for Old Testament prophecy).

But then Rahner and McCarthy both run into the inevitable problem: what is left as the difference between this kind of influence and the ordinary processes of writing? McCarthy is more straightforward:

> The divinely guided community produced texts as an integral part of a complex process in which was the very life of the community. Further, this process was the term

---

[3] Karl Rahner, *Inspiration in the Bible*, London 1961 (rev. 1964) pp. 22, 40, 51, 61.
[4] Dennis J. McCarthy, 'Personality, Inspiration and Society', *Theological Studies*, XXXIV pp. 553-576. My emphasis

of the special divine guidance different from providence, conservation and so on, which God must have exercised on the community. *Otherwise Israel was not the chosen people* in any meaningful sense and its history [was not] salvation history, for all peoples and all history are under ordinary providence. [My emphasis]

Rahner makes a similar point by distinguishing between *concursus* (the 'ordinary providence' of McCarthy) and the *formal predefinition* he claims to be operative in the case of the founding of the church and therefore in the 'inspiration' of the church's writings.

In fact what is at stake here is, once again, the problem of 'translating' coming close to 'doing-without'. Rahner, characteristically, chooses to begin from a dogmatic definition which includes, of course, a notion of God:

Our starting point is the doctrine of inspiration as established in its basic outlines by the teaching authority of the church and further explained and expanded by the theologians, not the bible itself and whatever it may have to say about inspiration.

This obviously involves him in a circular argument which he recognises (pp. 36-7). But it would be possible to leave out altogether from his account of the relation between the community and its self-expression any notion of God-as-agent.

One could simply say that when the Israelite group finds itself involved in a new situation in its history, it seeks to understand it, and the result is then a changed self-consciousness which finds expression in a normal cultural way. Since an integral part of the particular cultural configuration of this tribal community is a reference to their god, 'Yahweh' himself is partially re-defined in the process. In other words, Rahner's whole thesis reduces itself to *a parenthesis in a tautology*, as happens finally in the sentence already quoted:

The scriptures' (formally predefined) emergence from this vital context is what makes them scriptures. [p 61.]

This is a parenthesis basically of the same nature as Eagleton's detour through a Christian framework, noted above. Again, however, this is not directly to reject Rahner's thesis but rather to point to an essential element in theological thinking to which I shall return.

One can also gain illumination on the concept of revelation from somewhat similar approaches developed in two very different fields of theological inquiry: the Heidegger-Bultmann tradition associated with 'existential theology' and that which brings linguistic analysis and theology together, exemplified for my purposes here by Ian T. Ramsey. A key term in both these traditions is *dis-closure* or, for Ramsey, discernment.

The argument can be put only briefly here and many differences passed over, of course. A quotation from Magda King can make the basic point about Heidegger:

> The oldest name for truth in Greek-Western thought is *aletheia*. For Heidegger, the central meaning of *a-letheia* lies in *lethe*: hiddenness, concealment, coveredness, veiledness. The *'a'* has a privative function. The whole word can be rendered in English by expressions like un-hiddenness, un-concealment, dis-closure, dis-covery, re-velation. . . . the elemental Greek experience of truth (is) as a violent and uncanny spoliation, whereby things are wrenched from hiddenness and brought into the light to show themselves as they are.[5]

Bultmann is clearly in the same tradition in his prefatory remarks on the gospel of John:

---

[5] Magda King, *Heidegger's Philosophy*, Oxford 1963, p. 141. See *Being and Time*, §§ 44, 68

. . the basic meaning of 'truth' in *John* is God's reality, which, since God is the creator, is the only true reality. The emancipating knowledge of the truth is not the rational knowledge of the reality of that-which-is in general; such a knowledge would at best free one from the errors and prejudices occasioned by tradition and convention. . . So truth is not the teaching about God transmitted by Jesus but is God's very reality re-vealing itself —occurring!— in Jesus.[6]

and elsewhere:

By revelation is meant an event which concerns man, whose eyes are opened as regards himself so that he can once again understand himself.[7]

Ramsey's examples of what he calls 'discernment-situations' are not 'uncanny and violent spoliations' but, in true muted English fashion, occasions when 'the penny drops', 'light dawns', etc. For example:

Let us recall the setting of a High Court—all very impersonal, all very formal. The name of the judge is as suitably abstract as possible—Mr Justice Brown. The wigs and scarlet are meant to conceal the fact that Mr Justice Brown is after all a human being. Nor is the argument of the Court interested in persons. We have instead 'the Crown', 'the accused', and 'the prosecution'. Then, one morning, Mr Justice Brown enters the Court to see as 'the accused' the closest friend of his undergraduate days. Eye meets eye; astonishment; an odd word is uttered: "Sammy" — and the result is (as the papers will tell us next day) that the Court is 'electrified'. An impersonal

---

[6] Rudolf Bultmann, *Theology of the New Testament*, London 1955, II, p 18ff.
[7] Quoted from R. Schnackenberg, 'Biblical Views of revelation', *Biblische Zeitschrift*, VII (1963) pp 2-23.

situation has 'come alive'; Mr Justice Brown has seen in 'the accused' something he has never seen before . .[8]

This example obviously has affinities with the situation of the psychoanalyst who can literally see 'the patient' either as another human person or as an 'object' of care and attention (see for example R.D. Laing, *The Divided Self*), with Wittgenstein's notes on 'seeing-as' (*Investigations*, II, xi), and with Sartre's remarks on 'the look' of the other when we are caught in a compromising position, with an eye to a keyhole for example.

We can for the present adopt this terminology quite simply to denote the same process described by Rahner in terms of communal self-articulation: the kinds of events that force a new self-understanding on the part of the Israelites are for them discernment-situations, and what is 'disclosed' includes in their eyes not only a new way of seeing and experiencing themselves but also a partial re-definition of Yahweh. The same question arises again, of course, as to whether, with the Bultmann of 1929 (see Schnackenberg's article), we simply say that in fact man 'understands himself', or add, with Bultmann's commentary of 1953, that truth is God's 'very reality re-vealing itself. '

However we eventually answer that question—or make that choice—it seems clear that on any understanding of what constituted 'theology' for the Israelites it certainly included the notion of self-articulation as a community, of making sense of their own situation in terms that drew upon but also modified the self-understanding they had received from previous articulations. The new self-understanding is focussed round a new element in their historical experience, a new 'event': exodus, war, exile, or whatever, an event which does not fit wholly into the previous categories, a crisis of some sort which forces them to reach a new 'totalisation' which includes the old and the new in a

---

[8] Ian T. Ramsey, *Religious Language*, 1957, chapter I.

changed pattern.[9] If theology for the Israelites meant this attempt to understand, to make sense of, their history, it seems feasible that theology might still mean basically that for us today: the attempt to make sense of our history.

Yet between ourselves and the Israelites lies the Christ-event. (I use event in this phrase with an awareness of the problems involved but as an initially convenient shorthand). What difference does this make to our conception of theology? One role of the Christ-event is obviously that it acted as the new focus for the changed self-awareness of the Israelite community, or of the self-styled remnant of it that constituted early Christianity. For them, Christ was himself the new event that forced a de-totalisation and a re-totalisation. In particular, his resurrection, or the primitive community's experience of his 'resurrection', was the focal point of their new understanding: it was 'in the light of the resurrection' that his followers re-interpreted the writings of the old covenant.

Luke 24: 13-35 gives the basic elements of this process: after Christ has 'explained to them all the passages, starting with Moses and going through all the prophets, that were about himself' they broke bread with him 'and their eyes were opened and they recognised him' (a discernment situation): the two 'moments' in the process go hand in hand. (Rahner and others have in fact argued that Christ himself had to go through a process of self-understanding, in terms of the prophets and the law, before he grasped himself as the Messiah and the Son of God.) This resurrection-experience remains central, indeed the distinguishing mark of those called Christ-ians: if Christ has not risen, our faith is vain.

But the formation of the early Christian community is also characterised by another central phenomenon: the

---

[9] For the notion of totalisation see Jean-Paul Sartre, *Problems of Method*, London 1963. The following could also be borne in mind: T. S. Eliot, 'Tradition and the Individual Talent', in *Selected Essays*; Tillich's use of 'spiritual centre' in *The Courage to Be*; Augustine's discussion of miracles in *De Trinitate*.

extension of the good news beyond the bounds of the old Israel. This is indeed where the crucial struggle for a new understanding is fought out by the early Christians. To declare that the new covenant and the good news that made sense of it were to be available to all mankind was the decisive break with the Jewish tradition. We are perhaps only now beginning to appreciate what that break implies, in the discussion of the 'anonymous Christian' and even the 'anonymous Christ'.[10] To describe that struggle and the way its initial implications were gradually seen by the first Christians would be a lengthy process; here I can offer only some schematic comments.

In the New Testament, the fundamental statement about the extension of the new covenant is made in the context of the ascension, explicitly in the Lucan form and perhaps implicitly in the Matthean; the gospel of *Matthew* ends:

> Go, therefore, make disciples of all nations . . and know that I am with you always, yes, to the end of time.

Acts 1: 6-11, is interestingly different:

> Now, having met together, they asked him, 'Lord, has the time come? Are you going to restore the kingdom to Israel?' He replied . . 'You will receive power when the holy spirit comes upon you and then you will be my witnesses not only in Jerusalem but throughout Judaea and Samaria, and indeed to the ends of the earth.' As he said this he was lifted up . . and suddenly two men in white were standing near them, and they said . . 'This same Jesus will come back in the same way as you have seen him go there.'

There are problems implicit in this difference of accounts that cannot be discussed here but the Lucan passage at least is plain: the extension of the message is directly contrasted

---

[10] See, for example, Raymond Pannikar's *The Unknown Christ of Hinduism*, London 1964.

with any hopes within the Israelite tradition of expectation and is then associated with the ascension and with a different expectation. The theological point is clearly that the basis for the universal availability of the good news is the universal availability of Christ himself: the ascension is seen as the term of the resurrection.

The Council of Trent emphasised that what is characteristic of the risen Christ present sacramentally is that he can be present simul-taneously to every eucharistic community-event, to every eucharistic celebration. As Herbert McCabe has argued, a traditional and to some extent satisfactory way of putting this is to say that Christ is present whole and entire in every particle.[11] But what of the relation of the risen Christ, 'apart from' his sacramental presence, to the world?

Rahner has argued that resurrection, including our resurrection, consists essentially in a changed relation to the world.[12] Christ's risen relation to the world is certainly in one aspect a mode of presence to us as every other human being (the parable of the last judgement describes a discernment-situation). In some way Christ sees himself as 'me everywhere' (see below). Put in another way, the question about the relation of Christ's sacramental risen presence to his non-sacramental risen presence is the question about the relation of the church to the world. But to put the problem in terms of church and world reminds us that the ascension in Luke is not the actual beginning of the preaching to all men: that has to await the coming of the spirit.

In the Pentecostal experience, the 'founding of the church', a two-fold structure is established: the spirit sent by Christ, the *pneuma Christou* in Paul's terminology, is described as appearing as 'something like tongues of fire; these separated and came to rest on the head of each of them'

---

[11] Herbert McCabe, 'The Real Presence', *Clergy Review*, December 1964.
[12] Karl Rahner, 'Resurrection of the Body', *Theological Investigations*, II, 1963.

(*Acts* 2:3). Fire is an image of simultaneous presence without diminution, akin to the presence of Christ 'in every particle'; but this relationship exists only for the sake of the second: the relationship of the preaching disciples to the crowd, when their words were 'simultaneously translated' for all present, a relationship which echoes the relationship of the fire to the preachers themselves. (That it also echoes and reverses the Babel story should need no emphasis.)

In other words, the preaching to all men is an essential dimension of the church's existence.[13] Paul's 'mission to the gentiles' is the practical assertion and effect of this realisation. Put another way, the radical break that Christianity makes with Judaism lies in the further exploration of the notion the Jews had themselves had since the exile, that Yahweh was the 'Lord of History'. This is made clear by the startling words of *Isaiah* 45:1—the opening of the postulated Deutero-Isaiah of the exile period—'Thus says Yahweh to his anointed, to Cyrus': the gentile king is seen as Yahweh's instrument, a sense most fully expressed in the developed notion of the 'creator.'

Any specific historical situation is of course necessarily part of a wider contemporary history as well as a moment in the continuing history of the particular group involved in the attempt to understand it,[14] but for the newly Christian Paul the point about the gentiles is that they have to be included in the new totalisation not just passively as the instruments of the Lord of History, as factors to be taken into account, but on the same level as the older chosen people themselves: as sons of a father, as equal participants in the process of coming to know Yahweh. But Paul not only makes a connection between the first coming of Christ and an extension of salvation to all men. When writing of the warning signs that will precede the *parousia*, he makes a

---

[13] Cf. Paul Hitz, *To Preach the Gospel*, London 1963; Eugene Hillmann, *The Church as Mission*, London 1966.

[14] Cf. Henri Lefebvre's discussion of 'horizontal' and 'vertical' complexity, in 'Perspectives de sociologie rurale,' *Cahiers de Sociologie*, 1953.

second, almost reversed, connection between that extension and Christ's second coming. Joseph Sint briefly summarises this aspect of Paul's theology:

> Widespread apostasy, Antichrist, woes, on the one hand; diffusion of the gospel to the whole pagan world and whole-sale welcoming of the Jews into their Father's house on the other, must precede the coming.[15]

Rahner argues for the same point rather more philosophically:

> Insofar as God's self-communication is an historic phenomenon directed to all men, it must encounter every man before it reaches its end.[16]

One can perhaps even say—using Rahner's terms from his essay on 'inspiration'—that the 'resurrection' or even more the pentecostal event, marks the reversion to '*concursus*' as God's renewed relation to creation: the situation that prevailed 'before the fall', when 'the spirit moved over the waters', is now re-established. The need for a specific 'sacred sphere' or 'sacred people' is removed when Yahweh fulfils his promise as *go'el*; the redemption is for *all* humankind.[17]

John (whoever he was), writing after the struggle for inclusion of the gentiles was over, could begin his gospel with what is almost explicitly an account of a 'new creation', emphasising too that Christ is the Logos that enlightens every man. Rudolf Schnackenberg, however, makes the traditional point that 'revelation is something other than the natural disclosure of God through his visible creation (*Romans* 1:19f)'— because, in line with McCarthy and with

---

[15] J. Sint, S.J., 'Awaiting and deferment of the parousia in Paul' *Zeitschrift für Katholische Theologie*, 86: 47f.

[16] 'Christology and an Evolutionary World View', *Theological Investigations*, V, 1965.

[17] Compare arguments for Christianity as the source of 'secularisation'. For Rahner's use of *concursus*, see 'Christology and an Evolutionary World View', cited above.

Rahner's 'inspiration' essay, he wants to distinguish revelation from concursus. But with John's prologue in mind, we might now take instead the perspective mentioned more recently by Rahner himself, that:

> . . this world is no longer the milieu provided by God himself for man's activity, but . . man himself creates a 'second world' in the course of history. . .[18]

This 'second world' is, of course, familiar to us from many non-theological sources, for example:

> To act means to modify the figure of the given in such a way that a field is structured which, to the actor, constitutes a meaningful totality. This totality is the presupposition for any meaningful action within it; but man is constantly engaged in structuring the world as a meaningful totality.[19]

It is not only a 'second world' that we create by perception, language and work; we thereby create our-selves. Herbert McCabe has put this succinctly:[20]

> If we take seriously the notion of mankind as a structure of meaning, as distinct from a merely biological structure, then we have to admit that it does not yet exist. Mankind is in a sense a theoretical construction; we argue 'if all these particular human institutions are all human institutions, there must be behind them all, the institution of simply being human'. We are reminded of the kind of thinking that Wittgenstein attacks: 'if all

---

[18] 'Christianity and the New Earth', in Walter J. Ong, ed., *Knowledge and the Future of Man*, New York 1968.
[19] Ben Brewster, introducing P. Berger and S. Pullberg 'Reification and the sociological critique of consciousness' *New Left Review* 37. Paul Connerton's article, 'Alienation:the genesis of an idea', in *Slant* 20, gives a more specifically marxist acccount of this process.
[20] Herbert McCabe, *Law, Love and Language*, London, 1968, p.98.

these are games there must be some concept of game that applies to them all'.

The point about this is that we are all involved in giving significance to this world, but until the significance we create is in some sense a shared significance, the world we create is not a common world; nor are we 'fully human'. McCabe continues:

> If mankind does not form a single linguistic community . . this implies a defect of human communication not only in extension but also in intensity. The fact that mankind is split into fragments which are in imperfect communication with each other means that within these fragments, too, full communication is not achieved. Because I cannot express myself to all men I cannot give myself fully to any.[21]

To this we can add Sartre's remark in the *Critique of Dialectical Reason* that at present nothing can be said about men that is not a lie.

What I want, therefore, to suggest is that 'theology' — talking about (one) god — is, strictly speaking, impossible until that shared significance is achieved: 'theology' now can only be the attempt to achieve that shared significance. In other words, theology after the Christ-event is basically the attempt to make sense of all human history, and all humans, not just some chosen people, are involved in the realisation of a new totalisation, a new self-understanding. The Christian claim is that the Christ-event is the focus of that new totalisation, that the resurrection-experience is the key to the new self-understanding of humankind, *but we cannot understand that key till the totalisation is arrived at.* All men and women are involved in creating that totalisation, in their efforts at creating a common world; Christians too are necessarily involved in this, negatively or positively like all

---

[21] McCabe, *Law, Love & Language*, p.99 See Chapters 3 and 4 in full.

other men and women, but—it is claimed—the Christians also have a second function.

*

Both these aspects of my thesis require clarification: what meaning does 'making sense of history' have and, secondly, how can we describe this alleged 'second function' of Christians? 'Making sense of history' is obviously in one sense an activity we are all engaged in every time we think or act: we give the world around us significance (as emphasised in the work of contemporary semiologists), but in more explicit ways the concocting of autobiographies (written or otherwise, elaborately pondered or casually recounted) and the pursuit of academic disciplines (at whatever 'level' or condition of opportunity) are attempts to 'understand humankind' — ourselves or others or all humans.

One version of a total synthesis of these attempts would be the collapsing of the various language-games, the partial understandings, the single-angled descriptions and definitions produced by the present multifarious intellectual disciplines, into one language in which psychologists, sociologists, physicists, literary critics, biochemists, anthropologists, philosophers, etc., could not merely 'talk to one another' but indeed would in a sense be no longer distinct contributors—a situation in which the 'proper study of mankind' is, simply, humans. The problem here is not that of adding the various language-games together into one huge encyclopaedia-type description, but rather that of finding a methodology that overcomes the barriers or boundaries between the languages of distinct disciplines.

This, clearly, has not yet been done, but even now one can see something of what the attempt means. None of the examples can be analysed in detail here, but we can perhaps make some points. Contemporary history for most of us means the morning newspaper, but the newspaper is precisely an example of multi-genre writing: we feel no particular strain turning from politics and economics on page one, through art-criticism and book-reviews on page five to an essay (or sermon) on the leader page, to a joke on the back. If we want a more detailed grasp of a contemporary situation, say the recent history of Africa, we again find ourselves turning to a variety of genres: the *UN Year Book*, the autobiography of Albert Luthuli, the legal code of South Africa, the poetry of Senghor and the plays of Soyinka, the speeches of Verwoerd, the essays of Fanon and Nkrumah, analyses of Tanzanian economics, the studies of Worsley, Segal, etc. The same would be true of attempts to understand the housing problem or the Vietnamese revolution, and the volume of print covered in each case would be enormous.

Cathy Come Home and the Aldwych *US* were attempts to convey such multi-faceted situations in ways that transmuted the load of print; the television documentary play and the theatre of fact slide between the received literary categories, as do *The War Game* film or Edwin Dorn's *Rites of Passage*, in which fiction, essay, polemic, sociological analysis, etc. are combined in one work and one 'style'. Art may attempt this function—think of Eliot's comments on the smell of cooking, reading Spinoza, and falling in love—yet trying to get a single understanding of a situation cannot finally be only a matter of bringing sentences on a page or images on a screen together.

Another multi-genre form of activity is the symposium, the gathering of experts who publish their separate contributions between the same covers, but here the people are the main elements brought together. In the writing of the 1968 *May Day Manifesto*, for example, we can see that process extended: various groups and individuals come together to make contributions in an attempt to create a common analysis, a totalisation. The result is more than a symposium and, ideally, more than the sum of the individual contributions: it manifests, 'reveals', the situation more clearly than would have been the case had these groups not cooperated. A kind of reversal of this process occurs when a single author writes in different literary idioms in order to make one connected comment: e.g. Laing's *Politics of Experience* or, a more integrated example, Williams's *Modern Tragedy*, with its philosophical, critical, and creative sections.

When, however, more than one person is involved, each—no matter how much the group may 'have in common'—inevitably sees the common situation in a subtly individual way. This perhaps is one of the central problems still engaging contemporary novelists: how to convey the viewpoints of all their characters with the same degree of commitment. George Eliot's *Middlemarch* was concerned, at one level, with the problem of recognising another's 'equivalent centre of self, whence the lights and shadows must always fall differently'. Lawrence Durrell's *Alexandrian Quartet*, James Baldwin's *Go Tell It On The Mountain*, Raymond Williams's *Border Country*, are in different ways concerned with this avoidance of 'special pleading'. Oscar Lewis's *Children of Sanchez* comes close to contemporary fiction for this very reason: his use of a tape-recorder as a sociologist allows him to print the complementary autobiographies of Manuel, Roberto, Consuelo, and Marta without the distortion of being 'put through the sieve of a middle-class North American mind' (*sic!*).

The problem of special pleading arises because, in a very profound way, each person is impenetrable by another: each has a different structure of feeling, a different personal horizon, because each has a different history, a different memory. Probably the most sustained attempt by one man to 'understand' another is embodied in Sartre's biography of Jean Genet; that biography was one stage on the way to Sartre's final concerns and to some extent anticipated in practice what has since been articulated theoretically. The term 'totalisation' that I have often used throughout this article derives from *Questions de Méthode*, published as a kind of introduction to the *Critique de la Raison Dialectique* in 1960; *Questions de Méthode* adapts Henri Lefebvre's technique in the article cited above, and has been summarised by David Cooper as follows:

First: a phase of phenomenological description—observation informed by experience and a general theory. Second: an analytico-regressive moment—a regression backward into the history of the object to define and date its earlier stages. Third: a synthetic progressive moment which is still historico-genetic but moves from past to present in an attempt to rediscover the present, as elucidated and reconstituted in the light of the complete phenomenological analytico-synthetic regressive-progressive procedure.[22]

Again, Raymond Williams's *The Long Revolution* is perhaps a convenient example in English of something like this process at work: its three main sections fit clearly into the pattern outlined by Lefebvre.

But even given this complex and sophisticated approach, the 'felt experience' of a past age or of another person is not totally available to us. We can feel an age, share its structure of feeling, only if it is our age, simultaneously present to us as the milieu in which we move; but that shared structure of feeling is precisely what is partly unconscious and inarticulate — the capillary movements of everyday life; tone, accent, intonation, nuance, overtones, the 'slang-ness' or 'in-ness' of particular words and phrases, are the aspects of language that embody such a felt structure rather than the more formal and recordable aspects of language. In somewhat the same way, it is a commonplace that deep friendship or love can embody itself in a kind of significant silence, a silence that occurs always within some kind of linguistic framework but is not entirely assimilable to that framework.

This perhaps gives us a clue as to the second possible form that 'making sense' of history could take. Just as most people do not have to sit down and write an autobiography in order to achieve some degree of identity, to make sense of

---

[22] R. D. Laing & D. G. Cooper, *Reason and Violence*, London 1964, 43; for convenience and brevity I will cite this excellent summary rather than the original texts.

themselves, so the 'human race as a whole' may never have to 'make sense' of its history in any formal, encyclopaedic way, but in a process more like 'coming to terms with oneself'. One almost inevitably falls into pseudo-psychological terminology in trying to describe the development of humankind in general; perhaps we can gain a clearer picture of what a non-literary form of people in common 'knowing themselves' would be like by extending Marshall McLuhan's analysis of the demise of print, but that cannot be discussed here (though it is interesting in this connection that one of the latest attempts at a community arts centre, the Liverpool Great George's Project, is emphasising the visual-kinetic aspects of communal artistic creation rather than the verbal).

The description that in fact I find most useful in grappling with this problem is that of Sartre in the *Critique*, where, at the opening of Book II, he begins his discussion of the possibility of 'the group-in-fusion'. A quotation from Laing is probably the clearest brief summary:

> How does a series become transformed into a group? What happened on the 12th of July? Then, each member of what before had been a series reacted in a new way—neither as individual nor as other, but as singular incarnation of the commune. This new reaction has nothing in it of magic—simply the reinteriorisation of a lost reciprocity. At the Apocalypse there is a prophetic vision of the dissolution of the series in the group-in-fusion. This group is amorphous . . but everywhere it is here, not elsewhere, now, not then. Each person as third is absorbed into the totality. This is what happens in series that panic *en masse*. . . It is the error of many sociologists to take the group as a binary relation (individual-community) whereas it is always ternary— each member of the group being a third—totalising the reciprocities of each of the others and being included in the totalisations of the others as thirds in turn. The group-in-fusion is everywhere, not

elsewhere. In this ubiquity it is not that I am myself in the other—in this fused praxis there is no other. In the spontaneous praxis of the group-in-fusion, the praxis of each is realised by each as me every-where. [23]

Sartre's analysis is too complex to be further distorted by partial quotation, but even in this truncated form it can provide us with some idea of how a future common culture might be described structurally.

Various theological points could be made directly in terms of Sartre's analysis (e.g. the role of the episcopal college as 'third', or the relation of 'This is my body' or marriage to Sartre's 'me everywhere'), but I want here to add only two further quotations by way of transition to a consideration of the 'second function' of the Christian in the creation of such a postulated 'common culture'—the creation of which, needless to say, involves the kind of political activity *Slant* has consistently argued for. In discussing the relation of each-as-third to the group-in-fusion Sartre argues that:

> At the moment when the multiplicities of serial syntheses fuse somehow into an overall synthesis, uniting men for and by action, it has been easy for some sociologists to lapse into idealism—to postulate, in effect, a new transcendent being. But at this moment, it is each third, as himself, and not as other, who operates the syntheses, totalisations, and any unification of them, by interiorising the totalising designations in and through which other groups treat his group as a totality. . . There is no hyper-synthesis, no transcendent synthesis, no privileged synthesis of syntheses.[24]

This can be seen as a partial reply to the paradox Sartre himself once proposed:

---

[23] Laing and Cooper, pp. 130-32.
[24] Lain and Cooper, p.131.

'The War' (as a whole) exists only for God. But God does not exist.

Yet the war exists.[25]

The lapse into the postulation of a 'new transcendent being' which Sartre rejects is what Christians are in some sense asserting, except that their 'transcendent being' is not 'new'; it is the re-cognition of 'Yahweh'. But the Christian is not simply maintaining that in some mysterious way 'God' will 'appear' when the common culture, a fully shared humanity, is achieved. What Christians are asserting, as I remarked above, is *strictly unintelligible to them until that time arrives* (if it ever does arrive, of course). But the relation between what a Christian does assert now and the re-cognition of God can be to some extent articulated.

*

We can begin by remarking that the two forms of the common culture, total articulation or a kind of significant 'felt' silence (these are not necessarily alternatives: one can be the framework of the other), are precisely the options discussed by George Steiner in his collection of essays, *Language and Silence*. That he proposes those options arises basically from his own concern with making sense of an age which has gassed six million people (and is now starving many more); if art is a process of making sense of humankind, how does art tackle that action of actual men? It is out of considerations like Steiner's that a great deal of experimentation with multi-genre writing and art has

---

[25] In *The Reprieve*, using a method adopted from Dos Passos, Sartre's novel describes various simultaneous lives of characters who pass each other without ever knowing one another, but who help constitute a moment of a historicial period; the film *Four in the Morning* uses the same variant on the Durrell-Baldwin technique to tackle the problems of special pleading and structures of feeling discussed above.

developed, in both German and Jewish attempts to come to terms with the holocaust.[26]

The point I want to make is that this search for a methodology in art that can match the monstrosity dealt with is part of the process of repetition, of constant re-working, of an experience in order to assimilate it. This process is clearly akin to familiar processes in psychological development, and it also relates us back to Ramsey's discussion of discernment-situations. The second example Ramsey gives is:

> A party begins all stiff and formal; then it happens that someone's dinner jacket splits unexpectedly up the back; or someone sits sedately on a chair which collapses beneath her. At once the party takes on 'human warmth'; as we should say, 'the ice breaks'.

If we view this incident from the angle of the wearer of the dinner jacket or of the person who fell off her chair, it is precisely the kind of situation that tends to recur again and again in the memory of the person involved: the incident is gone over and over again, as compulsively as a tune 'in the head', until we can accept it as part of our personal history, acknowledge that it did indeed happen that way, that we did make a fool of ourselves on that occasion. If, as Freud pointed out, the experience is sufficiently traumatic it may take a total reorganisation of the personality to reintegrate the incident successfully, to accept and see ourselves without rejecting that aspect—and that often our maturity dates from that reintegration, although up to that point the incident has appeared as absurd or frightening.

John Robinson has adopted Ian Ramsey's term, 'discernment-situation', for the Christian sacraments; I would prefer to see the sacraments as almost neurotic 'repetitions', re-workings, of the original discernment-situation, the paschal 'event' from incarnation to Pentecost.

---

[26] Steiner has discussed some of these in his 'An Essay on Promethean Form', in *Essays for Ernst Bloch*.

The Christians repeat their sacramental self-articulation again and again, proclaiming the death of the Lord 'till he comes', but without essentially knowing what it is they are doing: their Christian actions are at present unintelligible to them (requiring a kind of suspension of dis-belief) since their full intelligibility rests on a context that is not available and that must be created (e.g. in what sense Christians 'repeat' the paschal event depends on the 'ontological' status of the 'resurrection', which we cannot yet know). We can extend the words of Charles Davis, quoted by Herbert McCabe in *New Blackfriars* (February 1967):

> Fortunately the great tradition of Christian teaching and the thought of the great masters of Christian theology and spirituality have been handed down to us by generations faithful to authority when much in what they passed on was not to them personally very meaningful.

What Christians basically proclaim and 'hand down' is 'the resurrection', which for them must embody a two-fold claim, *the first being finally intelligible only retrospectively, if and when the second has been vindicated.* The first is the very obvious claim that the 'resurrection' makes sense of, is the key to and basis of, the whole Christian endeavour. For the Roman Catholic Christian tradition this involves the kind of statements quoted from the Council of Trent earlier: that the risen Christ is present to every eucharistic community-event, that the words 'this is my body' apply to the Christian movement and also to the poor and oppressed, to every man insofar as he is in need (see Sartre on 'scarcity' below). But the second claim is even more fundamental, as the early Christians recognised: *Marana-tha!* 'Come, Lord!' In the terms adopted in this article, the basic Christian claim must therefore be that the 'resurrection' is also the key to, the focus of, the ultimate totalisation arrived at by human kind together.

Again, it is part of the point of this argument that the Christian *cannot know* 'what this means' until (and if) that totalisation is achieved: we are still compulsively repeating it and it will continue to look absurd until the re-focussing is achieved. We can, however, distinguish between a less and more radical way of trying to elucidate its meaning. If, for example, we take the phrase 'risen community', there are two ways of interpreting the adjective: as describing the quality of life enjoyed by that community, or as referring to a category of people who comprise the community. The first option might come very close to Sartre's description of a group-in-fusion but the second is obviously more problematic and here I can make only some brief converging comments.

Sartre sees the dissolution of the series into the group-in-fusion as the surpassing of the bonds of violence and fear,[27] but he pinpoints as the basis of seriality and violence the condition of scarcity, one radical scarcity being that of time; the creation of a fully authentic group-in-fusion would involve the surpassing even of temporal scarcity. After the 'apocalypse', whatever is meant by eternity?

Secondly, the technical problem of special pleading for the novelist is also the basic practical problem for the Christian: loving the other as yourself; the community of the risen would be both a community of love and one which includes in it every other as other, the subtly individual quality of each personal life being retained (the Trinity is our basic image of this paradox).

Thirdly, if we take relativity theories seriously, as the nineteenth-century church learnt to accept evolutionary theories, then humankind's conquest of time could be the correlative of our increasing control of matter and conquest of space; that one could hear another's voice a thousand miles away astonished the nineteenth-century, that we can hear another's voice from a dozen years ago (for example Oscar Lewis's tapes) no longer astonishes us; the creation of a group which would almost literally be 'me everywhere' is probably a biological possibility (recall the discussion of

---

[27] Cf. Laing and Cooper, pp. 133, 136, and see Adrian Cunningham on *shalom* in *Peace on Earth: The Way Ahead*, ed.Walter Stein, London 1966.

'cloning' techniques); we cannot, it seems to me, simply rule out *a priori* our eventual surpassing of 'temporal scarcity'.

This second version of the ultimate Christian claim obviously peters into impenetrability. But the Christian's inability to describe the future kingdom is hardly more marked than the relative silence of the radical humanist in describing any future 'Utopia'. Walter Stein's critique of Williams's *Modern Tragedy* points up some of the deeper problems facing any adequate notion of 'total secular redemption'. In the language of this article, one would simply say that, on the 'secular' alternative, humankind will achieve a totalisation in which in fact 'the resurrection' has no place, in which 'God' does not 'appear'; on this understanding 'theology' would finally be seen as a superfluous term, a detour.

At present, there is, for obvious reasons, no way of deciding between the two views, but I want to clarify the relation between the 'secular' and the 'Christian' viewpoints. If we see the final totalisation as a dis-closure, a discernment-situation, of the first kind described by Ramsey (the judge seeing 'the accused' as Sammy), then the Christian is not necessarily claiming to add anything to, for example, the marxist notion of the future community in its material aspects; a Christian is simply asserting (or claiming or hoping—it can be no more, ultimately) that when and if the creation of a common culture, an adequately human society, is achieved then a re-focussing will be possible, will occur, a de-mystification will take place, the final false consciousness be cleared away: it will be more like Wittgenstein's duck-rabbit example than like, say, the entry of a conqueror.

There are various ways of describing this in both the radical secular and the christian frameworks—for example, the description of 'de-reification' given by Berger and Pullberg is close to it:

> The clearest instance of de-reification is the overall disintegration of social structures, necessarily entailing a disintegration of their taken-for-granted worlds. History

affords a good many examples of how natural or man-caused catastrophes shook to its foundations a particular world, including its hitherto well-functioning reifying apparatus, bringing forth doubt and scepticism concerning everything that had previously been taken for granted. In such situations roles are suddenly seen as human actions and institutions revealed as humanly produced montages for these actions. Such 'times of troubles' (Toynbee) or 'axial times' (Jaspers) can be very conducive to a rediscovery of the world as an open human possibility.[28]

For the marxist, de-mystification is in part the realisation of the 'who' responsible for the historical process; the Christian claim is that the 'who' eventually re-vealed in the final shift of focus will be Yahweh, as visible to us as the divine can be, i.e., as Christ, as Logos made flesh, as integrally *within* the totalisation arrived at. One can here recall the structure of argument examined by Macpherson in Hobbes and Locke[29]: the final totalisation rests on an initial de-totalisation and is re-established because the sustaining premise, the focus, of the original totalisation in fact remains throughout. Within the Christian tradition there are various formulations that can be looked at only very briefly here. The New Testament speaks of the kingdom coming like a thief in the night, and like a lightning flash, but also of warning signs; it speaks both of the gospel being preached to the ends of the earth and of Anti-Christ — the totalisation arrived at but seen initially as only our own self-articulation.

The choice apparently facing us from Bultmann's writings—revelation as an event in which men's eyes are opened so that 'man can once again understand himself,' or as 'God's very reality revealing itself'—might be seen as a false choice. Rahner's thesis can basically be accepted, that the process of community self-articulation is the revelation of God, but at present, in 'these last times', we are caught

---

[28] See their article in *New Left Review* 35, cited above.
[29] C.B. Macpherson, *The Political Theory of Possessive Individualism: From Hobbes to Locke*, London, 1962.

between the beginning and end of a new totalisation in which we have no intelligible revelation of God. Rahner's starting point raises further questions but the final structure of his argument—a parenthesis in a tautology—is instructive: our task is to arrive at a kind of tautology and the Christian endeavour can almost be described as a simultaneously central and superfluous parenthesis within that process (a description that perhaps applies to cultural articulation as a whole). There are some aspects of Rahner's recent thought that in fact bring him close to the position I have tried to outline, for example in 'Christianity and the New Earth':

> It is possible that the Christian 'significance' and the final Christian root of an historical reality that is to come (social, political and so on) will first manifest itself when it is already present and thus can be interpreted reflexively.

There are of course, numerous points that could be developed from this article—a critique of Brian Wicker's 'radical gap' approach, for example, or a consideration of the meaning of personal faith—but I want to conclude by referring back to Terry Eagleton's articles I discussed at the beginning of the article.

I have argued, to put it briefly, that the basic meaning of 'theology' is an extended meaning (the other side, so to speak, of *Slant*'s use of an extended sense of 'politics'), that the Christian task of making sense of belief is an eschatological task and is inseparable from and even equatable with the shared human task of creating an adequate human self-understanding, a common world and a common culture. It seems to me that Eagleton's *Slant* articles could therefore be regarded as a kind of 'model' of this theological activity: the process of bringing together, of collapsing into one language, apparently disparate language-games in a way that not so much constitutes an argument as provides for a shift in focus. The alternatives today are: 'professional' deep-mining theology, which in practice is often mainly a contribution to society's general historical self-understanding, the study of the history of theological articulation, the attempt to grasp previous theologies, often themselves attempts to totalise the available contemporary self-understanding; or rhetoric, a traditional element in the community's self-articulation and still with a positive function (recall Stokely Carmichael's role in the Afro-American community); or a significant and active silence. But none of these alternatives can be isolated from the political context of 'carrying forward God's creation'—of humankind.

*

ABSENT CENTRE I [1]

Once upon a time, an honest fellow had the idea that men were drowned in water only because they were possessed with the idea of gravity. If they were to knock this idea out of their heads, say by stating it to be a superstition, a religious idea, they would be supremely proof against any danger from water. His whole life long he fought against the illusion of gravity, of whose harmful results all statistics brought new manifold evidence. This honest fellow was the type of the new revolutionary philosophers in Germany.

The quotation comes from the preface to *The German Ideology* by Karl Marx and Frederick Engels.[2] The point, obviously, is that it is something of a mistake to try to remove actual conditions of life by merely arguing, by changing someone's ideas about the subject. The theme is hammered home in various places in the same work, e.g.: 'The demand to change consciousness amounts to a demand to interpret reality in another way, i.e. to accept it by means of another interpretation,' and: 'You are in no way combating the real existing world when you are merely combating the phrases of this world'.

The alternative to such 'idealism' seems clear: e.g. 'The resolution of the theoretical antitheses is possible only in a practical way, by virtue of the practical energy of man. Their resolution is therefore by no means merely a problem of understanding but a real problem of life, which philosophy could not solve precisely because it conceived this problem as merely a theoretical one'.[3] The eleventh thesis on Feuerbach famously

---

[1] This essay is a version of a paper delivered at the December Group 1968 and stands largely as written for that occasion: much of it therefore raises problems in a somewhat introductory fashion; it may still, however, be useful to do precisely that in *Slant* itself.

[2] *The German Ideology*, ed. R. Pascal, New York 1963, p. 2.

[3] Karl Marx: *Economic and Philosophic Manuscripts*, 1844, ed D. J. Struik, New York 1964, p. 141.

clinches the point: 'The philosophers have only interpreted the world differently; the point is to change it.'

Alongside this we can put an interesting judgement passed on *Slant* some years ago. Raymond Williams, reviewing the *Slant Manifesto*, wrote:

> The more vigorously anyone seeks to persuade me that 'the Fall' and 'alienation' or 'redemption' and 'emancipation' are parallel and even possibly identical concepts, the more I believe I am dealing with men engaged in a search for rhetorical solutions to tensions of an understandable, perhaps intolerable, but certainly idiosyncratic kind, and the less I believe (as I strongly and patiently wish to believe) that I am dealing with fellow-socialists, who are also catholics, and who are above all confronting the common crisis of our society and the world. . . . What I look for is the active continuity of the critique, and what I do not look for and must reject, is a prolonged inquiry into the appropriation. [4]

To some extent Williams' criticism of *Slant* is that of Marx's against the Young Hegelians, but noticeably Williams is rejecting the theoretical bias of *Slant* not because it is theoretical as such but because it moves entirely within the realm of theory by seeking merely to connect two 'houses of theory', drawing the parallels. He is arguing for a participation in the process of 'criticising', which he sees as part of the practical activity of changing society.

The admission of theoretical critique as part of the practical engagement with social change recalls other elements within the main-stream of marxist writing. Marx can write:

> The conditions of life which different generations find in existence decide also whether or not the periodically recurring revolutionary convulsion will be strong enough to overthrow the basis of all existing forms. And if these material elements of a complete revolution are not present (namely, on the one hand, the existence of productive forces, on the other, the formation of a revolutionary mass,

---

[4] *New Blackfriars*, November 1966, 75.

which revolts not only against separate conditions of life up till then, but against the very 'production of life' till then, the total activity on which it is based), then, as far as practical development is concerned, it is absolutely immaterial whether the idea of this revolution has been expressed a hundred times already; as the history of communism proves.

but also, a few pages later:

The existence of revolutionary ideas in a particular period presupposes the existence of a revolutionary class. [*German Ideology*, pp. 29, 40]

This is a somewhat ambiguous statement, to say the least. In context, Marx seems to be arguing that ostensibly revolutionary thinkers will in practice be revealed as still themselves caught within the sustaining ideology of the ruling class whenever their ideas actually endanger the existence of that class of which they are part; only if the revolutionary thinkers can actually belong to a revolutionary class (requiring the conditions sketched above) can their ideas really be revolutionary. This raises interesting and apparently circular problems: e.g. if the 'ideas' of the ostensible revolutionaries do indeed endanger the unity and existence of the ruling class, then they are, in some sense, potentially revolutionary ideas, even if disowned or modified by the original thinkers (examples, including some from eastern Europe, are easily available).

Tucker's wry rejoinder is perhaps more to the point than we care to admit at the moment:

In actual fact, of course, and as many a revolutionist has learned by experience, the existence of revolutionary ideas in a given time and place implies nothing more for certain than the existence of one or more thinkers of revolutionary ideas.[5]

Neil Middleton's related point about *Slant*'s arguments being eventually arguments for the destruction of *Slant*, as within this church and this society, is also relevant, as is the title of his book:

---

[5] Robert Tucker, *Philosophy and Myth in Karl Marx*, Cambridge 1961, 180n.

that we have in this country no 'language of revolution' is indicative of the real absence of any revolutionary grouping. The problem can be presented schematically: to substitute theoretical formulation for activity directed towards changing one's society, is clearly to be rejected; yet, equally clearly, in Lenin's words (*What is to be Done?*) 'There can be no revolutionary movement without revolutionary theory,'—the problem is the inter-relation. In terms of specific responses to actual situations, the range is fairly wide. Marx, for example, described the position of the so-called 'True Socialists' in nineteenth-century Europe as follows:

> On the one hand we have the actual existing communist party in France with its literature, and on the other a few German pseudo-scholars who are trying to elucidate the ideas of this literature philosophically. The latter are hailed just as much as the former as an 'outstanding party of the age' . . . In this fashion Germany can show a whole horde of 'outstanding parties of the age', whose existence is known only among the small set of scholars, pseudo-scholars and literary hacks. They all imagine they are weaving the web of history when, as a matter of fact, they are merely spinning the long yarn of their own imaginings. On the basis of the philosophical belief in the power of concepts to make or destroy the world . . . they continually mix up literary history and real history as equally effective.
> [*German Ideology*, pp. 93-95].

This a sobering comment when one recalls the tiny groupings on the left, including in England, who all have their own journals, magazines and news-letters, known to (and often not read by) mainly other tiny groupings on the left, but not known to or read by, the broad public. *Slant* is one of these.

Mao Tse Tung's emphasis, in the China of 1930, allows the validity of theory, but with a firm warning:

> The method of studying the social sciences exclusively from books is extremely dangerous and may even lead one into the road of counter-revolution. Whole batches of communists who confined themselves to books in their study of the social sciences have turned into counter-

revolutionaries. Many who have read marxist books have become renegades from the revolution, whereas illiterate workers often grasp marxism very well. Of course we should study marxist books, but this study must be integrated with our country's actual conditions. We need books but we must overcome book-worship which is divorced from the actual situation.[6]

For Mao, in 1937, reflecting on the disasters of 1931-34, theory is basically learnt in practice, exists only as a response to a situation in which one is actively engaged:

Knowledge begins with practice and theoretical knowledge which is acquired through practice must then return to practice. The active function of knowledge manifests itself not only in the active leap from perceptual to rational knowledge, but—and this is more important—it must manifest itself in the leap from rational knowledge to revolutionary practice. [*Selected Readings*, p. 63].

Against this, the emphasis of Raymond Williams, in the England of 1958, represents a significant difference:

The evident problems of our civilisation are too close and too serious for anyone to suppose that an emphasis is a solution. In every problem we need hard, detailed, enquiry and negotiation. Yet we are coming increasingly to realise that our vocabulary, the language we use to inquire into and negotiate our actions, is no secondary factor, but a practical and radical element in itself. To take a meaning from experience, and to try to make it active, is in fact our process of growth. Some of these meanings we receive and re-create. Others we must make for ourselves, and try to communicate. The human crisis is always a crisis of understanding; what we genuinely understand, we can do.[7]

It was within that last perspective, primarily, that *Slant* began; and for an institution which is, crucially, an embodied belief-

---

[6] *Selected Readings from the Works of Mao Tse Tung*, Peking 1967 p.35.
[7] Raymond Williams, *Culture and Society*, London 1961, p. 324.

system, the church, an examination of held beliefs, of the house of theory which encloses and activates the daily behaviour and responses of the adherents, might be especially potent as an agent of change. To understand Christian belief anew, to argue towards a new theology, seemed, initally, a central task. Primarily that argument would be about the liturgy, the sacramental articulation of belief, the actions most properly demanding 'faith'. Yet this could not be the sole emphasis; Catholicism, particularly, is an embodied form of faith; from the start there had to be an engagement with the actual group of people one was simultaneously in continuity with and in opposition to.

The *Slant Manifesto*, in the actual arrangement of its contributions, attempted to meet the various demands of an adequate critique: a political-philosophical argument, linked to a historical analysis of a specific situation and worked through to a critique of the theology still sustained by that history. But to produce a manifesto is still mainly an attempt to understand; as such it does not meet the demands of Marx or Mao for 'practical' involvement. What must be the relation between the attempt to understand and effective action? How far has *Slant* taken the seriousness of the problem here? What are the possible mediating agents?

First we can note the extent to which *Slant* has provided a house of theory. Articles in *Slant* can now wield a formidable array of conceptual tools, of heavily-weighted footnotes, and it is arguable that this is not mere froth but a genuinely worked-through effort of understanding. But even granting this to be so, where is the point of contact between that framework, those articles, and the position of the majority of catholics in this country; how is the linkage to be made? Part of the answer to this would involve locating the questioners. *The May Day Manifesto* anticipated an objection thus:

> Who are these people anyway?—the conditioned response has been learned. In fact the answer is simple: people, like any others, all needing to be heard. Yet to state the principle now is the most absolute challenge. Every device of habit, pretended amusement, false political realism, interest in a job, will be deployed against it. Anything not in the system is

unofficial, voluntary, amateur or extremist, and so can be written down, and out. With a proper instinct for where they belong, the regular commentators, the men 'inside' politics, return public attention to such crucial matters as who is now Number Three or Number Four in the Cabinet; who, lately, has talked himself into or out of a job; how the interests, next Tuesday, and especially next Friday, are going to be balanced up; and, at moderate intervals, will the election be autumn or spring? It is in that drugged atmosphere that the struggle for new policies, for an effective democratic campaign, has now to be undertaken.[8]

In one sense, this is an appropriate response, but it is not a reply to that question: 'who are these people? ' only a rejoinder to the 'anyway'. One still wants to ask—and the people who wrote the *Manifesto* need to ask, in considerably more detail than that provided in sections 45 onwards—who are Clive Bell, Jim Bromwich, Michael Barratt Brown, Ian Christie, George Clark, Ken Coates, Brian Darling, etc.—those people listed as contributors? One asks, obviously, not in scorn or dismissal but with a serious insistence. One puts the question, as Alec Vidler put the question to the original *Slant* group some three years ago: what are your levers of power?

For a catholic on the left, there are two questions: who is he or she and what is his or her purchase on power within the catholic church in this country, now, and in the immediate future;[9] and secondly, who are the catholics in this country, and in what sense are they, as a group, a possible power for change in this society, now. Only by answering the first can a catholic found a personal strategy for effecting change in the church; only by answering the second can one see whether as a socialist it is worth bringing about a changed church. Of course, in

---

8 R. Williams (ed.), *May Day Manifesto*, London 1968, p. 146.

9 More accurately, perhaps, 'who should he or she be?' Our choice of job and permanent situation is closely related to the aristotelian notion of 'hexis' (habit) as the core of moral stance, or of revolutionary presence: being-present may redefine for another the situation in which one is present; recall the alleged 'futility' of demonstrations; in the eucharist, it is the sheer 'presence' of 'Christ' to the eucharistic group, rather than any specific 'activity', that is transcendent or revolutionary.

certain respects the second precedes the first: only by locating the catholic group in this country can a radical catholic, as such, locate oneself.

To a certain extent. *Slant* has attempted this kind of analysis: in the middle section of the *Slant Manifesto* and in one essay in the first *Slant Symposium*;[10] one can couple with these a few books like Monica Lawlor's *Out of this World,* a study of Roman catholic psychological attitudes; Adrian Cunningham's essay in the second *Slant* symposium, examining the influences stemming from *Action Française,* is also relevant.[11] But it is noticeable that, for example neither *Directions: Pointers for a post-conciliar church* nor *The McCabe Affair* nor even *First the Political Kingdom,* Brian Wicker's account of the catholic left, included any analysis of the historical and sociological situation of Roman catholics in England. It is perhaps also signicant of the same absence, operating at a different level, that no adequate information has ever been collated on who actually reads *Slant*: who are the readers?

*

An indication of the kind of detailed historical work that needs to be done might be — as a random example — the absence of any adequate critical survey of so-called 'spiritual reading' in England since 1900. Think of the following authors: Dom Marmion (*Christ the Life of the Soul,* 1922; *Christ in his Mysteries,* 1924; *Christ the Life of the Priest,* published as late as 1952); Abbot Vonier; Alban Goodier (*Public Life of Our Lord,* 1930; *Passion and Death of our Lord,* 1933); Edward Leen (*Progress Through Mental Prayer,* 1935); Eugene Boylan (*Difficulties in Mental Prayer,* 1943); Vincent McNabb; Cyril Martindale; Ronald Knox (Knox *New Testament,* 1945; *Retreat for Lay People,* 1955; *Pastoral Sermons,* 1960;

[10] A. E. C. W. Spencer, 'The Demography and Sociography of the Roman Catholic Community of England and Wales', *The Committed Church,* ed L. Bright and S. Clements, London 1966, pp.60-85.

[11] 'Culture and Catholicism: a historical analysis', in *From Culture to Revolution,* ed. T. Eagleton and B. Wicker, London 1968, pp. 111-147.

University and Anglican Sermons, 1963); Gerald Vann; Hubert van Zeller; etc.[12]

The tone and emphasis of these works, let alone their content, has helped form the sensibility and approach to 'religion' of most of the priests ordained up to, perhaps, as late as five years ago. Their influence, in derivative tracts, sermons, spiritual advice, confessional treatment, retreats, school devotions, etc., has pervaded the spiritual culture of two or three generations of English catholics; rejected or unread now, they yet represent a massive element in the received 'temper' of English Catholicism. Not only is there no adequate history of catholic spiritual practices and sources of devotion; there is simply no adequate history of the catholic church in England since 1900.[13]

This is not of course to say that *Slant* should, or could, have provided such a history, only to point to the crippling effect of its absence. But there are useful pieces of work *Slant* could perhaps do: on, for instance, the various groups now active: the London Ad Hoc Committee, the Pastoral Development Committee, the Catholic Family Weeks, etc; an analysis of how the national episcopal commissions have actually worked; an investigation into ecclesiastical wealth; some work on catholic papers, periodicals and publishing. There is simply a great deal to be done here, even in terms akin to those of Perry Anderson's cultural topography articles in *New Left Review*; but this paper can here only suggest and move on. A few quotations from Chairman Mao can make the point succinctly:

> As far as revolutionary movements are concerned, true revolutionary leaders must not only be good at correcting their plans, ideas, theories, or programmes, when errors are

---

[12] Cf. a brief essay by Elmer O'Brien, SJ, 'English Culture and Spirituality', in *Concilium*, November 1966, 72-77.

[13] David Mathew's *Catholicism in England*, (1935) has less than twenty pages on 1900-1935. See also the collection of essays edited by Dr G. A. Beck, *English Catholics, 1850-1950*; E. I. Watkin, *Roman Catholicism in England from the Reformation to 1950*, London, 1957; relatively little has been produced, in England, even on the English 'modernists'.

discovered . . . but when a certain objective process has already progressed and changed from one stage to another, they must also be good at making themselves and all their fellow-revolutionaries progress and change in their subjective knowledge along with it, that is to say, they must ensure that the proposed new revolutionary tasks and new working programme correspond to the new changes in the situation. In a revolutionary period, the situation changes very rapidly; if the knowledge of the revolutionaries does not change rapidly in accordance with the changed situation, they will be unable to lead the revolution.

and:

We are also opposed to 'Left' phrase-mongering. The thinking of Leftists outstrips a given stage of development of the objective process . . . they alienate themselves from the current practice of the majority of the people and from the realities of the day. [*Selected Readings*, 65]

Alongside this perhaps one can place without immediate comment a parenthesis in a circular from the 'open church' group: after analysing the composition of the 221 respondents to an appeal for an 'open church', Anselm Hurt added: 'There were no signatures from noted left-wingers at all.'

This raises directly the problem of who the 'noted left-wingers' are within the Roman catholic community. Recently the narrowness of *Slant*'s own basis, with, for example, a mainly university-educated editorial board, has been acknowledged in the newly-produced *Slant Bulletin*, whose first issue opened:

When *Slant* was first published, it was the outcome of particular needs and circumstances, as well as a response to the general conditions of the church in England at that time. Those who formed the original group came from a university and were concerned with producing a theoretical analysis of the position of Christians in the contemporary situation as much as they were anxious to start a kind of radical movement within the church. As the magazine developed, various conflicts of identity appeared: was it theory, journalism, or perhaps propaganda? There can at no point be a single statement of the magazine's aims, but, for better or worse, it has become a theoretical journal with a particular appeal and stable, predominantly academic (though in a wide sense of the term) readership. . . . This has led to the danger of intellectual elitism, which is contrary to the whole idea of church and society which led to *Slant* in the first place.

This seems to me a useful statement of one aspect of the problem. The key sentence is obviously the last. One could perhaps temporarily appropriate a term employed by Bernard Lonergan (in a clearly different sense) for the situation being described there: if there is a consistency of content in a statement, yet an inconsistency between content and performance, between what is said and the very fact of saying it, then that is a 'counterposition' rather than a contradiction. (It is a kind of counter-position, for example, for a Cretan to say that all Cretans are liars.)

It seems that *Slant* has drifted into a kind of counterposition, as all revolutionary elitist groups tend towards counterposition. There is, for example, a counterposition involved in arguing that all men (and women. .) must participate in the common creation of meanings yet withholding approval when 'democratic decisions' are reactionary ('undemocratic' often being the term of rejection!); the urgent plea for an 'educated' participating democracy can become the other side of the radical's assertion, recently caricatured as 'I am right, you are mystified.' The whole problem of the revolutionary party is obviously relevant here, but this paper cannot directly tackle that issue. The problem that I do want to follow up can be formulated by noting that when the marxist socialist reaches the point at which he wants to reject a proffered opinion of one of the exploited (a docker who believes, for instance, that Enoch Powell is the saviour of Great Britain), he resorts to the vocabulary of 'mystification', and to economic facts; when the radical Christian reaches a parallel impasse, on an intra-church issue, his appeal, it seems to me, must be to 'theology'. I have recently argued (*Slant* 22) that theology, in an eschatological perspective, is basically a process of de-mystification; I want at this point to explore briefly some connected, and even (dialectically!) opposed points.

*

In an essay entitled 'Criticism as Language', published here in 1963,[14] the French literary critic and semiologist, Roland Barthes, has this to say about criticism:

> Criticism's function is purely to evolve its own language and to make it as coherent and systematic as possible, so that it can render an account of . . the greatest possible quantity of, e.g., Proust's language. . . The task of criticism is purely formal; it does not consist in 'discovering' in the work of the author under consideration something hidden . . which has so far escaped notice (. . are we more perceptive than our predecessors?) but only in fitting together . . the language of the day (existentialism, marxism or psychoanalysis) and the language of the author . . If there is such a thing as critical proof it lies not in the ability to dis-cover the work under consideration but, on the contrary, to cover it as completely as possible with one's own language . . criticism is the ordering of that which is intelligible in our own time.

Whether this is an adequate account of literary critical method is perhaps debatable, but it does seem to offer an interesting way of describing what 'professional', in the sense of systematic or dogmatic, catholic theologians have up till recently seen their task as being: the attempt to cover previous formulations, both biblical and conciliar, of the Christian 'thing'. The problems of de-mythologisation and of 'doctrinal development' are clearly involved here, as are the 'further problems' raised by 'Rahner''s starting point' that I avoided in *Slant* 22; these still need exploration, but here I want particularly to fasten on one point Barthes makes; he goes on:

> Criticism deals not with the world but with the linguistic formulations made by others; it is a comment on a comment, a secondary or meta-language (as the logicians

---

[14] In 'Critics Abroad', a special issue of the *Times Literary Supplement*, 27 September 1963.

would say) applied to a primary language (or language-as-object). It follows that critical activity must take into account two kinds of relationship; the relationship between the critical language and the language of the author under consideration, and the relationship between the latter (language-as-object) and the world; criticism is thus defined by the interrelation between these two languages.

The second sentence in this quotation rests rather oddly alongside the others so far quoted (in terms of a standard philosophical problem, it slides from a coherence theory of truth to a correspondence theory), but Barthes then makes an important point in relation to criticism (and, here, theology) as a meta-language: he emphasises that while the language of the literary work before him is 'given', the language into which the critic attempts to transpose it is his own choice:

> The language that a critic chooses to speak is not a gift from heaven; it is one of a range of languages offered by his situation and time . . each critic chooses his necessary language, in accordance with a certain existential pattern as a means of exercising an intellectual function which is his and his alone, putting into the operation his 'deepest' self, that is, his preferences, pleasures, resistances and obsessions.

In so far as *Slant* has been involved in this kind of theology, it has, basically, said that the appropriate language which the meta-language of theology must employ is that of 'politics'. But the immediate insistence that it is the 'wider sense of politics' that is involved can be both positive and disabling: such an emphasis may be intellectually appropriate but strategically disastrous, for if the concern is to translate one's theological vocabulary into a vocabulary drawn from the political philosophies of Marx, Sartre and Merleau-Ponty (or, better, to speak theologically (in) the language of Marx, etc.), then this is perhaps useful, but it is not a translation into that kind of politics which is 'ordinary', and if the 'wider definition of politics' actually disables one from engaging with the narrow sense of politics, then something decidedly odd has happened to the word politics.

Obviously *Slant* and the people connected with *Slant* have engaged in the more narrowly defined political areas; but in what sense has the necessary theological translation been effected in connection with those areas? The absence, for example, of any close links between *Slant* and the Young Christian Workers may perhaps indicate that *Slant* is prevented by its own chosen language from arguing directly with those engaged in one form of 'narrow' politics (though there are, obviously, other factors involved). Again, at one level, the groups and people round *Slant* have been successful in opposing on some issues that area of traditional establishment theology which itself ought to connect directly with 'politics': so-called moral theology.

As a journal *Slant* openly rejected the Roman Curia's position on contraception from the start; it contributed to the argument on nuclear weapons; more recently Herbert McCabe's *Law, Love and Language* has directly tackled the whole problem of ethics; specific issues like that of violence have also involved moral theology arguments. But if the purpose of such engagement is to convince traditional catholics that their stance has to be on the political left, then it is fairly clear that that purpose remains badly unfulfilled—though one shouldn't ignore the 'percolation' effect. This is in part due, of course, to the choice of language made by traditional 'moral theologians' themselves: at few points has that language itself connected to people's ordinary linguistic experience. Only the contraception issue has in any sense closely involved the energies and anxieties of the majority of catholics in this country—and as that issue broke upon us again recently *Slant* as a journal was curiously uninterested.[15]

Heidegger remarked once that 'Our being is in language, but language occurs only in conversation'. The problem of mediation between theory and praxis, between those who are 'right' and those who are 'mystified', is the problem of conversation, of finding a common ground with people with

---

[15] It should be emphasised that my querying of the strategy of *Slant* applies to it as a journal; individuals on the *Slant* board did of course respond publicly to *Humanae Vitae*: Eagleton in *Tribune*, Redfern and Bright in *Newman*, Middleton in *New Christian*, Pyle in his new edition of *The Pill and Birth Regulation*, etc. This is a useful occasion to recall that *Slant* editors do have other jobs and personae, a point frequently omitted during criticisms of a vaguely-defined '*Slant*'.

whom you want to engage in common action—and that conversation involves a strategic choice of language.

*

So we have circled back to the problem from which we began: what can serve as mediation between theoretical analysis and praxis? I want in the second half of this paper to look tentatively at two areas, probe two possible responses to this persistently difficult problem, about which I feel somewhat unsure; but one response to the question can be given immediately, with rather more confidence. In my view there needs to be a recovery of an emphasis that *Slant* used to have to a considerably greater degree than has been recently apparent. I have already quoted Marx's comment on the 'True Socialists' mixing up 'literary history and real history' as equally effective. Adrian Cunningham has recently put basically the same criticism to the catholic left, in the symposium *From Culture to Revolution*: he characterises the 'final continuing British catholic tradition' as 'aesthetic' and comments:

> I use this word neutrally as the most accurate description I know. The aesthetic is obviously denoted first by its distinction from the realm of socio-cultural analysis, sociological and historical imagination, which at its finest one finds in the field of religion represented by Troeltsch. Its contrary strengths are that creative sensitivity, finely discriminated sense of values, and exacting standard of relevance to the task in hand which follows from the literary critical discipline especially in the hands of a practitioner like Leavis. Its abiding temptation is the simple appeal to the literary world as a court of appeal to clinch rather than illustrate arguments—all geared to the paradigmatic instance of the literary fact. The characteristic reference is not to events or socio-historical analysis or political self-understanding but to imaginative schemes and their interpretations which often ends as an appeal to a stratified world of values beyond appearances. . . the aesthetic is less a concern for the historicity and structural intelligibility of the object it surveys and the problems for religious thought raised by such a view, than for the pattern of significance of

a literary-critical kind that may be lifted from them. Salvation history is particularly amenable to the aesthetic mode and is emphasised to the exclusion of almost any other sense of the term 'history'. [pp. 144-5]

Cunningham ends his essay with the perceptive comment:

> One of the most pressing of current difficulties is that the most interesting and awkward problems in catholic culture are those of the historic, and the most potent answers and tools of analysis available are aesthetic. [p. 147]

Adrian Cunningham's own option, expressed in his choice of academic position, is for the 'historic', including the kind of analysis I mentioned earlier. This at present seems to be increasingly the dominant option within the *Slant* movement. I want here, while fully accepting that perspective, to recall some of the real strengths and purpose now of the 'aesthetic'.

Perry Anderson has examined at some length the historical reasons for the emergence of a radical socialist critique in this country not from marxist or classical sociological sources but directly from the literary critical tradition of dissent coming through Arnold, Orwell, Leavis to Williams.[16] Anderson comments: 'The detour that Williams had to make through English literary criticism is the appropriate tribute to it.' It is the emphasis of 'detour' that I would like here to question. If one looks now at the sources of critical opposition and dissent in our society, in western and even soviet-communist society generally, the central importance of creative literary work is clear. For example, Stuart Hall's useful survey of America's 'new revolutionaries' constantly notes the influence of 'literary' sources:[17]

---

[16] Perry Anderson, 'Components of the National Culture', *New Left Review* 50, pp. 3-57.

[17] *From Culture to Revolution*, pp. 182-222. This is not of course to deny that currently the actual experience of change is increasingly the motor of further change.

In the beat poets and beatniks of the early and middle fifties was signalled the first real generational breakaway. Affinities between the beat poets, novelists, and 'fellow-travellers' and the hippies of the sixties are worth noting.

And:

> In this period the underground developed an image of the american socio-political system which owed more to *Howl*, *An American Dream*, *The Naked Lunch* and *The Fire Next Time* than it did to Daniel Bell's 'end of ideology', Seymour Lipsett's panegyric to the 'pluralist society' or J. K. Galbraith's 'countervailing power'.

Kerouac, Ginsberg, Ferlinghetti, Corso, Mailer, Baldwin, even figures like Salinger, have helped form much of the root protest-consciousness of the American new 'movement'; even a social theorist like Paul Goodman has perhaps been most influential in his semi-novels, an inter-mixture of fact and fiction, rather than in 'straight' analysis. In Germany, too, since the war the main thrust of opposition has been articulated as much by people like the Gruppe 47 (Gunter Grass, Heinrich Böll, Peter Weiss, Martin Walser, etc.) as by the sociologists and political theorists; Enzensberger's attack on the German establishment was, again, initially in terms of its actual linguistic habits; since the early 1960s the work of the Dortmunder Gruppe has tried to bring even more closely and obviously together literary work and social analysis, in their brand of 'industrial literature'.[18] Even in Spain it is a satirical magazine, *Codorniz*, that most publicly offers a kind of critique of the Franco regime, while in France and the USSR the linking of political commitment and creative work, though in different forms, has been extensive.

In England, the change of mood in the fifties was partly reflected, partly crystallised, partly provoked by the so-called Angries (never, of course, a homogeneous group); a new sensibility has appeared in films, television, novels, which articulates and therefore spreads a mood; recently, the 'pop & poetry' scene and the theatre of protest, the arts lab and the

---

[18] In this context one might mention the continuing relevance of Hochhuth's work, with his present play, *Soldiers*.

freak-out, have had close links with the growth in a kind of political awareness that recalls the free-wheeling unstructured 'do your own thing' early days of the American movement. It may seem difficult at present to give full assent to many aspects of this scene (these scenes); but the argument that revolutionary activity is precisely that of forcing a society towards restructuring by the insistent attempt at re-integrating its excluded margins applies not only to dispossessed and socially crippled people but also to those areas of activity and fields of experience that cannot be accommodated within the straitjacket of a society that defensively terms itself permissive.

*

If *Slant*, then, as a journal of some 'sophistication', is to choose, deliberately, tactically, a language within which its theological concerns can fruitfully interact, not just for the personal satisfaction of those who write for it, but, consciously, as a way of reaching and shaping a wider audience, it seems to me arguable that its main co-thrust, in harness with historico-sociological inquiry, should become (or become again) critical in the sense of directly literary-critical. This would involve an attempt to analyse the kinds of literary productions, from pastorals and sermons through to the work of 'catholic writers' this century, that in a sense 'the church' has itself produced, as well as an attempt to come to grips with the wider literary-cultural scene, in particular the literature and music of contemporary protest. This, if you like, is the emphasis represented by Terry Eagleton's analysis of contemporary poetry in *New Left Church* or his argument in *Shakespeare and Society*, or the essays of Brian Wicker and Walter Stein, in say, *Theology in Modern Education* (1965). Yet that strand has almost disappeared from the pages of *Slant* itself and even from the arguments centred on the *Slant* position (though Paul Francis's analysis of newspaper reporting of the Grosvenor Square demonstration, in *Slant* 11, was a good example of what might be done).

If the language *Slant* as a journal deliberately chooses to employ, as a strategic, political act, is more that of direct criticism of widely available creative works, then to conduct an argument for radical change and to talk, in some sense, theologically, in terms, say, of Baldwin and Mailer, the Stones and the Doors, rather than explicitly in the vocabulary of Heidegger and Merleau-Ponty may be immensely more difficult and may to a certain extent restrict the particular contribution of each piece of work (still, if Lenin could begin from a glass of water . . .!). To engage with literature, films and pop music as the public or at least published language of Christian left theology should not mean, obviously, a mechanical appropriation of such work—as seems to have happened in some efforts at theology-and-literature explorations in the States. Some quotations can underline the problems but also the possibilities here. In the essay cited before, Barthes argues that:

> A work of literature is never quite meaningless (mysterious or inspired) nor ever quite clear; it is, so to speak, suspended meaning: it offers itself to the reader as a declared system of significance, but as a signified object it eludes his grasp. This kind of disappointment or deception inherent in the meaning explains how it is that a work of literature has such power to ask questions of the world (by undermining the definite meanings that seem to be the apanage of beliefs, ideologies and commonsense) without however supplying any answers: no great work is dogmatic.

and also remarks:

> The major sin in criticism is not to have an ideology but to keep quiet about it.

Perry Anderson, again writing of *Scrutiny*, comments:

> Suppressed and denied in every other sector of thought, the second displaced home of the totality became literary criticism. With Leavis, English literary criticism conceived the ambition to become the vaulting centre of 'humane studies and the university'. This claim was unique to England: no other country has ever produced a critical discipline with such pretensions. They should be seen, not as reflections of megalomania on the part of Leavis, but as a symptom of the objective vacuum at the centre of the culture.

What Anderson seems to forget somewhat is that the 'objective vacuum' is still to a large extent present. There is, in England, now, still no major body of marxist or sociological writing upon which a socialist critique at a theoretical level can be based with any hope of a wide constituency. With the various paperback appearances in the wake of the 'student revolt' this is perhaps just beginning to change but to a very great extent *Slant* seems still to be conducting a (fascinating) conversation with postulated nowhere-men living in some nowhere-land.

[A retrospective postscript: It was partly upon the model of the publishing house associated with *Slant*, Sheed & Ward, which had specialised in translating 'continental theory' —of a theological kind— that Anderson established New Left Books, later Verso, which did indeed aim to foster a 'major body of marxist or sociological writing' in English—albeit much of NLB's initial output was also translated. The first NLB book was actually co-published with S&W. And Terry Eagleton of course went on, not quite single-handed, to establish a major and influentially accessible body of marxist literary criticism. As it ironically happened, the second part of my 'Absent Centre' appeared in *Slant* 25, an issue which also included Terry Eagleton's essay 'Reluctant Heroes: the novels of Graham Greene', shortly to be incorporated into his first widely read critical book, *Exiles & Emigrés*, Chatto & Windus, 1970. Much of the rest of programme I sketched remains, of course, unwritten and unachieved.]

*

ABSENT CENTRE II

In the first part of this paper, I said that I wanted to offer two possible responses to the difficult problem of the interrelation between understanding and practice, comprehension and strategy, from a christian-left point of view, concerning which I felt 'somewhat unsure.' That uncertainty remains, and what follows is therefore offered, as it was at the December Group, tentatively and for discussion and criticism.

The connection between theology and culture as art has led directly, in the general debate, into the problem of the relation between theology and culture as a whole way of life, and thence into the question of the relation between eschatology and a common culture. Various strands have entered this debate, among them the problem of tragedy and with it the notion of 'radical gaps' in human existence bridgeable only at the *parousia*; a different emphasis has been on the disjunction between two modes of language and rationality: the discursive and the dialectical; a further strand has been the argument that culture and liturgy are 'ordinary'.[1]

I now want to look briefly and in a rather scattered way at an area of human existence which seems to me peculiarly relevant to most of the strands in this debate: the realm of the humorous. Immense efforts have been made to carry the weight of our times on an adequate theory of tragedy, yet comedy has scarcely entered the debate. Yet, clearly, comedy, laughter, has been a crucial element in protest, recently and traditionally, through satire and ridicule. If, too, we are looking for a shared culture, an area of human creativity to some extent shared by all members even of our society, the area to explore would be that of comedy.

---

[1] See in particular the work of Brian Wicker, *Culture & Liturgy*, London, 1963 and *Culture & Theology*, London, 1966.

Everybody, I should imagine, glances at the cartoon in whichever paper they happen to read: the sense of humour, the particular tone and reference, may be different, but the feature is common; even in *Slant* more people, I'm sure, read *The Real Thing* than read the articles; in the *New Statesman* many turn first to *This England*, etc. If, in other words, one tries to locate that elusive entity, the 'structure of feeling' of a period, one place to look is in the humour of the period: back numbers of *Punch* are perhaps the most difficult of all literature to read in their entirety.

Again, if one is looking for an activity which combines the discursive and the dialectical, and is therefore an image of the common culture society, surely nothing could serve the purpose better than a joke: the whole point of a joke is that it be told in discursive fashion, with a straight face, and then suddenly—to manipulate some phrases of Terry Eagleton—explodes in a non-discursive flash, in immediate manifestations of self-enacting truth. One sees the point, it's a disclosure-situation. The structure of a joke is basically the bringing together of contrary expectations, the fusion of two disparate structures of feeling, the intrusion of the absurd into the surd, etc. It is a variant of the basic technique of art: transcendence by metaphor.

Yet again, the point has been rammed home in *Slant* that (on the good authority of Wittgenstein) a dog cannot lie; it's also relevant that a dog cannot laugh: only humankind is *risibilis* as well as *rationalis*. It is then an interesting comment on our society that in Claude Lelouch's film *Un Homme et Une Femme* the sheer exuberant energy of a dog is the only available image for the spontaneous joy of the man and the woman: in our society sheer human joy and laughter are rarely available to us; further, when they are, they tend to startle, even to shock, challenge and 'offend' those who accidentally witness them (see Lucy's characteristically sour and depressive reaction to Snoopy's occasional delirious flapping in *Peanuts*).

In particular, the two places in our society where we still feel peculiarly restrained, hesitant about speaking and oddly afraid to laugh (or at least where we run the most risk of 'offending' if we do) are museums or art galleries and churches: a kind of internal censorship takes over. Yet joy, humour, laughter, should surely be part of both: culture and liturgy may be ordinary, but they shouldn't be flat; culture, after all, is enjoyable too. Art as play is, indeed, being cautiously rediscovered against an ingrained habit of reverence—in primary schools, in community art centres, in the post-Pop Art departures. But it remains an apposite comment on the present condition of the church that Rosemary Ruether, in *Contraception and Holiness*, should find it natural to use the following analogy for the dehumanisatlon created by the official 'rhythm method':

> Suppose one were not allowed to smile when one really felt happy. The smile was not allowed to function as a spontaneous expression of *joie de vivre*. Rather the smile was treated as if it were some kind of appetite which had to be kept in check, although being a forceful appetite, one must condescend and satisfy it periodically. The satisfaction of the animal smiling-drive was linked by some Grand Inquisitor with a lunar stop-watch which flashed red and green at intervals. When it flashed green the person could smile, when red he must stop. . . The person lived in constant dread of smiling at the wrong time, in which case he would be hit on the head with a ten-ton block. [2]

Anyone who has been through certain traditional kinds of catholic retreat (the epitome of spiritual effort) will recognise the atmosphere.

Yet even within the rather angst-ridden theological tradition of the last century, the connection between Christianity and humour has not gone wholly unremarked. Gregor Smith, in his book on Hamann, contrasts the different viewpoints of Hamann and Kierkegaard:

---

[2] Rosemary R.Ruether, *Contraception and Holiness*, London 1965, p. 80.

For Kierkegaard there is another stage, the stage of directness, of the 'single one' separated from the world, which is beyond humour. For Hamann there is no stage beyond the indirect-ness of faith, which is grounded in the whole life of the world and history. . . . Hamann understands the relation of God not as something in and for itself, separate from the world, but in and through the world. He remains a 'humourist'; there is no religious stage beyond that of humour. That is to say, his faith includes and never gives up scepticism. He combines believing and not believing within the conditions of this world. For Hamann the duty and art of concealment expresses his conviction that directness is never possible, that the witness can never point to his own achievement, that humour is therefore the final stage, even in faith. For Kierkegaard 'humour is the last stage of the inwardness of existence before faith.' The point at which Hamann and Kierkegaard part company is precisely that where Kierkegaard, wishing to come out into the open, walks into a wilderness of his own making; whereas Hamann, remaining in the world, knows that in so doing he is at the same time a voice crying out in the wilderness. But it is the wilderness which is at the same time full of hints and signs of our calling. Hamann's 'humour', that is to say, is bound up with a radical pessimism, or more precisely a Christian realism about the condition of man: you can be a Christian only in rags, you have really nothing. [3]

I would not be happy with some of the emphases here, but there is certainly a connection to be explored between humour, in the richer sense of laughter, and a kind of scepticism allied to faith, an awareness of 'the real situation' that is also a way of pricking the mystifications of our world. Bernard Lonergan is one of the few contemporary theologians to have considered laughter (though Hugo

[3] R. G. Smith, *J. O. Hamann*, London 1960, pp 19, 109.

Rahner's *Man at Play* is also relevant); in certain sections of *Insight* Lonergan makes points akin to those of Hamann:[4]

> The dramatic subject, as practical, originates and develops capital and technology, the economy and the state. By his intelligence he progresses, and by his bias he declines. Still, this whole unfolding of practicality constitutes no more than the setting and incidents of the drama. Delight and suffering, laughter and tears, joy and sorrow, aspiration and frustration, achievement and failure, wit and humour, stand not within practicality but above it. Man can pause and with a smile or a forced grin ask what the drama, what he himself is about. His culture is his capacity to ask, to reflect, to reach an answer that at once satisfies his intelligence and speaks to his heart.

Later he develops this point in more detail :

> Satire breaks in upon the busy day. It puts printers to work, competes on the glossy page of advertisement, challenges even the enclaves of bright chatter. It enters not by argument but by laughter. For argument would presuppose premises, and premises that would be accepted easily also would be mistaken. But laughter supposes only human nature, and men there are. Moreover, as it is without logical presuppositions, so it occurs with apparent purposelessness: and that too is highly important for, if men are afraid to think, they may not be afraid to laugh. Yet proofless, purposeless laughter can dissolve honoured pretence; it can disrupt conventional humbug; it can disillusion man of his most cherished illusions, for it is in league with the detached, disinterested, unrestricted desire to know. Satire laughs at, humour laughs with. Satire would depict the counter-

---

[4] Bernard Lonergan, S.J., *Insight*, London 1987, pp. 236, 626f.

positions in their current concrete features, and by that serene act of cool objectification it would hurry them to their destiny of bringing about their own reversal. In contrast, humour keeps the positions in contact with human limitations and human infirmity. It listens with sincere respect to the Stoic descriptions of the Wise Man, and then requests an introduction.

Lonergan acknowledges, of course, the difficulties of the satirist or the humourist :

But the significance of satire and humour is, I suggest, out of proportion to their efficacy. Because counterpositions commonly keep shifting their ground, the satirist is likely to clip one head off the monster he attacks only to witness another sprout in its place. Again, because the point of humour is transcendent, it is apt to be missed.

Leswek Kolakowski, from a very different tradition, makes some parallel points both about the function and the risks involved in being what he terms a 'jester':[5]

In every era the jester's philosophy exposes as doubtful what seems most unshakable, reveals the contradictions in what appears obvious and incontrovertible, derides common sense and reads sense into the absurd. In short it undertakes the daily chores of the jester's profession together with the inevitable task of appearing ridiculous.

At present the efforts of protest in this country are simply hung up on the incorporation of demonstration as a sports-feature on weekend TV, their assimilation by the '*société du spectacle*'.[6] The response to being so snookered may be an escalation of violence as a means to more effective demonstration. Yet this is to enter a deadlock situation, to fight with a weapon drawn from a system of institutional violence we reject as inhuman, to collapse into another kind

[5] L. Kolakowsi, *Marxism and. Beyond*, London 1969, p.54.
[6] See Guy Debord, *La société du spectacle*, Buchet / Chastel, Paris, 1967.

of counterposition. The problem of violence is an acute one for the Christian: can the Christian accept violence, in this society, as a mediation between analysis and change, as the appropriate language of theological conviction? Brecht's lament captures the paradox:[7]

> Even the hatred of squalor makes the brow grow stern.
> Even anger against injustice makes the voice grow harsh.
> Alas, we who wished to lay the foundations of kindness
> Could not ourselves be kind.

And another of Brecht's poems adds:

> What a strain it is to be evil.

But his *Messingkauf Dialogues* give what seems to me might, now, in England, conceivably be a contrary emphasis. The dramaturg says to the philosopher:[8]

> This game of preference, this cooking up of things for the audience (to learn, to criticise, to judge) can only be conducted in a cheerful, good-tempered mood, a mood where one's disposed to fun. You place art just right when you pointed out the difference between the work of a man who's responsible for pushing five buttons on a machine, and a man who juggles with five balls. And you linked this ease and light-heartedness with extreme seriousness in one's attitude to one's social task.

> *The Philosopher* : However much of what's considered essential to the art of the theatre we may wish to abandon for the sake of our new aims, there is one thing which we must, in my view, preserve at all costs, and that's its quality of lightness and ease. The whole thing has got to retain its natural cheerfulness if it isn't to be just silly. You can achieve any amount of seriousness

---

[7] See 'To those who come after', in Bertolt Brecht, *Selected Poems*, Grove Press, 1959, p. 177, and 'The mask of evil', p. 165.

[8] Bertolt Brecht, *The Messingkauf Dialogues*, XXXX, London 1965, pp.90, 94.

within such ease, none at all without it. A theatre that can't be laughed in is a theatre to be laughed at. Humourless people are ridiculous.

It is perhaps difficult to see exactly in what ways humour (rather than satire) is to be activated as an alternative to violence within a form of demonstration, as a means of revealing the contradictions of our society. We can recognise that a joke does bring together contradictions and may thereby reflectively reveal them, but how in practice do we 'enter by laughter rather than by argument'?

Laughter, at least satirical laughter, has not been absent from the arena of protest, however. In England, the recent line from *TW3* through *Private Eye* to Alf Garnett and *If there weren't any blacks we'd have to invent them*; in the States, Dick Gregory standing for President, the mocking applause for Wallace as the sole way to silence him; in the Sorbonne, the absurd slogans (*Je suis un marxiste—après Groucho*). Laughter sheerly by itself can infect even one's opponent: the anti-Nixon TV advert in the presidential campaign which simply showed a beaming Nixon with the sound-track: 'This man for President'—followed by a pause, then a low chuckle rising to hilarious laughter; or the brief moments during the Cambridge installation of a Vice-Chancellor when a tape-recording of *Goon Show* laughter began to infect even the staid and solemn (ridiculous) procession itself.

Such attempts can only hope for precarious success but are symptoms of a style of protest that should perhaps be particularly attractive to Christians who are socialists. If socialism is allied to a relaxed being-with, to care and concern and 'grace', as capitalism is linked to a tensed being-against, to dominance and will-power, then the appropriate life-style of a socialist is surely more one of joy, relaxation, humour—and the necessary reflection of that in the kind of demonstration, protest and criticism he or she engages in: the medium is part of the message, the life-style is part of the critique.

This does not preclude sheer hard work nor does it ignore insistent daily tragedy—the interstices and disjunctions are just as available for tragic dislocation as for comic absurdity. But it does lay an emphasis relevant to a *Slant* that once had a reputation for a certain kind of humour—an emphasis on imaginativeness, on laughter-making as well as on love-making instead of anger-provoking as a mode of protest. The Dialectics of Liberation Congress sought to explore and to some extent establish as an available style some of these connections. Indeed, David Cooper's characteristic question at congress-style discussion groups, 'What would unify this group?' can most positively be answered by: 'A joke. '

*

One could continue even *ad nauseam* about jokes: their relation to the unconscious, naturally, but also to the wonder that Charles Hartshorne finds at the basis of belief (the problem of beauty—what Stendhal defined as the promise of happiness—rather than the problem of evil), or even jokes in the Old and New Testament (Jonah, the Samson tales, the man born blind in John, or the fig-tree told to dry up), but it is more important at this stage briefly to go back and qualify an earlier statement.

There is, as I remarked, something basically shared in the humour of a period, yet, equally obviously, jokes can be among the most private areas of language: one has to be 'in' on the joke, which often means being 'in' the group which makes the joke, the 'in-joke.' One might, for example, have to be a fairly regular reader of *Slant* to recognise immediately that T.E.'s report of the 'Anti-Medicine Congress' (*Slant* 22) was a joke. Mis-reading the extent to which a group shares the presuppositions of your joke can lead to simply being 'fool-ish'. This obviously raises further problems for any strategic use of humour, but, more positively, it can lead directly into the second connected area of possible response to the original problem of mediation between theory and practice.

Freud, in his *Five Lectures on Psycho-Analysis* [9] tells a joke about two wealthy but crooked businessmen who have had their portraits painted by a well-known artist and hold a reception to unveil them.

> The two hosts themselves led the most influential connoisseur and art critic up to the wall on which the portraits were hanging side by side, in order to extract his admiring judgment on them. He studied the works for a long time and then, shaking his head, as though there was something he had missed, pointed to the gap between the pictures and asked quietly, 'But where's the Saviour?'

Freud comments that the connoisseur made a remark that seems at first sight strangely inappropriate and irrelevant but which we recognise a moment later as an allusion, to the insult he had in mind and as a perfect substitute for it.

This seems to me a fairly apposite way of describing the liturgical activity of Christians: an activity which at first sight seems strangely inappropriate and irrelevant. If you like, the liturgy is a kind of family joke, the point of which is rather lost on an outsider: during a meal someone picks up a piece of bread and says 'This is my body'—it must be some kind of a joke. One could say of the liturgy, as of other people's 'in-jokes', what Wittgenstein says of dreams: [10]

> It is characteristic of dreams that often they seem to . . call for an interpretation. There seems to be something in dream images that has a certain resemblance to the signs of a language. As a series of marks on paper or sand might have. There might be no mark which we recognised as a conventional sign in any alphabet we knew, and yet we might have a strong feeling that they must be a language of some sort: that they must mean something.

[9] S. Freud, *Two Short Accounts of Psycho-Analysis*, Pelican, 1962, p. 57.
[10] Wittgenstein, *Lectures and Conversations*, Oxford 1966, 45.

Wittgenstein continues, interestingly:

> When a dream is interpreted we might say that it is
> fitted into a context in which it ceases to be puzzling.
> In a sense the dreamer re-dreams his dream in
> surroundings such that its aspect changes.

A family joke perhaps reverses this: it is often the re-telling
or re-performance of an original situation, which requires
knowledge of the original situation to make sense of it, to
respond appropriately by laughter: it relates back to and recalls a remembered significant situation in which the
particular point was first made in quite that way. In the case
of Christians this originating situation is the life and death of
'Jesus the Christ': the liturgy is a kind of memorial of his
transitus. (In this connection it may not be irrelevant to
recall Marx's qualification of Hegel in the *Eighteenth Brumaire*:
'Hegel observed somewhere that all great historical events
and individuals occur in a manner of speaking twice over.
He omitted to add: once as tragedy, the second time as
farce.')

In recent years, however, the emphasis on rediscovering
the eucharist as 'encounter with Christ in his transitus' has
rather obscured the pre-requirement of encounter with
Christ that traditional theology locates first in the sacrament
of baptism; it is primarily in baptism that we are taken up
into his death, that we die and rise with him; and it is, or
should be, that dying and rising—our own dying and rising
as well as, and in, his—that we recall and celebrate, re-affirm
as well as expect, in our eucharistic activity. So strongly
does the church emphasise this that for a non-baptised
person to take part in the eucharist is, traditionally, a non-
viable action. It strikes me that one of the pressing problems
in the revival of Christian life in the catholic body in this
country is the need to locate and root catholics in some lived
experience of what it means to be, or come, together in
Christ, and I would suggest that it should be in a revival of
baptismal theology and practice that such a rooting
experience should be located. Yet for many catholics their
baptism is simply not a crucial experience they recall in the
eucharist (despite Easter renewals of baptismal promises,

etc.). The consequences, for ecclesial existence and structure, of attempting to make it so could be many, and moreover link directly to problems of a Christian left strategy.

For a socialist Christian what sort of experience should 'baptism' be? Obviously, in some sense, on any contemporary theology of baptism, it should be entry into a community; but a socialist would immediately want to insist that the church cannot and must not exist as a self-sufficient community, in a privatised, narcissistic way; at most it must be, as the eucharist is, an inter-mittent community, acknowledging as its context the absence of adequate community in the world as a whole. The 'church' of the baptised must not be a society parallel and alternative to ordinary society, with its own schools, buildings, territorial divisions, diplomats, etc.; but rather be a detour (perhaps akin to that crucial detour which is theology), an exit-and-return, neither an opting out nor an opting in, but a way of coming to see in a changed way the actual ordinary society in which one does, ordinarily, live.

Obviously, these are now generally available ideas, shared by many, and practical attempts have been made in recent years to recapture something of the essential relation between baptism and the Christian body as a whole; with the reintroduction of baptism during the eucharist, especially the Easter eucharist, a sense of incorporation has been given. But the Christian project is not, after all, in my view, so much an incorporation into some pre-existing community, as the worked-through attempt to make community together—admittedly linked to a base in a continuing, wider community of communities. The wanderings of the Israelite people—a collection of liberated tribes becoming a people—is our model for this, traditionally and liturglcally, but we can also give some account of this process in various available secular and socialist terms.

Research on autistic children has clearly shown the extent to which personality develops through active response, by the experience of provoking reactions, from bawling for food to talking.[11] Yet once the establishment of self-certainty has been achieved through response, that element of response begins to enter a new phase, one given its basic description by Hegel in the section on 'Lordship and Bondage' in the *Phenomenology of Mind*. Marx developed his basic analysis of alienation from this passage, while Williams's term 'the dominatlve mode' clearly recalls it. But for Williams 'un-learning' the dominative mode, like any other process of seeing things in a new and fully appropriated way, involves a reorganisation of experience that is a real kind of pain, a sort of death.[12]

> It is . . to every man, a matter of urgent personal importance to 'describe' his experience, because this is literally a remaking of himself, a creative change in his personal organisation, to include and control the experience. This struggle to remake ourselves—to change our personal organisation so that we may live in a proper relation to our environment—is in fact often painful. Many neurologists would now say that the stage before description is achieved, the state of our actual organisation before new sensory experience is comprehended, the effort to respond adequately while the new experience is still disorganised and disturbing, is biologically identical with what we call physical pain.

I would want to argue that baptism should today be, literally, a process experienced by a group, a process of growth-together towards genuine being-with as an overcoming in common of master-slave patterns of relationship, an un-learning of the dominative mode. It would thereby, necessarily, involve a real kind of death, what both Hegel and the New Testament call a losing of one's life—of that ego-centric area we jealously, tensely, guard as ours and ours alone. Further, as Terry Eagleton has put it in discussing, not baptism, where I would want to locate the process primarily, but the eucharist :

---

[11] See also Jacques Lacan, 'Phase of the Mirror,' *New Left Review*, 51, and R. D. Laing's discussions of 'ontological security'.
[12] Raymond Williams, *The Long Revolution*, London 1961, p. 26.

Barriers—the existence of other subjects as threats to the free autonomy of the self—become horizons: other subjects become the language of individual identity, the syntax of a we-being. [*Slant* 22]

That dying and rising to each other in a process of communal baptism has three further aspects to it, each of which has a theological resonance.

*

Williams, in speaking of the actual pain of re-organising one's experience, had directly in mind the attempt to describe adequately one's experience. This, clearly, is an element present throughout the process I have sketchily indicated. In particular, it is precisely and only in interpersonal relations, the specifically human situations, that we can, as children, learn how to use such non-ostenslve words as 'perhaps' and 'if', 'today' and 'maybe', those words which characterise a specifically human experience, that, for example, of time not just as duration but as expectation and intention. We need the experience for the language to 'mean' anything to us. Wittgenstein makes the further point that a shared conception of truth points basically beyond or through a shared language to a shared form of life:[13]

It is what human beings say that is true or false; and they agree in the language they use. That is not agreement in opinions but in form of life.

The process of reaching baptism communally, creating a baptised community, could be described in terms of holding a conversation in establishing a common form of life— learning the Christian language, appropriating the Word.

---

[13] Ludwig Wittgenstein, *Philosophical Investigations*, 241.

Lacan's description in *Écrits* of a psychoanalytic cure also links the overcoming of alienating self-other relations and the 'conversation' of the 'talking cure':

> The subject begins by speaking about himself without speaking to you, or by speaking to you without speaking about himself; when he is able to speak to you about himself, the analysis will be finished.

When we can learn to speak genuinely to one another as Christians we may begin to realise what the Christian language means. Paul Connerton has made the point that we need to feel our way into a grasp of 'a cluster of resonant words' that are peculiarly the product of a specific age in order to share its characteristic world-view. Being baptised involves grasping, as means of communication, certain key Christian terms (not in isolation, as single entities, but as crucial foci of the whole Christian language-game), terms like 'God', 'grace' and 'resurrection', phrases like 'he who raised the Christ from the dead', 'this is my body' and 'till he comes' —terms in the same mode as 'if', 'perhaps', 'possibly', and so on: we need the experience in order to need the language.

For a Christian these must presumably resonate beyond the language available from other traditions and areas of experience. It seems to me that, for example, Terry Eagleton's recent articles on the eucharist[14] are, from one angle, exploring the inadequacies of the marxist response to Marx's own analysis of the root phenomenological alienations in the 1844 *Economic and Philosophical Manuscripts*, and the extent to which a 'resurrection' language meets those inadequacies. But the basic Christian language is intimately linked to the sacramental articulation of Christianity: what the Christian is 'trying to mean' beyond what can be described in terms drawn from other traditions, is ultimately expressible only in symbols and action: baptism

---

[14] See Terry Eagleton, 'Language, reality and the eucharist', *Slant* 21, June-July 1968, 18-23, and *Slant* 22, Aug-Sept 1968, pp 26-31.

leads naturally into the eucharist, through the creed. (There are, of course, further problems I cannot here discuss: particularly that of horizontal and vertical continuity between groups who have, in personal ways, appropriated the Christian language: hence the problems of conciliar definition, of ecumenism, of heresy, of ecclesial structures and the sacrament of structure or order—indeed, in the New Testament writings themselves, the presence of different '*Sitz im Leben,*' group-rooted, theologies).

*

Sharing the Christian language means sharing a mode of life. Learning the Christian language involves overcoming the dominative mode of life, coming through to a way of being characterised by forgiveness, openness, relaxation, listening. The early Heidegger puts this in typically Heideggerian fashion:[15]

> Listening to . . is Dasein's existential way of Being-open as Being-with for others. Indeed hearing constitutes the primary and authentic way in which Dasein is open for its own-most potentiality for being. Being-with develops in listening to one another.

But in his later writings he, too, is beginning to find a more adequate language for the mode of life and awareness one is postulating here:[16]

> Our relation to technology will become wonder-fully relaxed and simple. I would call this comportment towards technology which expresses 'yes' and at the same time 'no' by an old word: releasement towards things: *Die Gelassenheit zu den Dingen.* [*Gelassenheit* is the word used by Meister Eckhart for composure, calmness, unconcern and specifically for 'letting the world go for God']. Releasement towards things and openness to the mystery grant us the possibility of dwelling in the world in a totally different way. They

---

[15] Martin Heidegger, *Being and Time*, Oxford 1967, p. 206.
[16] Heidegger, *Discourse on Thinking*, New York, 1966, p. 54].

promise us a new ground and foundation upon which we can stand and endure in the world of technology without being imperilled by it.

Lonergan too has his own characteristic comment, in the remarks on 'Openness and Religious Experience' in *Collection*[17]—though my context would take them beyond the concentration on the individual and on primarily intellectual openness:

> Openness as a fact is the pure desire to know. It is referred to by Aristotle when he speaks of the wonder that is the beginning of all science and philosophy. Besides openness as a primordial fact, there also is openness as achievement, which is the self in its self-appropriation and self-realisation.

But an important element in the Hegelian master-slave relationship is the mediation of things, material reality. Any adequate coming-together in Christ—as a lived, group experience—might also involve the attempt to establish a common, if temporary, material environment for the group: creating an at-homeness. One's own room, a room of one's own, is a kind of me-everywhere: insofar as you have personally chosen the colour scheme and the furniture, the carpet and the curtains, the room is you insofar as such things can express you—you are at home there; marriage involves building a shared home; a common culture would be a society in which such public meanings had been created, in which there was a kind of we-everywhere situation, actually in terms of the architecture, the material environment, even the street furniture (compare the role of advertising hoardings in present capitalist society). It is perhaps in this light that we ought to re-consider our notions of the *ecclesia*, the church, as a building of God's home for those called out to meet in him.

These two elements in the baptising experience relate to another, to the term Sartre uses for scarcity, the central feature of our present pre-resurrection situation; to be *de trop*

---

[17] Bernard Lonergan, *Collection*, London 1966, p. 186.

also means to be unwelcome, to be, as Sartre says, one too many, to be an unwanted guest, not to be at home, to feel out of place. There is an interesting link here between the kind of situation I have sketched and one way in which it seems possible to make some sense of the resurrection: if the crucial fact is that we do not die any more, that death has been overcome, this reflects back on our existence: we are no longer being-towards-death, time is no longer scarce, we are not 'in a hurry' with no time for others, we are relaxed, at home, open, available for the exploration of each other, able to enjoy, laugh, play. Insofar as being baptised means experiencing something of what resurrection means, it is perhaps along these lines that we should seek it (and this would clearly involve the creative use of the contemporary arts as part of the sacramental experience—a feature notably absent in much heavily-theologised liturgical 'renewal').

These are only sketchy ideas, meant to root the argument for fundamental change in baptismal procedures within the wider perspective demanded by the richness of the theological penumbra round baptism, and it would be relatively easy to pursue such ideas into other fields of Christian experience. For example, seminaries could be seen precisely as communities learning a language, in the worked-through experience of establishing a common form of life, with crucial emphasis on encounters with those human situations (now accounted for in what is tepidly termed 'pastoral practice') which force us, painfully, to re-organise our slack and half-honest reactions to people, to question deeply the adequacy of our language (including our automatic Christian language) to negotiate the human experiences of illness, crime, poverty, deprivation and death, anxiety, loneliness and madness.

*

We can return directly to the discussion of baptism by recalling the statement: 'Wherever two or three are gathered in my name, I will be present to them'. The experience of forging presence to each other in forgiveness and acceptance would, if the Christian belief in the presence of the risen Christ has any validity, mean that Christ would in some sense be present to that group: among the meanings they would 'in part receive, in part re-create' would be an ability to talk of and to 'what we call God'. But we have already seen that the church of the baptised cannot be self-enclosed and static: the creation of a limited community, in the baptismal group, should not become an attempt at a permanent home; the group must deliberately dissolve its own achieved community. But what then would be the relation between the experience of the baptismal group and the after-life of the baptised, if you like, between 'being baptised' and 'the faith of the church'?

Perhaps we can put the matter in these terms. The presence of Christ to the group is from one angle a precarious presence: it rests on their presence to each other. When the group breaks up, dissolves (marking that dissolution by their first eucharist, perhaps), a kind of death of Christ is involved (the eucharist re-enacts his death). The best way I can convey what I mean here is by another quotation from Sartre (though, to reinforce a point made earlier, I think it is the language of the novelist rather than Sartre's own philosophical vocabulary that reaches us here):[18]

> I have an appointment with Pierre at four o'clock. I arrive at the café a quarter of an hour late. Pierre is always punctual. Will he have waited for me? I look at the room, at the patrons, and I say: He is not here. Is there an intuition of Pierre's absence? . . Do we not say: I suddenly saw that he was not there. Is this a matter of misplacing the negation? Let us examine this a little closer.
>
> In perception there is always the construction of a figure on a ground. No one object, no group of objects, is specially designed to be organised as specifically either figure or ground; all depends on the direction of my attention. When I enter the café to search for Pierre, there is formed a synthetic organisation of all the objects in the café, on the ground of which Pierre is given as

---

[18]   J-P. Sartre, *Being and Nothingness*, London 1957, p. 10.

about to appear. The original nihilation of all the figures which appear and are swallowed up in the total neutrality of the ground is the necessary condition for the appearance of the principal figure, which here is the person of Pierre. This nihilation is given to my intuition:

I am witness to the successive nihilation of all the objects I look at—in particular of the faces, which detain me for an instant (Could this be Pierre?) and which as quickly decompose precisely because they are not the face of Pierre. Nevertheless if I should finally discover Pierre, I should be suddenly arrested by his face and the whole café would organise itself around him as a discrete presence.

But now Pierre is not here. This does not mean that I discover his absence in any precise spot in the café. In fact Pierre is absent from the whole café; his absence fixes the café in its evanescence; the café remains ground; it persists in offering itself as undifferentiated totality to my only marginal attention; it makes itself ground for a determined figure; it carries the figure everywhere in front of it, presents the figure everywhere to me. The figure which skips constantly between my look and the solid real objects of the café is precisely a perpetual disappearance! It is Pierre raising himself as nothingness on the ground of the nihilation of the café. It serves as the foundation for the judgment: Pierre is not here. My expectation has caused the absence of Pierre to happen as a real event concerning this café.

This should, among other things, remind us that the initial Easter-day statement is 'He is not here' and that the initial eschatologlcal statement is 'This is not the Christ', when men say 'He is here, he is there'— indeed, that the initial pericope of John's gospel is also concerned with this kind of statement: 'When the Jews sent priests and Levites from Jerusalem to ask the Baptist, "Who are you?" he declared quite openly "I am not the Christ".' Heidegger's account of finding something missing is also apposite—and presumably underlies Sartre's account:[19]

> When something ready-to-hand is found missing, though its everyday presence has been so obvious that we have never taken any notice of it, this makes a break in those referential contexts which circumspection discovers. Our circumspection comes up against emptiness and for the first time now sees what the missing article was ready-to-hand with and what it was ready-to-hand for. The environment announces itself afresh.

A death in a family has precisely this effect: the patterns of relationship re-organise themselves, painfully; new roles are assumed, new responsibilities are undertaken, involving a new self-definition and self-awareness on the part of the remaining members. Christ's death and ascension forced the re-organisation of his disciples, to form a new body of Christ; Christ remains the 'unforgettable one' sought for, present now by his felt absence.

This experience of absence is akin to the effects of John Cage's early music of silence, particularly *Four Minutes and 33 Seconds* which forces us to realise and listen to the disorganised sounds which are the daily ground of our auditory existence; and also to certain kinds of abstract painting, which seem to offer us a ground that demands, but does not present a focussing figure. It is another way of putting what I have argued for in terms of 'focus' and 'totalisation' (*Slant* 22).

Faith is, then, not quite a state of mind, or a disposition, or an activity, but that peculiar human experience that comes between them: a searching for, an active seeking out, a being-on-the-alert, a concentration and expectation; it is an experience of the organised dis-order of this world, but a refusal of that negation as final: evil is an absence, the absence of the figure which orientates the ground.

---

[19] Heidegger, *Being and Time*, p. 105.

Faith is thereby akin to certain other specifically human experiences and activities of this nature. Valéry's approach to poetry, discussed by Marcuse in *One-Dimensional Man*, is concerned with an activity very like the sense of faith I am trying here to suggest:[20]

> Paul Valéry insists on the inescapable commitment of the poetic language to the negation. The verses of this language 'ne parlent jamais que de choses absentes'. They speak of that which, though absent, haunts the established universe of discourse and behaviour as its most tabooed possibility—neither heaven nor hell, neither good nor evil, but simply 'le bonheur'. Thus the poetic language speaks of that which is of this world, which is visible, tangible, audible in man and nature—and of that which is not seen, not touched, not heard. Creating and moving in a medium which presents the absent, the poetic language is a language of cognition—but a cognition which subverts the positive. In its cognitive function, poetry performs the great task of thought: 'Le travail qui fait vivre en nous ce qui n'existe pas'. Naming the 'things that are absent' is breaking the spell of the things that are; moreover it is the in-gression of a different order of things into the established one — 'le commencement d'un monde. '

With this we can link the passage from Barthes I used in the first part of this essay: 'a work of literature . . offers itself to the reader as a declared system of significance, but as a signified object it eludes his grasp', and, too, the remarks used earlier of Hamann (the wilderness that is full of hints and signs) and of Wittgenstein (the marks in the sand which produce 'a strong feeling that they must be a language of some sort').

---

[20] H. Marcuse, *One-Dimensional Man*, Sphere edition, London 1968, p. 66.

In *Zettel* [21] Wittgenstein often approaches the problems involved in this kind of activity. One can perhaps leave most of his remarks without comment: their theological resonance within this model should by now be clear enough.

> 67. An expectation is embedded in a situation from which it takes its rise . . .

> 68. Fulfilment of expectation doesn't consist in this: a third thing happens which can be described otherwise than as 'the fulfilment of this expectation', i.e., as a feeling of satisfaction or joy or whatever it may be. The expectation that some-thing will be the case is the same as the expectation of the fulfilment of that expectation. (Marginal note: Expectation of what is not).

> 54. It seems as if the expectation and the fact satisfying the expectation fitted together somehow. Now one would want to describe an expectation and a fact which fit together, so as to see what this agreement consists in. Here one thinks at once of the fitting of a solid into a corresponding hollow. But when one wants to describe these two one sees that, to the extent that they fit, a single description holds for both.

Obviously, in trying to make sense of faith along these lines I am also recalling Moltmann's argument in *Theology of Hope.* Again in *Zettel* (469), Wittgenstein tackles precisely the notion of hope in a way that recalls that process of learning key words in conversion through a shared form of life that I discussed earlier:

> Imagine someone saying 'Man hopes.' How should this general phenomenon of natural history be described?—One might observe a child and wait until one day he manifests hope; and then one could say 'Today he hoped for the first time.' But surely that sounds queer. Although it would be quite natural to

---

21 Wittgenstein, *Zettel*, Oxford, 1967.

say 'Today he said "I hope" for the first time.' And why queer?—One does not say that a suckling hopes that . . . nor yet that he has no hope that . . . and one does say it of a grown man—Well, bit by bit daily life becomes such that there is a place for hope in it.

*

If the experience of communal being-baptised were an available memory for us yet not a permanently available context for life (one is baptised only once), then the temper of our existence as Christians would be, precisely, one of expectation, of hope; looking for and remembering, occasionally celebrating. The church would be a movement, a movement towards, witnessing by its style of expectation.

Yet how are we to describe what such a movement would be compulsively looking for? In a sense, one would accept, with Heidegger, that 'in waiting-upon we leave open what we are waiting-for' (*Discourse on Thinking*, p. 68) but the ideas of 'being at home', in a we-everywhere situation expressed in the material environment as well as in 'being welcome', and of a state in which the figure of Christ, again visible in his parousia, most fully reveals to us the 'ground' of our being, the Father, have strong roots in the traditional notions of 'heaven' and the 'beatific vision.' In the *Summa*, (Ia, 12.3, ad 2) Aquinas quotes Augustine as follows:[22]

> It is extremely likely that we shall then see the bodies that make up the new heaven and the new earth in such a way as to see God present every-where in them, governing everything, even material things. We shall not merely see him as we now do when 'the invisible things of God are made known to us by the things he has made', but rather as we now see the life of the living breathing people we meet. The fact that they are alive is not something we come to believe in, but something we see.

---

[22] Aquinas, *Summa Theologiae*, Dominican English translation, volume 3, *Knowing and Naming God*, ed. Herbert McCabe, London 1964, p. 13. My emphasis.

That is the future. Is it even partially realised in the present: is the model of baptism I have sketched at all available now, in England? There are some scattered, concluding points to be made here.

In one sense, what I have been describing should surely be the real meaning of 'Christian education', a prolonged period in which we explore our relations to each other and the adequacy of our language for describing, and changing, those relations, as a way of learning what it is to be a Christian. In sheer practical terms, a massive redirection of our educational effort into what is beginning again to be called the catechumenate would be part of the programme here, but any programme based on this model would go much further than current plans for the catechumenate!

But it is hardly 'official programmes' that one is envisaging. If the church is genuinely to pass through a death and resurrection moment, this will involve the kind of re-patternings, re-definitions and emergence of a new self-awareness that were mentioned in relation to death above. It will mean that those who demand a changed church will have to realise themselves as being that changed church. To a perhaps surprising extent this is, simply, happening—in Holland, clearly; in the 'underground church' in the States; in England, in the growth of the informal 'institutions' cited by Herbert McCabe in that famous editorial— Spode House, the December Group, the Downside Symposia, *ad hoc* groups of various kinds, and, increasingly, in the para-liturgical groups and anti-parishes scattered across the country; *Slant* groups in particular might embody this model.

It is these groupings which come closest to the kind of baptismal format that I have in mind, and they have their secular parallels in attempts like Villa 21, in the kind of educational process envisaged by Williams in *The Long Revolution* which would include as crucial the experience of participation in democratic decision-making, and, in more specifically political terms, the emergence of *équipes* and communes and in the strategy of 'red bases' under consideration by activists in the German SDS, etc. In this connection it is perhaps amusing to quote a footnote in a recent discussion of 'red base' strategy in *New Left Review* 53, p. 31:

> Such a movement could enter not just the factories, but also the cultural institutions of the working class. For example, should it follow the example of the early Bolshevik party and send groups of specially trained comrades to work within the religious sects which have a working-class membership and elements of an anti-capitalist ideology?

Marcuse's argument at the 'Dialectics of Liberation Congress' also connects here: he maintains that the present stage of technological civilisation demands a revolutionary perspective that focusses on the creation of new needs, the need for a surpassing, in personal and group experience, of the dominative and aggressive urges in capitalist man.[23] (Fergus Kerr's recent articles in *New Blackfriars* have also examined some of the theological implications of this argument.) The history of radical protest in the 19th century is indeed riddled with backward glances into history, to the organic community or the rural idyll; today the problem remains: in Charles Taylor's terms, there is still no counter-environment in which to root one's experience of a fuller life; parties, sit-ins, picket-lines and marches are each limping experiences of that. If the church is the *Ur-Sacrament* in her structure, if her sacramental articulation is part of her communication of the word, then it is time we looked seriously at the potentialities of baptism for providing and rooting an experience of new needs, in the creation of being-with.

There are various strands remaining, but we can recapitulate briefly. The problem of mediating between theory and practice, analysis and action, is acute for *Slant*: the language it has adopted till now has been political philosophy; it needs to locate itself in order to talk

---

[23] See *Dialectics of Liberation*, Penguin, 1968.

adequately, through historico-sociological studies, but it also needs to use that more widely available mediating language of literary criticism. I have suggested too an exploration of the possibilities of laughter and humour, as a language, as counterpoint to the deadlock of violence; and finally, in a different sense of 'locating', if the church as a whole is to re-root itself in experiences which can sustain the socialist critique of society, then 'baptism' ought to be re-examined. What further links these last two areas is the realisation that no language, no argument, can now sufficiently erode the standpoint of the mystified (see Marcuse's notion of 'repressive tolerance'), but we can perhaps undercut and challenge, by laughter and by active experience of new needs, a new sense of the absent centre, our own and others' inadequate self-comprehension—which is where we start.

*

TOWARDS A POLITICAL THEOLOGY OF MARRIAGE:
—*Corruption Begins at Home?*

Anyone sensitive to symbolism must normally shudder at the words of eucharistic consecration. Not because of the current English translation. Something that cuts deeper: the priest takes the chalice and says: 'And when supper was ended, he took the cup, saying: This is my blood. . .' Most chalices are still lined with gold, a mark of respect, the most precious metal alone allowed to touch the consecrated wine. Yet that gold, enshrined at the heart of our celebration of love and peace, is also, still, at the base of the international monetary system. More specifically, it underpins the economy of South Africa, the world's largest gold-producing country: the blood that is relevant here is also the blood of apartheid. The hasty response, that a gold-lined cup is a mere container, can only be dubious in the light of a sacramental theology that recognizes the sign-value of form. More honest to admit the contradiction, acknowledge indeed the wider interlocking of the eucharistic community itself with that systematic exploitation revealed in a minor, everyday detail.

The other words of consecration, 'This is my body', have resonance for another sacrament: matrimony. Bellarmine traced a further echo: 'The sacrament of marriage . . is similar to the Eucharist, which likewise is a sacrament not only in the moment of its accomplishment, but also as long as it remains.'[1] But the eucharistic bread, one might argue, can decay and corrupt; it may not 'remain'. An opening, by analogy, towards divorce perhaps appears: individual relationships may cease adequately to measure up to the form of marriage; the core corrupts, the sign decays. Perhaps. But, further, what if the form, the shape and structure offered to receive the marriage, is already unfit? A

---

[1] *De Controversiis III (de Matrimonio)*, cont. 2, c. 6; quoted by Pius XI, *A.A.S.* 11 (1930), p. 583.

sharper parallel with the eucharist emerges, as we begin to ask political and theological questions in conjunction.

Political theology is still stuttering towards strategy, the practice of politics, seeking points of intersection. The current clash between Italian State and Italian Church over a Divorce Bill reminds us that marriage is such an intersection—the point at which Catholic ideology, the ordinary, everyday experience of most adult members of the Church, and a crucial political structure meet.[2]

That married life embodies ordinary, majority experience is important: the twin dangers of opposition strategy, either working towards a 'change of heart' without structural transformation, or labouring at legal reform and shifts in income-distribution without the creation of 'the new man' [sic], can only be avoided by mining the intermediate area, of lived experience. The incorporation of Labour Party 'parliamentary socialism' and Trades Union Congress 'organized labour', both lacking internal structures within which democracy and solidarity can be lived, is sufficient warning. Marriage is an activity which fuses an intensely personal and intimate experience and an immediate participation in a total social complex; it offers itself as an area in which 'new needs' may be generated, demanding transformed patterns of personal and social life.

Certain points about marriage and family, within the context of a political theology, are clear: for example, the use of metaphors drawn from family experience to block radical change: within a family modifications in individual's attitudes are normally adequate to overcome internal disagreements; if not, since the family is 'naturally' hierarchical, the only option is to leave. By speaking of Church and society as 'families', ecclesiastical and political leaders (themselves of course cast as father-figures) can play on deeply disabling mechanisms.[3]

---

[2] This article develops my concluding remarks in 'Revolutionary Intersections?', *The Newman*, 5, 3, July 1970.

[3] See T. Eagleton and A. Cunningham, ed. *Slant Manifesto*, 1966, pp. 42-45; A. Cunningham, in *The Christian Priesthood*, 9th Downside Symposium, ed. N. Lash and J. Rhymer, 1970, pp. 261-3.

More specifically, in England, the role of 'the Catholic marriage' in preserving not just a 'unity of faith' but an adult life held within the sub-group confines of a still 'immigrant' body (that being the presumed basis for a retained faith) parallels the similar function, for children, underlying the Catholic educational system. Monica Lawlor has reminded us of how highly 'keeps the marriage laws of the Church' can rate as a (theoretical) criterion of 'the good Christian' in English Catholics' value-systems—and also how much higher than by adult Catholics this criterion is rated by Catholic schoolgirls raised in that educational system.[4]

As with most characteristic organizational forms of an immigrant social group caught uneasily between assimilation and self-preservation, 'Catholic' marriages are differentiated from other marriages in English society by some marginal aspects (particularly in the socially invisible sphere of contraception) but in general conform to the standard model offered in England of the normal marriage. And that is where the precise question of this article is located.

We tend both to accede to and yet be slightly jolted by the obviously economic treatment of marriage in, say, a description of Bedouin marriage:

> The more settled the domicile, the stricter are their conditions of ownership. Therefore, among the half-Bedouin (small livestock-breeders) and those of fixed abode, the economic bonds of the family-group are firmer than among the full Bedouin (camel-breeders), and much more stress is laid on the bride-price than among the latter. Because of the higher bride-price, divorce is more difficult and less frequently resorted to among the nomads than among the Bedouin. On the other hand, the high bride-price easily becomes an object of tribal speculation, and therefore tends to prevent freedom of choice in marriage, which is more prevalent among the full Bedouin.[5]

---

[4] M. Lawlor, *Out of this World*, 1965, pp. 71-73.
[5] Quoted by J. F. Thiel, in *Concilium*, May 1970, p. 15. The whole issue (vol. 5, no. 6) is devoted to 'The future of marriage as an institution'.

Yet we characteristically take Western European forms of marriage for granted, part of the 'natural' way of life, the economic ramifications mentally invisible. Christians happily equate 'Christian marriage' with Western European forms, forgetting the long process of gradual fusion that had to take place in this area of life when Christianity was imported into Europe—forgetting it, particularly, when we try to export European marriage-forms as part of a package-deal Christianity. Many missionaries are now acutely concerned with this problem.[6]

But awareness of what one might call horizontal plurality in forms of marriage also raises the question of historically vertical plurality: would we be happy, now, to sacramentalize a form of marriage which seemed culturally and socially out of date, were it proposed—would a parish priest now be willing to have solemnized in the parish church a marriage which was clearly an 'arranged' marriage in the sense in which some mediaeval and Victorian marriages were? More interestingly, what would be his reaction to a proposed marriage which was felt to be culturally 'in advance' of the present accepted forms—and on what criteria do we judge such a claim?

That last question is, clearly, part of the wider question of the criteria of general social advance. One tradition concerned with such problems is the Hegelian-Marxist-Leninist line, and it is at least interesting that one of the earliest passages in Hegel where one finds the germ of his later concern with surpassing master-slave relations, in all their complexity, is in a fragment 'On Love' in his early theological writings.[7] Marx, in his early philosophical and economic writings, not only developed the analysis of master-slave relations generally, but also pinpointed marriage as a central index of social development:

> The immediate, natural, necessary relationship of human being to human being is the relationship of man to woman. In this natural species-relationship man's relationship to

---

[6] E. Hillmann, 'The development of Christian marriage structures', *Concilium*, V. 6.

[7] Hegel, *Early Theological Writings*, Harper edition, p. 304ff.

nature is immediately his relationship to man, as his relationship to man is immediately his relationship to nature, to his own natural condition. In this relationship the extent to which the human essence has become nature for man or nature has become the human essence of man is sensuously manifested, reduced to a perceptible fact. . . In this relationship is also apparent the extent to which man's need has become human, thus the extent to which the other human being, as human being, has become a need for him, the extent to which he in his most individual existence is at the same time a social being. . . From this relationship one can thus judge the entire level of mankind's development.[8]

In the early phase of the Russian Revolution, this last sentence was given a practical edge by some socialists, in experimenting with various forms of marriage—though the more important factor in the temporary shaking of traditional marriage foundations was arguably the Civil War; by the time of Lenin's death, the older forms had recovered.[9]

Among the several kinds of reason for the extremely short-lived nature of this experimentation in new forms of relationship (not least of which was Lenin's opposition to 'free love' as bourgeois), it could be argued that the need for a stable economic unit during the New Economic Policy was an important underlying factor. In post-revolutionary China the attempt to forge a new economic unit, while respecting and maintaining traditional forms of marriage, resulted in the Agricultural Producers' Cooperatives (1955-57), then the Commune system (1958 onwards). But the tensions between traditional forms of 'personal' relationships and new social-economic structures has put obvious strains on this attempt; only in the course of many generations can such tensions be resolved; a 'cultural revolution' may be one means of forcing the

---

[8] *Writings of the Young Marx on Philosophy and Society*, ed. Eastern and Guddat, p. 303. The awkward use of generic 'man' here needs no comment.

[9] Cf. E. H. Carr, *Socialism in One Country 1924-3926*, Penguin ed. 1970, I, 37-48; Sheila Rowbotham: 'Alexandra Kollantai', *The Spokesman*, nos. 4, 5.

pace.[10] The same elements of tension and strain in a post-revolutionary situation are beautifully presented in Tomas Alea's film from Cuba, *Memories of Underdevelopment*, in which a relationship between an intellectual bourgeois and an unsophisticated Cuban girl is presented as both index to and metaphor of the wider problems of Cuban advance.

Obviously, however, family-structures are interlocked with economic and political problems not only in revolutionary situations. Among black Americans, the interaction between matriarchal patterns, male unemployment, divorce rates, loss of ancillary earning relatives, domestic tensions from ghetto conditions, and the 1967 'riots' has been clearly brought out.[11] The role of particular conceptions of the 'decent' family in maintaining the dominant conservative 'milieu' of Western Germany is a theme in Carl Amery's *Capitulation*. In Britain the general situation with regard to the political role of the family-home is, it seems to me, very close to that in Western Germany. It is this general British situation that I now want to sketch, as a prelude to raising again the theological question. We can then, perhaps, approach the problem of how marriage might serve as a political activator among the Christian minority in England.

In Britain we are all aware of some of the general interlocking between the 'domestic' area and the social, economic, political system as a whole. But a reminder of some broad connections might be useful. For example, the present Tory Government's policy of cuts in private taxation at the expense of public and welfare services clearly militates against the low-income, 'lower'-class families, and acts in favour of high-income, middle-class families. The differences in sources of family income, degree of dependence on welfare services and proportion of income spent on domestic necessities makes this clear.[12]

---

[10] See, for example, *China Readings 3*, ed. F. Schurmann and O. Schell, Penguin, 1968, pp. 87, 176-188, 452.

[11] See *Report of the National Advisory Commission on. Civil Disorders*, Bantam, 1968, pp. 251-265,280.

[12] See *Trade Union Register I*, 1969: John Hughes, A Note on Low Pay, pp. 133-138, and Table 3: Household income and expenditure, pp. 334-335. Cf. also the arguments of the Child Poverty Action Group—e.g.

Class differences in family income and expenditure are related to the role of the family in the class structure generally: parental occupation is, still, a main index of social class. At one end of the social pyramid 'family connections' and 'family firms' still permeate dominant sectors of society.[13] At the other, we have the 'home-centred society', to which not only expenditure but leisure is increasingly oriented, resulting in the narrow circle: more comfortable home, so more leisure spent in home, especially in watching TV, which in turn—through domestic consumption advertising and the pervasive models of 'the home' present in plays, comedy, serials and toothless 'family viewing' generally—reinforces the urge for domestic expenditure and home-centred activity.[14] This further encourages 'housewives' to enter employment, for the sake of 'the home', so that the main group of working women now are wives, and by 1973 one estimate puts the total at nine million, of whom over 60 per cent will be married.[15]

This perhaps indicates an interesting minor contradiction in the present system: though most girls are still geared towards marriage as the obvious and natural main role of adult life[16] (and women who are restricted to domestic concerns, besides providing an immense unpaid labour-service,[17] tend also to

---

in *Poverty* No. 7 and *BRPF London Bulletin* No. 18; also K. Coates and R. Wilburn, *Poverty: The Forgotten Englishman*, Penguin Special, 1970.

[13] 30 per cent of the top 116 U.K. companies still have family boards. See M. Barratt Brown, 'The Controllers of British Industry', in *Can the Workers Run Industry?* Sphere & Institute for Workers Control, 1968.

[14] See M. Abrams, 'The Home-Centred Society', *The Listener*, 26 Nov. 1959; R. Fletcher, *The Family and Marriage in Britain*, 1966, ch. 5; J.H. Goldthorpc, et al.. *The Affluent Worker in the Class Structure*, 1969, esp. pp. 50, 99-105, 152-53.

[15] See H. Gavron, *The Captive Wife*, 1968, p. 43. For class differences in motivations of working wives, cf. pp. 112, 117f, 125f.

[16] T. Veness, *School Leavers*, 1962.

[17] Figures are not available for U.K., but one estimate for Sweden points out that while industry uses 1,290 million labour-hours annually, housewives donate 2,340 million unpaid domestic labour-hours annually.

provide the Conservative Party with a crucial habitual vote),[18] nevertheless as more women enter paid employment and become unionized, besides raising the important issue of equal pay, their electoral support for the Conservatives should wither.[19] Perhaps then we would not have a Tory Government so busily cutting family social services.

This point of contradiction is not, however, a very pressing one: it is simply an aspect of the general contradiction in capitalism between consumption and production, and for the most part the family and 'the home' serve not to exacerbate social contradictions but to mute them, to maintain them at a non-explosive level. Some of the specific ways in which the family currently maintains economic and political 'stability' are worth noticing. For example, in terms of the production/consumption contradiction at a very simple level, the role of 'the wife' is partly to provide a domestic manager who will desperately 'make ends meet' (often at cost to herself in food, health, personal spending money, time) in a situation of wage-depression, partly to provide economic slack to be taken up when production booms. But the most general contribution of the family to the maintenance of political stability and stagnation is its socialization function for children; in the present society, as Ralph Miliband points out:

> The working-class family tends to attune its children in a multitude of ways to its own subordinate status. And even where, as is now ever more frequently the case, working-class parents are ambitious for their children, the success for which they hope and strive is mostly conceived in terms of integration at a higher level within the system and on the latter's own terms; and this is most likely to lead them to try to persuade their children that the path to success lies not in

---

[18] See figures in P. Anderson, *Towards Socialism*, 1965, pp. 276-277. Without the female vote, England would have had a continuous Labour government since 1945.

[19] See Janet Blackman, 'The Campaign for Women's Rights', in *Trade Union Register I*; for the effect of unionization on voting, cf. Anderson, p. 262f.

rebellion against but in conformity to the values, prejudices and modes of thought of the world to which entry is sought.[20]

Within this general pattern, various mechanisms can operate, below the level of any specific intention. The narrowly privatized home described by the Goldthorpe team in Luton reduces any political or trade union awareness to a minimum, leaving only a passive acceptance and inactive expectation of collective 'integration at a higher level', and a limited perspective on individual advance.[21] This connects with traditional working-class passive acceptance of neighbourhood groups, leaving no tradition of the social skills necessary actively to establish new relationships in a changed setting.[22] More deeply, the absence of those social skills is closely related to the generation by certain family-structures and patterns of parental authority, typical among the working class, of importantly restricted linguistic capacities, the confinement of perception and expression within an immediate 'world', an inability to make the necessarily complex connections involved in grasping our society as a whole.[23]

It is in the interacting combination of all these factors, with the working-class family home as their meeting point, that one could most feasibly locate the wide-spread political apathy of the working class in Britain over the last generation or so. In other words, the characteristic British family-structure, far from contributing to political disturbance, as in the case of an oppressed minority in America, operates mainly to maintain ingrained inaction among a subordinate and complacent majority.

---

[20] R. Miliband, *The State in Capitalist Society*, 1969, pp. 263-4.

[21] Goldthorpe, *et al.*, *op. cit.*, ch. V, pp. 116-156.

[22] See J. M. Mogey, *Family and Neighbourhood*, 1956, and Richard Hoggart, *Uses of Literacy*, 1957. Gavron, *op. cit.*, ch. 11, 'Social Contacts', and Goldthorpe, *op. cit.*, ch. 4, 'The pattern of sociability'.

[23] See Basil Bernstein's work, most easily available in the Routledge series *Primary Socialization, Language and Education*, or, summarizing the work up to 1967, D. Lawton, *Social Class, Language and Education*, 1969.

At this point the theological question re-emerges. If it were a case, say, of a specific family which was clearly generating acute psychological disorientations in its children,[24] it would seem distinctly odd to claim that this family was a 'means of grace' or 'a point of entry of God's love into the world'; if one could reasonably predict that a particular marriage would produce schizophrenics, it might be questionable whether one could confidently solemnize such a marriage as a sacrament of grace. For anyone concerned with developing a fusion between theology and revolutionary socialism (and I presume that many readers of *New Blackfriars* would at least respect that option), the wider question presses: whether, given the role of the family sketched above, some current theological reflections on marriage can be endorsed at all.

How, in this light, can we accept, for example, Edward Schillebeeckx's remarks that 'never before in the history of man has married life been led back in such a remarkable way to its original, authentic shape and form as it has today', that marriage as a sacrament is 'a sacred sign' in which 'God's activity becomes visible to us all in faith' and that it can be 'the appointed means of revealing and expressing, in a human religious manner, God's covenant of grace with men in Christ'?[25] Or Denis O'Callaghan's conclusion:

> As a human institution marriage associates man and woman in a family unit in which they achieve their identity and fulfilment and rear new life to responsible adulthood in an atmosphere of loving communion. As a Christian institution marriage is a sacramental and consecrated state in which the various elements of natural wedlock are given a redeeming force and are directed towards the realization of the Kingdom of God. Against this background marriage consent

---

[24] See R. D. Laing's work, especially *Sanity, Madness and the Family*, 1964.

[25] E. Schillebeeckx, *Marriage: Secular Reality and Saving Mystery*, 1965, vol. I, pp. 1, 18, 170.

is the dedication of man and woman in partnership to a Christian mission in Church and world.[26]

Even fairly recent theological writing on marriage has tended to see only the internal problems (mainly contraception).[27] O'Callaghan at least is more concerned with the role of marriage in the realization of the kingdom, but his article seems to ignore almost all other problems.[28]

Schillebeeckx is aware of the problem of marriage-structure, but his theological comments echo a 'change of heart' strategy: the christianization of marriage is, for him: 'the making Christian, not of the secular structure of marriage, but of its natural and human inter-relationships, although these are always experienced within ordinary secular patterns of life', and 'permeated by Christian charity, the ordinary secular relationships of the family were not cancelled out, but subjected to a complete metamorphosis. Love achieved authority.' It is significant for our point that Schillebeeckx then adds: 'A parallel process took place in the "natural" relationship of the master to the slave existing in the society of those days. This relationship too was inwardly transformed by Christian love—it became so permeated by the new spirit that in the long run, with the coming of new economic situations, slavery itself could be abolished. '[29]

Whatever truth there may be in this emphasis, we need —just as in the case of slavery—to take more seriously the form of the institution of marriage as such; we cannot take a family squabble as the model for restructuring the form of the family itself.

At present, much of the debate in the Church is centred on celibacy and contraception, both of which are only fully intelligible in the context of two wider debates: on the connection between the mission and structure of the Church in

---

[26] 'Marriage as Sacrament', *Concilium*, V. 6, p. 103.

[27] For example, L. M. Weber, *On Marriage, Sex and Virginity, Quaestiones Disputatae 16*, 1964.

[28] Vatican II's rhetoric on marriage is equally irrelevant—e.g. *Documents of Vatican II*, ed. Abbot, pp. 249-258.

[29] Schillebeeckx, *op. cit.*, vol. I, p. 197-199.

relation to secular structures, and on the nature of marriage itself. If we take seriously the notion of marriage as 'directed towards the realization of the Kingdom of God', those two wider debates begin to fuse. If celibacy is claimed as 'superior' to marriage because, either 'theologically' or practically, it is regarded as more appropriate to a life directed towards the kingdom, then it is possible to respond in terms of an emphasis on marriage more theologically and practically directed towards the kingdom. Yet our present theology of marriage is largely irrelevant to any practical concern with building anything more than a private 'kingdom upon earth', while our practice of marriage conforms utterly to the modes sketched earlier. Can we attempt to see beyond these present forms and debates? This article is concerned to suggest a fresh context rather than to present a fully worked-through 'solution', but at least one can begin.

From flirtation to communion—via communes?

It is already possible to see some of the political significance of contraception and celibacy: the argument that the absence of a fear of unwilled propagation, of offering an involuntary 'hostage to the State', has already had its deep psychological impact on Reich-minded students, releasing them towards the 'festival of the oppressed' in the Paris *événements*, is familiar; so is the spectacle of South American guerillas embracing celibacy or North Amerian blacks rejecting a married Stokely Carmichael. Other political connections with 'the family' assert themselves: we should obviously take seriously both the Women's Liberation Movements and the 'generational conflict' as potential levers.[30]

Each of these is concerned with 'liberation' and if we look more closely at two 'liberation zones' in present English society,

---

[30] See the ironic 'Discourse on Birth Control', by Ipousteguy, in *Reflections on the Revolution in France, 1968* ed. C. Posner, 1970; Juliet Mitchell, 'Women; the longest revolution', *New Left Review* 40; Sheila Rowbotham, *Women's Liberation and the New Politics*, May Day Manifesto Pamphlet no. 4; E. R. Leach, *A Runaway World?*, 1968, ch. 3; etc.

a more immediate opening appears. For many people the period between school and marriage remains in memory as a brief interlude of peculiar freedom; parties crystallize and later re-enact that sensation. What both that period and parties share is an element of flirtation, a flexing or exercising of relational skills. But flirtation and serious courting are problematic today: the sense of linguistic decay in terms like 'walking out', 'courting', 'going steady', 'dating' and even 'in love' is an index. The young are caught between an older pattern of encoded courting, with fixed and socially approved 'stages' (first date, first kiss, meeting the family, engagement, etc.) and a variant on the spontaneous combustion theory of love, a 'romanticism' that invites a promiscuous pattern of first meeting/first sex. The move has been rapid from the Monotones' 1958 question in *The Book of Love*:

> I wonder, wonder, who
> wrote the book of love,
> was it someone from above ?
> Chapter One says you love her
> love her with all your heart
> Chapter Two you tell her
> yer never, never gonna part
> Chapter Three remember
> the meaning of romance
> In Chapter Four you break up
> but you give her
> just once more chance . . .

to Roger McGough's 'At Lunchtime: A Story of Love':

> When the busstopped suddenly to avoid damaging a mother and child in the road, the younglady in the greenhat sitting opposite was thrown across me, and not being one to miss an opportunity i started to makelove with all my body.
> At first she resisted saying that it was too early in the morning and toosoon after breakfast and that anyway she found me repulsive. But when i explained that this being a nuclearage, the world was going to end at lunchtime, she

tookoff her greenhat, put her busticket in her pocket and joined in the exercise, etc.

(Compare poor Clough's 'Natura Naturans' for a Victorian reaction to the same opportunity!) Some pop music can still operate in the old mode (e.g. Siren's coy *God Bless the Bride*, 1970) but intelligent rock has long recognized the incredible difficulty of contemporary 'love', and its links not just with a sense of the nuclear shadow but with deep psycho-social frustrations: the Rolling Stones' *Satisfaction* and *Backstreet Girl* are early examples.[31]

A sense of fragility has replaced conventional confidence; silent fumbling has replaced assertion; solipsistic or anarchic movements have replaced pre-patterned dance. Two related assumptions are openly opposed: the immense social pressure towards marriage as an ending, almost a full-stop in the novel, and the cessation of alternative relationships after marriage.[32] One response is to try to re-discover a gradual growth in relationship, in which sex (and perhaps formal marriage) is only one stage, implying still only partial commitment—as for some tribal societies[33]— and, secondly, the attempt to establish almost a new form of tribal grouping, the commune as a wider context within which that gradual growth can be given 'space' and a variety of types and levels of immediate relationship can be exercised.

Communes, located in cities rather than the 'back to the land' experiments of an earlier generation, again offer themselves as an available structure for marriage, and their political intentions are often explicit, whether in German SDS communes or the Blackheath Commune. To view them as peculiarly appropriate carriers of Christian marriage is not to argue for communal sex: most communes are, in fact, a context for monogamous relations, despite predictable press sensationalism. Though they

---

[31] See Michael Parsons, 'Rolling Stones', *New Left Review* 49, for an analysis of *Backstreet Girl*'s 'contradiction between the overtly arrogant and patronizing words and the gentle tenderness of the melody'.

[32] 'Only one couple in the sample still went dancing, though 81 per cent of the wives mentioned it as their favourite activity before they were married', Gavron, *op. cit.*, p. 110.

[33] Examples in Hillmann, *Concilium* V. 6, p. 29.

provide a 'situation' in which the traditional ethical considerations, narrowly preoccupied with sex, may be raised in new ways, it is the political and social significance of their form that I want to emphasize. They provide a socializing context for children which may more easily escape the inculcation of passive modes and restricted codes; they dislocate present standard ratios between income and household expenditure, in the shared consumption of 'goods' ranging from washing-machines to newspapers, remedying the extravagant under-utilization of some items, making available shared 'luxury' and leisure items hardly within the scope of one family income; and they accommodate a wider range of differentiated living space, etc.

Above all, they can offer the experience of communal living, of democracy and solidarity painfully achieved and precariously maintained, in which atrophied social skills can be re-discovered; and they release members for alternative 'production': the gradual production, through social work, political agitation, area projects, of a society in which to live as a community is the social experience. In Marx's terms, they can surpass the struggle for certain fetishized needs, leaving energies free for the recognition of new needs, for the sensitive realization of others as needs, and for the necessary response to the needs of others, both within and beyond the commune-group. One of the needs that might be genuinely felt within such a group would be the need for an adequate language and celebration of community, the need to say, socially, with full recognition, 'This is my body' and 'This is my blood'. Communes are, potentially, permanent liberated zones.[34]

One could spell out further the ramifications of communes (the headaches for the Inland Revenue or Housing Committees, e.g.) but they are not the only possibility. The concluding point is therefore simply one of principle—theological principle. At present, the Churches and cultural Christianity are among the important blockages on experimentation with married forms of life; in that sense they help to legitimate a shell—the pre-packaged family home as economic unit of capitalism—which

---

[34] See also my remarks on baptism in 'Absent Centre', *Slant* 25, pp.15-20.

142

militates against the anticipated establishment of the 'kingdom', one stage on the way towards which is a socialist society, and which in any case (if one refuses that particular eschatological interpretation) shores up a system directly and immediately repressive.

Yet one aspect of Jesus's divorce saying was to break through an inherited view of marriage, not simply by undercutting a legalistic 'contract' view of it and restoring it to a context of 'covenant', but by emphasizing a mutuality, an assertion, if you like, of women's emancipation: 'a man can be answerable to his own wife as an adulterer (cf. *Luke* 16, 18a)—the obligations of a woman to her husband, formerly one-sided, are now mutual. Man and wife are shown to be equal partners with equal rights.'[35] In English law a double standard, as between husband and wife, concerning the grounds on which each could sue for divorce remained till 1923.

Now that one breakthrough implied in the divorce saying has been belatedly recognized (albeit inversely), perhaps we can begin to grasp the wider implications for us, now, of Jesus's refusal to accept the form of what was not, in his day as in ours, just a 'religious' structure but also a crucial social and political structure. We might also take seriously two other sayings: Jesus's rejection of the excuse 'I have just got married and so am unable to come' (*Luke* 14:20), and his enigmatic comment about the kingdom: 'For when they rise from the dead, men and women do not marry' (*Mark* 12: 25).

*

---

[35] Paul Hoffmann, 'Jesus's saying about divorce and its interpretation', *Concilium* V. 6, p. 53.

METAPHOR AND METAPHYSICS

Brian Wicker has written a very curious book.[1] A rough summary of its contents will indicate the obvious sense in which it's curious: the second part consists of six critical studies, of Lawrence, Joyce, Waugh, Beckett, Robbe-Grillet and Mailer; the first, theoretical, part includes an analysis of metaphor and analogy in relation to Saussure and Chomsky, a comparison of homeopathic and contiguous magic with myths and fairly-tales, an excursus on causality in science linked with comments on angels and ecology, and a chapter that brings together discussions of religious language, Whitehead and Teilhard, and the differing narrative structures of Old and New Testament stories.

It's a brave author and publisher who can expect a readership for such a work. But it's the kind of argument that links these components that I find really curious, since I remain very unclear just what Wicker is arguing for. There are two major difficulties: the overall argument seems to be trying to establish a kind of natural theology, a queer kind of proof that God exists, though Wicker's formulations of his case never quite commit him to this; and secondly some of his basic arguments seem to me so dubious that, given my respect for Wicker's previous work, I can only conclude that one of us is deeply muddled but remain uncertain which.

In chapter I Wicker outlines the familiar post-Saussurean parallel polarities: language / speech, code / message; paradigm / syntagm; selection / combination; substitution / context; similarity /contiguity; metaphor /metonymy. He

---

[1] *The Story Shaped World. Fiction and Metaphysics: some variations on a theme*, Athlone Press, London, 1975. Some of the variations have appeared in *New Blackfriars* (Dec '72, Jan '74, May '74) and in *The Prose for God*, ed. Ian Gregor and Walter Stein, Sheed & Ward, 1973.

then suggests that (Thomist) analogy is to be located with the second term in each of these polarities: Aquinas in applying 'healthy' to both 'person' and 'urine' is using a kind of 'metonymic' relationship: healthy urine is both a sign and a part of a healthy person; that it is a reliable sign of a healthy person indicates a causal relationship (healthy person causes healthy urine). Wicker notes that some metonymic relations have 'causal historical' links ('White House' for 'President' is one he offers) but then makes a crucial move:

> it is necessary to my hypothesis . . . that a causal connection underlies the items on the 'syntagmatic' side [of the polarities]. (p.17)

In other words, the causal basis of Thomist analogy is also discoverable in all these terms. In the structure of a sentence, the kind of 'cause' operating is systemic or a matter of 'mutual contextual determination': in 'John hits Jim', 'John' is a subject *because* 'hits' is a verb and *vice-versa*. By contrast, a Humean associationist notion of cause-effect excludes mutual, simultaneous causes. Further, Wicker states, again against Hume, that 'a cause . . is not a relationship but a thing: an agent that brings about some effect by the exercise of what can only be called its own "natural tendency" to behave in a certain way' (p. 20).

To me the whole book seems to be based here, and to flounder here. It is based here because Wicker later states (p.76), and often implies, that all metaphors depend on an underlying analogy (a causal relation), that transitive causality is necessary for grasping the ecological balance of Nature, and that it is the relation between analogy and metaphor that allows the possibility of a religious language that reconciles talk about the 'God of the philosophers' and the 'God' of biblical faith (e.g. pp. 87, 96f).

Why I think that the argument flounders here is that Wicker's basic terms seem unclear. He wants a notion of a cause that is 'simultaneous' and one-way, as against Hume's which is temporal and one-way, and he can suggest a two-way 'simultaneity' in the case of a sentence-structure (systemic cause); but in the case of metonymic analogy it's unclear whether the causality is only one-way (the healthy person causes healthy urine but not vice-versa) or two-way (healthy urine as a reliable sign 'requires' a healthy person, as verb 'requires' subject).

Further, in the case of sentence-structure, Wicker adds: 'the grammar of the whole system in which the sentence . . exists ensures' the systemic 'mutual determination' (p.18). He elaborates this, via a citation of Chomsky,[2] into the claim that:

> beneath the level of mutual contextual determination . . there is a fundamental and one-directional causal relation linking that particular utterance to something that might be called its creative source: namely the language itself . . [as] . . a system of generative processes. (p. 19)

But is the kind of 'causal' 'generative' 'link' here other than systemic: a relation of whole to part of a definitional kind, a system constituted by mutually requiring processes? Moreover, such terms as 'generative', 'creative source', 'the language itself', and perhaps 'ensure' and 'system' too, would seem to be either metaphorical or metonymic-analogical; if metaphorical they would presumably, for Wicker, depend upon an 'underlying analogy' or metonymy; but then is the metonymy involved itself simply a definitional matter, a systemic two-way relation of whole and part (as another of Wicker's metaphors implies: language as 'an active in-gredient', p.19)?

The introduction of transitive causality as meaning 'a thing: an agent that brings about some effect' doesn't really help here, since I'm not sure in what sense 'grammar' or 'language' or 'competence' (or, another, political example, 'the two-party system') is a "thing", since what Wicker seems

2 Wicker cites Noam Chomsky, *Aspects of the Theory of Syntax* (1965) pp. 3-4, which is, however, only a brief summary of the conclusions of *Current Issues in Linguistic Theory* (1964). Wicker neither examines nor defends Chomsky's arguments in that (early) work.

to want to mean by "thing" is some X distinct from and 'outside' its effects (i.e. not related as whole:part), whereas the thrust of his analysis of metonymic analogy leads only to a notion of an X which is 'internally' structured (though in any case I'm not sure that his account of other examples of metonymy as resting on a 'causal historical' link really demands either).[3]

The problem is not, perhaps, the intelligibility of what he is trying to assert but rather the way he argues it, so that the use of Chomsky's competence' or 'the two-party system' leaves it unclear whether they are themselves analogies of proportion (competence is to subject / verb as two-party system is to opposition / government) or metonymic analogies (cf. 'aspects of a single idea', p.17), or illustrations, similes, metaphors, examples, or what? Which is one of the reasons why I'm not very sure what Wicker is arguing for.

He links this theoretical discussion to a literary-critical inquiry (Part II) which explores the fact that various novelists agree that 'to adopt a metaphorical style is to adopt a metaphysical world-view' (p. 4), or 'to admit the validity of metaphor at all is *ipso facto* to admit a whole metaphysical system.' (p. 7) But these two differing formulations indicate the problem: my 'adoption' of a metaphysical world-view says nothing about the validity (truth) of that world-view, while in the second formulation unless (as is possible) the notion of 'validity' itself demands a particular metaphysical system, my 'admitting' a metaphor (and its metaphysical system) may be more like 'suspending disbelief'.

Since what is at issue between the crucial two of his novelists is that Robbe-Grillet wants to eradicate metaphor (and metaphysics) while Mailer exploits the metaphorical play of language (thereby keeping open a metaphysical

---

[3] Wicker quotes Herbert McCabe, appendix 2 to the Dominican English translation of the *Summa Theologiae*, vol. 3 (1964), but McCabe's formulation seems to me both subtly different and more satisfactory: 'A cause is thus a thing exerting itself, having its influence or imposing its character on the world.' (p. 102)

dimension), the possibility of my merely 'adopting' or 'admitting' metaphorical language would make Wicker's teasing out of the analogical underpinning either curiously irrelevant (I 'adopt' that too) or itself only an example of how *his* use of metaphors ('generate', 'creative source') commits him to a metaphysical system—which isn't the point at issue but rather the premise that Robbe-Grillet and Mailer develop different attitudes towards.

It is therefore the notions of 'adopt', 'validity' and 'cause' that require examination—but Wicker neither shows that such an examination is impossible without using metaphors and analogies (and he clearly wants to retain some notion of 'literal' statement) nor fully attempts to examine them. Quite possibly this circular tangle betrays my confusion rather than Wicker's, though there is a third possiblity I will try to suggest later.

Some discussion of two related sections of the book may first clarify my dissatisfaction. Wicker's analysis of Hopkins's poem *God's Grandeur* (pp. 23-28) is interesting in a number of ways. The poem is divided into an octet and a sestet and Wicker argues that the opening octet poses a question ('Why do men now not reck his rod? ') in metaphorical terms ('The world is charged with the grandeur of God', etc.) which is answered in the sestet in analogical terms:

> Because the Holy Ghost over the bent
>   World broods with warm breast and with ah!, bright
>   wings.

Wicker suggests that the octet shows God as both present in the world (and therefore should be recognized, reckoned with) and yet 'blotted out' since 'all is smeared with trade' (the 'growth-processes that were once the true signs of God's creative power' are now invisible, absent). To say that the world is 'charged' with the grandeur of God is to employ a rich metaphor that brings God 'into' the world but leaves open the question whether this phrase is 'only' a metaphor—perhaps simply for non-divine processes of the world. The final lines state how God is still present in the

148

world though apparently blotted out: as the sustaining generative power of the Holy Spirit.

For Wicker, the final lines assert 'an underlying causal relationship between God and the world.' They obviously do: the 'because' is explicit. But, Wicker comments:

> When we say that God is the cause of the existence of the world . . . the word is being used analogically. But this does not mean that (as with metaphor) we want to deny the literal truth of the statement. On the contrary, the point of such analogical language is that, if the theory of analogy is true, we can stretch the meaning of the word in question to cover things which, in everyday talk, we do not have in mind. (p. 26)

It is obvious now why Wicker needed a concept of a cause that was 'one-way' and 'simultaneous', to allow for the use here of 'because' as meaning God as 'creative source' of the world, neither simply part of the world nor temporally prior to it but an X distinct from yet sustaining it.

Two problems seems to hover: if the meaning of 'cause' (its 'literal truth'?) is already established as 'one-way and simultaneous', why are we 'stretching its meaning' to cover the case of God; and if the use here is analogical, then in what sense is it 'metonymic'— unless God's causality is the 'whole' of which other causes are a 'part' (which again makes God's kind of causality the 'literal' meaning of the term)? But rather than pursue these termino-logical tangles,[4] I want to point to two features of the poem itself.

By dividing the poem between the octet and the sestet, Wicker can make the claim: 'This second part of the poem is one single, complex causal proposition corresponding to the single metaphorical proposition of the octave.' (p. 28) But

---

[4] Wicker's first *Note* (p.107) acknowledges that 'The justification for analogous usage . . itself depends on an analogous use of *'cause'*, and that 'This argument is clearly circular'—but his attempt to deny that the circle is vicious seems to me finally self-destructive.

what happens if we instead divide the poem differently, as line-divisions, sentence-structure and rhyme-pattern all allow us to, and then quote the middle part as a *whole* poem:

> Generations have trod, have trod, have trod;
>   And all is seared with trade; bleared, smeared with toil;
>   And wears man's smudge and shares man's smell: the soil
> Is bare now, nor can foot feel, being shod.
>
> And for all this, nature is never spent;
>   There lives the dearest freshness deep down things;
>   And though the last lights off the black West went
> Oh, morning, at the brown brink eastward, springs —

It's a less interesting poem, certainly, but it's only that curious dash at the end which indicates that anything is missing.[5] This poem, like the world it depicts, is sufficiently self-contained.

The opening four lines and the last two of the 'longer version' can suddenly seem arbitrarily supplementary, mere assertion; they perhaps demand each other, the rest of the poem doesn't demand them. In other words, there is no essential connection between the two statements the poem can be seen as making: the 'shorter version' simply asserts the abiding creativity of nature; the longer version adds an opening question which implies an answer (which together constitute another assertion) but the formulation of the question as metaphorical and of the answer as analogical doesn't explain or clarify the god-less (and 'literal'?) statement they enclose. In other words, neither the octet nor the sestet is 'a single, complex proposition' but rather each is two assertions, one god-less, the other 'god-full'. The relation between them is something I'll come back to.

Secondly, as Wicker rightly notes, Hopkins's final lines have developed from three other texts: *Deuteronomy* 32:11

---

[5] My treatment of this poem clearly raises problems of whole/part relations ('organic form'?) and 'quality' (why is either version a good poem?) that Wicker doesn't examine. Note that the 'shorter version' could almost have been written by a Robbe-Grillet.

Like an eagle watching its nest,
Hovering over its young,
He (Yahweh) spreads his wings out to hold him,
He supports him on his pinions,

echoed by *Genesis*:

God's spirit hovered over the waters

and then adapted by Milton

Thou from the first
Wast present, and with mighty wings outspread
Dove-like satst brooding on the vast Abyss
And mad'st it pregnant
(*Paradise Lost*, I, 19-22)

The awkward presence of 'waters' in *Genesis* contradicts the
notion of *creatio ex nihilo*, so Milton modifies the metaphor to
'impregnating' the 'Abyss'. But, as Wicker points out, 'such a
metaphor can only apply to a process *within* the world' and
Hopkins, recognising this, uses the image precisely for the
mode of God's presence within the world.

But the point that seems insistent here is that Milton's
inability to grasp the nature of *creatio ex nihilo* in a metaphor
and Hopkins's adaptation to express God's sustaining-
creative power both bring into play again the related
concepts of time and cause. Hume's concept is of cause as
temporal and one-way; Wicker wants a one-way causal
relation which I (and he) earlier termed 'simultaneous'. But
that 'simultaneity' needs questioning. Wicker touched on
the problem:

in the case of a simultaneously co-existing structure such
as a sentence or picture, there is no question of one part
preceding another in time. (Of course, a sentence will
take time to utter or write or read; and a picture will take
time to paint or scan fully: but once there it is a

simultaneous whole, a 'gestalt' that exists in a comprehensive present.) (p. 18)

Yet 'simultaneous' here surely means a-temporal not 'existing at the same time': the *structure* of a sentence is not temporal in any normal sense. The term 'once' in 'once there' is, however, temporal, since it is linked to 'there' (and seems to refer at best to the painting as an object). In his other example, a different phrase occurs with similar intent:

> Given the two-party system, both propositions [party A is the opposition (because) party B is the government] are true, although in a Humean sense, neither can be said to be either 'effect' or 'cause'. (p. 19).

But the 'given' here is a logical term, as is 'true'—there is a valid relation between premise and conclusion (a point Hume wouldn't deny). What is clearly at stake here, I think, is the relation between logic ('given') and time ('once') in causality: whether a cause is temporally as well as logically 'prior' to its effect. Wicker's use of 'once' and 'simultaneous' obscures that problem, while his 'given' seems almost to suggest that the two-party system is a *creation ex nihilo*![6]

Wicker's second chapter raises related problems. He sees a parallel between similarity (metaphor) and homeopathic magic: the 'idea of bringing about an effect in A by doing the same [*sic*] thing to a similar object B in a similar situation'; and between contiguity (metonymy) and contagious magic, which 'depends on actual contact between B and A' (p. 41). Homeopathic magic 'would have to be formulated as A brought about F in B', contagious magic in the form 'C because D' where A and B stand for things, but C and D for clauses. In contiguous magic

---

[6] Compare Wicker's earlier odd use of 'causal-historical' to account for some metonymies; what is involved there is the relation between logic and history (e.g. the relation between Hegel's *Logic* and Marx's *Capital*). This reference to the 'two-party system' is, surprisingly, one of the very few to politics—unless one so regards the discussion of ecology.

the events which are described in each of the clauses (say, *Cinderella's pumpkin turned into a golden coach* because *the fairy godmother waved her hand*) are in themselves quite intelligible. We can 'visualize' them without raising any questions as to their explanation. What is not intelligible is precisely their connection, that is to say the relation denoted by 'because'. (p. 42)

I am puzzled. Someone waving her hand is perhaps quite intelligible (she may think she's a fairy godmother, e.g.) but a pumpkin turning into a golden coach is not 'in itself quite intelligible' and I for one can't 'visualize' it without raising questions as to its explanation (and if anyone else said they were 'describing' what had happened, I would probably say they'd *only* visualized or imagined it). It's *not* the 'because' that bothers me in the sentence; it's 'turned' and 'fairy godmother'.

Further, Wicker says:

> in a proposition of the other sort (say, 'the fairy godmother brought about the form of a golden coach in the pumpkin') the *whole* of what is being described [*sic:* imagined?] is strictly speaking unintelligible.

But Wicker now seems almost to have reversed his earlier position: he had characterised 'transitive causality' as indicating 'an agent that brings about some effect by the exercise of what can only be called its own natural tendency to behave in a certain way' (p. 20) and cited Herbert McCabe where McCabe formulates transitive causality as 'A brings it about that F is in B.' McCabe also says:

> when you know what something is you already know what it is likely to do—it is indeed the same thing fully to understand the nature of a thing and to know what it will naturally do . . to understand the cause is just to understand that it naturally produces this effect.

—in that sense, I might fully understand, 'fairy godmother' as a literary convention within a fictional genre.[7]

But the problem is that Wicker's homeopathic magic is both transitive causality and strictly speaking unintelligible —so I'm not sure whether the argument in Chapter I employing 'transitive causality' was itself 'intelligible'. However, for Wicker, homeo-pathic magic, like all 'metaphor' poles, depends upon its 'metonymic' pole:

> Propositions describing homeopathic magic are always reducible at their critical points to propositions about contagious [contiguous?] magic and such propositions are themselves simply propositions that combine two clauses in a single context, the special feature of which is that the contextual relation signified by 'because' is in principle wholly beyond explanation. But 'magic' is not the only case of this kind: the *creatio ex nihilo* whereby, theologians say, God brought the world into existence (and indeed whereby he keeps it in existence too) is another instance of the same principle of sheer contiguity. (p. 42)

The re-entry of *creatio ex nihilo* seems to redeem Wicker's consistency: *all* transitive causality is 'strictly speaking unintelligible' because (?) it depends upon God's causality, the causal processes in the world require God's creative-causal act.

Yet now I'm not sure that consistency is retained in another respect: if *creatio ex nihilo* is a kind of contagious magic, then it is to be formulated as '*E because F*' in which

---

[7] See also Wicker's discussion in chapter 4 of 'Yahweh' as a literary 'character'; the question of the *cognitive* force of literature underpins the whole book, but I'm not sure that it can be solved along Wicker's lines here, that 'stories are good, and sometimes necessary, to think with.' Perhaps related to this are the questionable phrases 'description, and *in a sense*, explanation' (p. 43) and 'a coherent religion cannot do without a *philosophical belief* in God' (p. 99n)—both emphases mine.

there are two clauses both of which are 'in themselves quite intelligible'; but E would contain the phrase '*ex nihilo*' and F at least the subject ' *God* '. But I don't find either of these terms 'in themselves quite intelligible' and I'm not sure that Wicker would claim to (and what would it mean for God to be the subject of a clause anyway?). To put it mildly, when he goes on to say that 'magic is a metaphor for creation' (p. 43) he seems to be back in a circle. To put the problem in terms of *God's Grandeur*, the relation between the god-less and the god-full statements or 'clauses' in the sestet is finally only one of juxtaposition (mere contiguity); the 'because' of the last two lines is not the link but part of a detachable assertion; the real link is an enigmatic '———' .

*

I don't want to pursue Wicker's argument further, though the rest of the book contains many interesting sections and problems, What needs to be noted instead are two overall points. First, that in sketching certain queries above I have in a sense been playing the *naif*. I know, of course, that many of the problems I crudely gesture at have received extensive treatment by Aquinas, among others. The various possible relations, e.g., between creation, *creatio ex nihilo* and the (non-)eternity of the world were seen differently by Maimonides, Albert, Aquinas and Augustine—not to mention Hopkins's Scotus (cf *Ox.* 11, 1, iii, 19). The difficulty is that Wicker's mode of argument raises these issues and both implies and rests upon, as well as using, something like Aquinas's answers. But he doesn't argue for the validity of the Thomist metaphysics; nor does he argue for the validity of Chomsky's claims.

Instead, he seems to use Chomsky as a premise from which to re-build certain features of Aquinas's metaphysics. He seems to suggest that if one wants to work with the dichotomies of paradigm / syntagm and metaphor / metonymy you *must* be led to a belief in the existence of God: i.e. that way of grasping the structure of a linguistic utterance leads, if fully followed through, to a recognition of the need for a First Cause in a non-Humean sense. But I've tried to show that, as it is presented, this argument slides over problems; it holds, if at all, I suspect, only if the whole range of Thomist responses to other problems is available to shore it up, only if, in other words, the reader has *already* accepted a Thomist metaphysical system.

Which leads to my second point, fairly drastically compressed. Fergus Kerr, in a number of articles in recent years, has been suggesting that, in the wake of Heidegger and Derrida, we need a post-metaphysical theology.[8] His case can't be re-presented here, but two particular texts of Derrida are worth recalling. In *White Mythology: metaphor in the text of philosophy*, Derrida probes the problems in Aristotle's definition of metaphor, a definition 'the whole surface of which is worked by metaphor'. (*Marges* p. 276) Derrida eventually concludes:

> Metaphor, then, always has its own death within it. And this death is undoubtedly also the death of philosophy, But this 'of' has a double meaning. Sometimes the death of philosophy is the death of a form (genre) belonging to philosophy in which philosophy itself is reflected upon and summed up, recognizes itself in fulfilling itself; sometimes the death is of a philosophy which does not see itself die and never again finds itself. (p. 323)

In an earlier text, 'Ousia et Grammè', Derrida analysed Aristotle, *Physics* Bk IV, on 'time'. Part of his argument there states:

> The entire weight of Aristotle's text is shored up by a tiny word, one scarcely visible. . . What sets the text

---

[8] See *New Blackfriars*, Dec. 1973, Aug. & Oct. 1974, July 1975, and Feb. 1976. Wicker's essays on Joyce, Beckett and Robbe-Grillet seem to me the least satisfactory; Derrida has affinities with all three.

going and hinges the whole discourse, what from then on will constitute the linch-pin of metaphysics, this little key the play of which both locks and unlocks the history of metaphysics, this skeleton which supports and shapes every conceptual move in Aristotle's discourse, is the tiny word *hama*. (*Marges*, p. 64)

hama [ἅμα] means 'together', 'all at once', 'both together', 'at the same time', 'simultaneous'. Its use as a crucial term in the argument about 'time' allegedly begs the question of the relation between 'two *nows*' since *hama* itself involves concepts of time, duality and contiguity. Its use is not, perhaps, fully recognized in Aquinas's *Commentary on the Physics*, but in the light of the similarly hingeing use Wicker makes of the term 'simultaneous' (as both 'mutual' and 'at the same time') and his closely related uses of 'once' and 'contiguity', a re-reading of the *Physics* and the *Commentary* (and perhaps Hegel's *Logic* and Heidegger) seems worthwhile.[9]

Put that another way: in Fergus Kerr's words (*New Blackfriars*, December 1973),

The flight to biblical studies and patrology, or to sociology and poetry, so typical of the opposing wings in the new generation . . must lead to an *impasse* in the long run unless we face up to the philosophical problems that all these various disciplines ignore.

An article cannot do more than raise again those problems, and this is not the occasion on which to probe Derrida's own text for non-metaphysical god-talk possibilities, but in recording my gratitude to Brian Wicker for tackling philosophical problems in relation to both biblical studies and the creative language of literature, I still remain without

---

[9] [I finally attempted a critical reading of Derrida's 'Ousia et grammè' in 1985, eventually and reluctantly published in *Theory After Derrida: essays in critical praxis*, edited Kailash C. Baral & R. Radhakrishnan, Routledge, 2009. See also my *Time Pieces*, 2015.]

much illumination as I ponder once again Nietzsche's original broken thought:

> 'Reason' in language: oh what a deceitful old woman: I fear we are not getting rid of God because we still believe in grammar....
>
> (*Twilight of the Idols*)

*

MARXISM AND BEYOND:

On historical understanding and individual responsibility,

by Leszek Kolakowski.

—a review

The films of Roman Polanski and Andrzej Munk, the poetry of Zbigniew Herbert, even the criticism of Jan Kott, have made many aware of the cultural revival in Poland since the 1956 'October'. The accompanying philosophical mutations are less recognized. Before 1939 Poland was famous for its logical and analytical school, flanked by the phenomenology and aesthetics emphasis of Cracow and the Neo-Thomist inquiries of Lublin. Those strands continued their conversation under the blanket of official Marxism during 1949-56, and their offspring is clearly Leszek Kolakowski. Trained by Tadeusz Kotarbinski, deeply engaged in debate with Catholic philosophy in his early career (*Essays on Catholic Philosophy*, 1955), and himself a playwright and critic, Kolakowski not only symbolizes but partially provoked the Polish October.

The three earliest essays in this collection, 'Intellectuals and the Communist Movement', 'Permanent and Transitory Aspects of Marxism', and 'The Concept of the Left', were influential prompters in 1955, moving from a plea for renewed theoretical bases of Marxism to a critique of 'Office Marxism', and thence to an attempt to spell out the criteria of a true 'Left'. The second essay in particular shows Kolakowski applying to the Party a critique previously developed in relation to the Church; Catholic readers can easily re-translate.

At this stage many Polish thinkers were 'living in a perpetual translation' (see Brandys's *Memories of the Present Time*). After Gomulka's accession, debate was far more open. The four linked articles from 1957 that, under the title

'Responsibility and History', make up a quarter of this collection, reflect immediately the turmoil of this period. The first takes in part the form of a dramatic dialogue, between Clerk and Anti-Clerk, who speak for opposed tendencies that preoccupy Kolakowski throughout the volume, variously formulated as ethical socialism and Stalinism, 'sterile' utopianism and 'opportunist' realism, etc. Already in 'The Concept of the Left', Kolakowski had declared:

> The intellectual and moral values of communism are not luxurious ornaments of its activity, but the conditions of its existence. (p. 102)

In the notion of 'ethical socialism' he begins to explore directly the connections between moral evaluation and history:

> Can we formulate a general principle regulating the inter-relationship between our knowledge of historical necessity and our moral convictions? Between the world of being and the world of values? (p. 130)

One must either accept as logically prior some moral criteria of progress, which may lead one to oppose 'history', or pre-define whatever happens in history as 'progress'. Kolakowski attempts to show the practical contradiction of any anti-evaluative determinism by pointing to the normative character of negations of ethical norms; this leaves him able, with Marx (for example, discussing the British Raj), to judge an action as morally wrong yet historically progressive; but it leaves the sources of ethical criteria still un-founded. Despite this, we must, he asserts, be communists on moral not 'theoretical' grounds:

> . . when we have to accompany our theories with an act of practical choice, which means a pledge, then we act out of moral motivations, not theoretical concerns . . practical choice is a choice of values, that is, a moral act,

and that means an act for which everyone bears his own personal responsibility. (p. 162)

The urgency of this assertion reflects its context: 'Only on this basis were we able to try SS men.'

It was in 1957 that the period of 'concentration camp literature' in Poland (it was that or silence) came to an end; but the extermination of one-fifth of Poles burned into the moral fabric of the period:

History's skeletons are recorded in round figures
A thousand and one becomes just a thousand
The odd one might never have existed
    (Szymborska)

That old woman who leads a goat on a string
is more necessary and more precious
than the seven wonders of the world
whoever thinks and feels that she is not necessary
is guilty of genocide
    (Rozewicz)

This agony of awareness of the individual crushed within history was still the context for the appearance of Sartre's article 'Marxism and Existentialism' (later published as *Questions de Méthode*) in a special number of *Tworczosc* in 1957, and for the responses of Adam Schaff and Kolakowski:

Everyone can if he wishes interpret himself historically and unearth the determining factors that made him what he is—his past—but he cannot do the same for the self he has not yet become. (p. 176)

—that self is an existential choice.

What that period of confused cross-fertilization had 'not yet become' is indicated in the two most recent essays in the collection. 'In Praise of Inconsistency' argues for an acceptance of the humanly necessary gap between belief and behaviour; the alternative is the logical fanaticism of

161

Stalinism or the Final Solution. 'The Priest and the Jester' also eventually asserts the necessity of de-absolutizing allegiances, but in the first part of this essay—perhaps the most striking in the volume—Kolakowski circles back to his pre-1955 preoccupations, not now polemically but with an awareness that the old theological problems —nature/grace; faith/reason; incarnation; revelation; trinity and person—are pre-forms of the real questions engaged with in the intervening years in political-ethical areas. Kolakowski thus finds himself thinking alongside colleagues in Poland (Malewska, Mazowiecki) and Czechoslovakia (Machovec, Prucha) more directly involved in the Christian-Marxist dialogue.

The problem of locating ethical criteria remains (for both). In 'Responsibility and History', one response was to ask for simple acceptance of the social fact of moral evaluations, as a co-determining factor in any current political stance. In 'Karl Marx and the Classical Definition of Truth' (1958) this is explored further in an interesting examination of the epistemological grounds of the 1844 *Economic & Philosophical Manuscripts*. Kolakowski's recent work, particularly his major book *Religious Consciousness and Church Affiliation* (1965), has developed this strand towards a sociology of ideology—and again the parallel with Christian exploration is revealing.

While Schaff has also developed from the 1957 breakthrough, with books on existentialism, semantics and language, leading to his explosive *Marxism and the Human Individual* (1965), Kolakowski seems uniquely to fuse both that development and the current movement within Christian theology. George Vass, S.J., commented of the Marienbad Paulusgesellschaft meeting: 'While the progressive Marxist philosophers try to work out the transcendent meaning of human life, Christian theologians are preoccupied in defining the historical role of their beliefs and institutions in an immanent perspective.' Kolakowski's stature is indicated by his deep concern with both.

One hopes that this collection will usher in English publication of his other work (*The Alienation of Reason: A*

History of Positivist Thought is already available in a U.S. edition). Perhaps with the next collection the editors will indicate chronology more adequately; the essays in this volume are best read, not as printed, but in the sequence indicated above, as a developing engagement with different forms of basic human questions. But in whatever order, they should, emphatically, be read.

*

NOTES AFTER FOUCAULT [1]

. . the slightest alteration in the relation between man and the signifier. . . changes the whole course of history by modifying the lines which anchor his being.

It is in precisely this way that Freudianism is seen to have founded an intangible but radical revolution. No need to collect witnesses to the fact: everything involving not just the human sciences, but the destiny of man, politics, metaphysics, literature, art, advertising, propaganda, and through these even the economy, everything has been affected.[2]

Lacan: The Unconscious as Language

The original 'slightest alteration' underlying Freud's intangible but radical revolution can be conveniently dated to 1898, when Freud, travelling to Herzegovina, turned to ask a travelling companion whether he had ever seen the famous frescoes of the 'Four Last Things' in Orvieto Cathedral, painted by ——— : the painter's name would not come; 'Botticelli' and 'Boltraffio' came to mind instead. Freud's account of why he had failed to recall the right name, 'Signorelli', contains the core of his later theories. 'Signorelli' had been replaced through a series of transformations: '*Signor—*' into '*Herr*', recalling both *Her*zegovina-and-Bosnia and an anecdote about attitudes to death and sex in which the sentence 'Sir (*Herr*), what is there to be said? ' had been the punch-line.

This anecdote had linked to an earlier incident when Freud, while staying at Trafoi in the Tyrol, had heard of a patient's suicide because of an incurable sexual disorder. Thus, the 'forgotten' 'Signorelli' produced 'Herzegovina-

---

[1] This article began as a review of Michel Foucault's *Les mots et les chases: une archéologie des sciences humaines,* Gallimard, 1966; English translation: *The Order of Things,* Tavistock, 1970.

[2] Jacques Lacan, 'L'instance de la lettre dans 1'inconscient, ou la raison depuis Freud', *Ecrits,* Editions du Seuil, 1966, p. 527.

and-Bosnia', '*Bo*-snia' conflated with '*-elli* ' to produce '*Bo*-ttic-*elli*', 'Herzegovina', via 'Herr', indirectly produced 'Trafoi', which conflated with '*Bo*-snia' to produce '*Bo*-l-*traffio*'. The trigger for this process was the suppression by Freud of part of the anecdote about sexual attitudes, itself an aspect of his wanting to forget the news that had reached him at Trafoi. Instead of 'forgetting' that news, it had re-emerged in the displacing of a name he wanted to remember.[3]

It is the connexion between Freudian analysis and linguistic structures, apparent in this simple example, that has been revived in recent years by Jacques Lacan.

Lacan has grasped the parallels between Freud's terms, *Verdichtung* (condensation) and *Verschiebung* (displacement), and the ancient terms of rhetoric, metaphor and metonymy, recognizing that the processes apparent in the interaction of 'conscious' and 'unconscious' are those already familiar as stylistic tropes—that, indeed, the unconscious is structured as a language.

The 'unconscious', in fact, speaks to us: an incredibly alive and endless patter which obeys no conventional rules, but puns outrageously, strings chains of echoes, leaps to connections by assonance, rhyme and association, flows and spirals round obscene and absurd meanings; its discourse is the language of poetry, of dreams, of insanity. But it is also a structured language that the unconscious speaks: a structure given not by the logic of linear, rational discourse, but by the deeper structures of the entire language, grasped as a simultaneous totality, a system—and not a system of words only, but that whole order of signs and symbolic codes into which we are born.

This account of the unconscious offers the possibility of re-thinking the model of the interaction between conscious and unconscious. We tend to take Freud to mean something

---

[3] S. Freud, *The Psychopathology of Everyday Life*, Standard Edition, Vol. VI, ch. I.

like two 'levels', with all the dangers implicit in that of using misleading terms like 'inner' and 'outer'. Lacan's work suggests a different model, which a simple example might help to illustrate.

Consider that I am now typing this article from a handwritten version, amended and corrected in places, which is being dictated by someone else, though I can also read the manuscript from which she is dictating. At the same time, the news is coming over the radio and there is a conversation going on near me. I am, in other words, following more or less attentively a number of simultaneous discourses. Some of these discourses reduplicate each other—where the manuscript, the dictation and the typescript coincide; others diverge or clash—where I glance at one version of the manuscript while the corrected version is being dictated, or where my attention is caught more by a news item than by what is being dictated and I am typing; I then find myself, for example, typing a word prompted by a phrase in the news that has no place in the article at all. I am also, of course, trying to follow various 'rules': grammatical rules, stylistic considerations, typing conventions and even rhythms.

It seems to me that it is this kind of simultaneous presence of multiple discourses in the same 'field' that offers us the best model for the interaction of conscious and unconscious. The strings of nonsense we hear talking to us as we slip asleep, obstinate tunes in the head, or getting two stations at once on the radio, are cognate analogues or even examples. Indeed, in Lacan's view, we are almost like radio receivers, open to multiple wave-lengths at the same time; we are no longer primarily transmitters, as a theory based on the *Ego* of the *Cogito* would have us believe; man is ex-centric to himself, sunk inescapably in an autonomous medley of verbal threads, of spirals of signifying chains.[4]

---

[4] See Lacan, 'Fonction et champ de la parole et du language en psychanalyse'; 'L'instance de la lettre'; 'Le stade du miroir comme formateur de la fonction du Je', in *Ecrits*. 'Le stade du miroir' is translated in *New Left Review*, 51. For some of the philosophical

Here Lacan's work intersects with that of Lévi-Strauss, who can write of the 'inversion of the relationship between the sender and the receiver since, in the end, the receiver reveals himself as signified by the message of the sender.' To investigate the 'sender' in the case of myths is not, for Lévi-Strauss, 'to show how men think the myths, but rather how the myths think themselves out in men and without men's knowledge.'[5]

Lévi-Strauss began his major revaluations by finding in *The Elementary Structures of Kinship* codes and rules of exchange governing marriage which, without the knowledge of the partners involved, 'thought themselves out' in their complicated kinship relations, by an almost algebraic logic. The inquiries of the later *Mythologiques* are directly concerned with the logic of myths, and again the structures we see emerging are those of condensation, displacement, transformation; the permutations of language are figured in the endless re-patternings of mythic elements. But myths, like dreams, 'run up against a lack of taxonomatic material for the representation of such logical articulations as causality, contradiction hypothesis, etc.'[6]

In general, 'the purpose of myth is to provide a logical model capable of overcoming a contradiction (an impossible achievement if, as it happens, the contradiction is real)' and, Lévi-Strauss would claim, 'we may be able to show that the same logical processes operate in myth as in science, and that man has always been thinking equally well; the improvement lies not in an alleged progress of man's mind,

---

context and history behind Lacan's de-centring of the subject, see Paul Ricoeur, *Freud and Philosophy: an essay on interpretation,* trans. D. Savage, Yale U.P. 1970, pp. 42-55.

[5] Levi-Strauss, *Mythologiques I: le cru et le cuit,* 1964, 'Ouverture'.

[6] Lacan, 'L'instance de la lettre.'

but in the discovery of new areas to which it may apply its unchanged and unchanging powers'.[7]

Formulae of Exclusion

At this point the work of Michel Foucault becomes relevant, for a number of converging reasons. Part of the project common to Lacan and Lévi-Strauss is that of trying to penetrate and understand forms of discourse which are, at first reading, incomprehensible (the language of myth or the language of the unconscious, the discourse of the deranged and the insane), to restore their meaning, recapture their sense.

Foucault's first book, *Madness and Civilisation*,[8] tried to recapture the meaning of madness in a different way: the historical and social meaning of the way in which different periods have defined and classified madness. He begins from the fact that 'from the High Middle Ages to the Crusades, leprosaria had multiplied their cities of the damned over the entire face of Europe'; then, at the end of the Middle Ages, leprosy disappeared from the Western world; but though the leper vanished, almost, from memory, those leprosaria remained, waiting from the fourteenth to the seventeenth century. Then, 'often, in these same places, the formulas of exclusion would be repeated, strangely similar. . . Poor vagabonds, criminals, and "deranged minds" would take the part played by the leper. With an altogether new meaning and in a very different culture, the forms would remain.' But what logic classified *together* the poor, the criminal and the insane in their shared confinement? At the origin of this 'abusive amalgam of heterogeneous elements', argues Foucault, 'there must have existed a unity which justified its urgency; between these diverse forms and the classical period that called them into being, there must

---

[7] Levi-Strauss, *Anthropologie structurale*, 1958, ch. 11.
[8] *Histoire de la folie à l'Age Classique*, Plon, 1961, abridged translation by. R. Howard, *Madness and Civilisation*, Tavistock, 1967. Cf. also *Naissance de la clinique: une archéologie du regard médical*, P.U.F., 1963.

have been a principle of cohesion.' 'To inhabit the reaches long since abandoned by the lepers, they chose a group that to our eyes is strangely mixed and confused. But what is for us merely an undifferentiated sensibility must have been, for those living in the classical age, a clearly articulated perception.'

Foucault finds that that principle of cohesion 'organizes into a complex unity a new sensibility to poverty and to the duties of assistance, new forms of reaction to the economic problems of unemployment and idleness, a new ethic of work, and also the dream of a city where moral obligation was joined to civil law, within the authoritarian forms of constraint'. It was the moral condemnation of idleness that provided the generic category: the treatment of the poor, the criminal and the insane is in continuity with the suppression of beggars as the economic revival of the early seventeenth century got under way; the Great Confinement can be dated from 1656.[9]

The coherence of the classification held until the end of the eighteenth century, when, slowly, poverty became detached, assumed its place within a different and mainly economic set of connections: 'Men had seen unemployment assume, during crises, an aspect that could no longer be identified with that of sloth' or of transgression. The confusion of moral and economic interpretations of poverty continued to haunt the nineteenth century, but the decisive break within the categories of confinement had been made. New classifications emerged to cover criminals, while madmen became conflated for a time with, for example, 'marauding beasts' (in the Revolution's laws of 1790). By the end of the nineteenth century, Freud could begin to claim that madness was, after all, only madness—a phenomenon in its own right, an object deserving its own science, its specific analysis.

---

[9] In the late sixteenth century, Paris contained 30,000 'beggars' in a total population of 100,000; by 1650 a large part of this indigent population had been evicted or forced into work, but the 1656 Decree still resulted in the confinement of about 6,000.

But there a complex paradox awaited. In recognizing the locus of madness in the dislocation of discourse between the sane and the insane, the doctor and the patient, Freud also recognized that the barriers of classification between the sane and the insane would barely hold, would have to be re-drawn. The paradox was already latent: the Age of Reason had been logical even in its madness; Paul Zacchias (*Quaestiones medico-legales*, 1660) had uncovered the logic of the insane: a syllogism in a man letting himself starve to death: 'The dead do not eat, I am dead, hence I do not eat'; induction extended to infinity in a man suffering from persecution illusions: 'A, B and C are my enemies; all of them are men; therefore all men are my enemies'; enthymeme in: 'Most of those who have lived in this house are dead, hence I, who have lived in this house, am dead'. Zacchias concludes: 'From these things, you truly see how best to discuss the intellect'.

From Freud's slips of the tongue, we too began to see how best to discuss the intellect. But—bearing Lévi-Strauss in mind—not only the individual intellect. If the classical age operated with such alien categories of classification in its response to a madness which reflected its own logic, what are we to make of its other categories of classification— those self-confident sciences of Enlightenment. It is this question that pre-occupies Foucault in his second major work, the difficult but important *Les Mots et Les Choses*.

Separating Nature from Word: The end of Resemblances

If *Madness and Civilisation* wrestled with the problem of excluding the Other, *The Order of Things* struggles with defining the Same. The work, Foucault reveals, first arose out of a passage in Jorge Luis Borges, which quotes 'a certain Chinese encyclopaedia' as classifying animals into:

(a) belonging to the Emperor, (b) embalmed, (c) tame, (d) suckling pigs, (e) sirens, (f) fabulous, (g) stray dogs, (h) included in the present classification, (i) frenzied, (j) innumerable, (k) drawn with a very fine camel-hair brush, (1) *et cetera*, (m) having just broken the water-pitcher, (n) that from a long way off look like flies.

The obvious problem is that we cannot *think* (with) that classification, cannot grasp the underlying order, the principles of categorization. In Foucault's terms, we do not share the *epistémé* of the alleged Chinese encyclopaedist; his categories are not, for us, situated within a common space that would allow us to grasp his distinctions, we do not share the conditions, the way of ordering the world, that make that kind of classification, that kind of theory, that kind of knowledge possible. Put simply, we could have no shared premises from which to argue with him against that incredible list.

Yet, normally, theoretical arguments can occur. In Foucault's view, we 'must constitute the general system of thought whose network renders an interplay of simultaneous and apparently contra-dictory opinions possible. It is this network that defines the conditions that make a controversy or problem possible.' He argues that there are two discontinuities in the conditions for Western knowledge, one about the mid-seventeenth century, another at the close of the eighteenth century. Across those discontinuities, blank incomprehension is possible: the *Encyclopaedia Britannica*, for example, speaks of Aldrovandi, the great botanist of Bologna (1522-1607), as totally lacking 'the critical faculty', since his work indiscriminately lists both 'scientific facts' and fabulous beliefs. Aldrovandi's *Historia serpentum et draconum* is indeed arranged under the headings:

> equivocations (the various meanings of 'Serpent'), synonyms and etymologies, differences, form and description, anatomy, nature and habits, temperament, coitus and generation, voice, movements, places, diet, physiognomy, antipathy, sympathy, modes of capture, death and wounds caused by the serpent, modes and signs of poisoning, remedies, epithets, denominations, prodigies and presages, monsters, mythology, gods to which it is dedicated, fables, allegories and mysteries,

hieroglyphics, emblems and symbols, proverbs, coinage, miracles, riddles, devices, heraldic signs, historical facts, dreams, simulacra and statues, use in human diet, use in medicine, miscellaneous uses.

In 1657 Jonston's *Historia naturalis de quadrupedibus* has a section on 'The Horse' sub-divided into: name, anatomical parts, habitat, ages, generation, voice, movements, sympathy and antipathy, uses, medicinal uses. Linnaeus (1707-1778) proposed in his *Systema naturae* regular chapter-divisions for each animal of: name, theory, kind, species, attributes, use, and, as a final category, *Litteraria*—the appropriate traditions, beliefs, poetical figures, etc.

At first sight, Aldrovandi might seem simply to include Jonston's categories, and Linnaeus to restore the *Litteraria* omitted by Jonston. But the real difference is located elsewhere: in the separation that occurs between Aldrovandi and Jonston and is maintained by Linnaeus—the separation inserted into Aldrovandi's interwoven texture between what the animal *is* and what is *said about it*. For Aldrovandi shares in a non-Classical *episteme* in which all reality is 'legend', is to be 'read', whether the Book of Nature, the Book of Books (the Bible), other books, or books on books (the great Commentaries). His world is structured by *resemblances,* an order of similitudes, visible in cosmic signatures and graffiti, natural blazons and emblems; nature and word intertwine as one great text, to be interpreted by the interlocking signs of *convenientia, aemulatio, analogia* and sympathy. Knowledge is one unbroken weave of endless addition, asymptotic commentary.

Attribution / Articulation : Designation / Derivation

The episteme shared by Jonston and Linnaeus, however, establishes a different relationship between nature and word, that of *representation* : a gap appears between thing and name; instead of resemblances, the quest is for identities and differences, to be pinned down and classified in a new taxonomy. In the fields of *General Grammar*, and *Analysis of*

172

Wealth, as in *Natural History*, Foucault traces the Classical period's new conditions of knowledge. Each field can be configured as a quadrilateral, its corners occupied by the techniques of attribution, articulation, designation and derivation.

In Natural History *attribution* rests on the visible characteristics of individual animals, in General Grammar on the function of the verb in a proposition, in Analysis of Wealth on the objects which are reckoned as needs. These combine with the modes of *articulation* (in the double sense of linking and differentiating) by, respectively, descriptive classification, specific naming, and economic exchange, to allow the crucial notions of each discipline to emerge: the 'structure' of beings, the '*ars combinatoria*' (the hoped-for universal language, clear and distinct precision), the 'value' of things. *Designation* and *derivation* combine in a similar way: in Natural History, designation of species and the juxtaposition of beings together produce 'generic characters'; in General Grammar, primitive names and *tropes* (degrees of rhetorical and other displacement from the original norm of precision) engender encyclopaedias; in Analysis of Wealth, the monetary pledge operates with circulation of trade to make notions of price possible.

Natural History, then, occurs in the connexions between animal structure and generic character, General Grammar tries to combine universal language with encyclopaedic accuracy, Analysis of Wealth exists between the poles of price and value.

But these two central concepts in each discipline are not directly linked: the justification for their connexion is not internal, scientific, but rests on metaphysical beliefs: in the belief that things can be represented (that attribution and derivation are compatible—that, for example, objects of need are involved in the circulation of trade) and in the belief in an unbroken continuum of beings (that articulation is not divorced from designation—that, for example, the reliance on money within exchange is justified, or that no describable monster will appear that can't be fitted into a form of species).

It is, of course, difficult to *think* these connections (and impossible to summarize them adequately)[10] but not just because they are complicated and multiple. We also cannot think them directly, because the episteme they indicate can only be thought *within* one field or another: in itself it is an *a priori* of thought, a tacit condition of theory and connection. Moreover, we now operate in a different episteme, one that—as Foucault also demonstrates—has re-patterned the quadrilateral of conceptual techniques, linking (in the sciences of Philology, Biology and Political Economy) articulation rather to designation and attribution to derivation. The metaphysical spaces left open by the Classical episteme have been closed, by phonetics, comparative anatomy and the analysis of production on one side and by syntax, physiology and the analysis of distribution on the other.

Again, summary is vain, but Foucault's brilliant analysis allows us to see where new philosophical problems have now been opened up (since, perhaps, the 1840s?), resulting in attempts (in hermeneutics) to link signification and history ('designation' and 'derivation') and (in structural-ism) to forge a fusion between formal ontology and formal logic ('articulation' and 'attribution').

The transformation of deep structures of thought: from Man to Language?

The evidence used by Foucault may be unfamiliar, the mode of argument even more so.[11] But his achievement is clear: he has provided an exact account of what is so often felt, in the study of a period, as a set of common presuppositions, assumptions and premises, within which, but not about which, major theoretical disagreement is possible. It is this kind of inquiry, into what might also be called the deep

---

[10] The closest Foucault himself comes to summary is on pages 214-221 (English translation, pp. 200-208).
[11] Foucault examines his own method in *L'Archéologie du savoir*, Gallimard, 1970.

structure of thought in a period, that he terms 'archaeological' analysis; it undercuts the history of opinions, history of ideas, intellectual history—merely 'doxological' inquiry. An archaeology of the sciences takes us to an area of embedded 'logic' that recalls Lévi-Strauss's analyses, not just in their method but also in their conclusion:

> Not that reason made any progress: it was simply that the mode of being of things, and of the order that divided them up before presenting them to the understanding, was profoundly altered.[12]

Put very crudely, Foucault's is a kaleidoscopic view of the intellect in history: shaken at certain points, it re-settles in a new pattern, with variations on the same problems inter-connected in changed ways (some problems as 'solved', some as newly 'open'). The logic of Foucault's own position has led him not only to assert that 'Man' no longer has his classical place in our episteme (he, like Lacan, de-centres 'Man'), but also to an attempt to uncover the foundations of the *whole* Western episteme, including its periodic transformations.

In *L'Ordre du Discours* (1971) Foucault suggests his future lines of inquiry, and they ultimately involve a return to that abortive episteme-ological break that we can recognize in the Sophists. The 'sophisms' rejected by Greek philosophy—of the kind contained, for example, in Borges's categories, (h) and (l) above, or examined in Lacan's first important article[13]—rest on an episteme we cannot think (with), for it refuses our distinctions of true/false and same/other and proposes an alternative logic. Were we to recover that episteme, or arrive at a transformation of it (rather than yet another transformation of the episteme underlying Aristotle and his progeny), then, Foucault hopes, we might demolish the dominance of the signifier over the

---

12 *Les Mots et les choses*, p. 14 (ET, p. xxii).
13 'Le temps logique et l'assertion de certitude anticipée: un nouveau sophisme', *Cahiers d'Art* (1945), pp. 32-42.

signified (see Saussure, Freud, Lacan) and admit the event of discourse to a new place, no longer squeezed between thinking and speaking.

To see what is involved here (and perhaps to indicate the difficult notion of 'discourse') we can gropingly extrapolate from the present growing role of linguistic models sketched above. For language itself to displace Man, the subject, from the centre of our episteme is not entirely inconceivable. We can see something of the possibilities in the return to Freud's discovery of the autonomous discourse of the unconscious, but also in some insights of Marshall McLuhan and in such literary phenomena as found poetry, Beckett's *Lessness* and Burroughs's cut-ups. The prospect is terrifying perhaps, for we are prone to feel overwhelmed even by our present half-awareness of the buzz of discourse. Yet the possibility is not entirely without a kind of precedent: Marx's analysis of the reification of money or the fetishism of commodities perhaps marks the beginnings of a similar process, now familiar, of Man dominated and displaced by the Economy.

Why does the kaleidoscope shake? The imprisonment of Désir

But to mention Marx is to raise a query against Foucault. Marxism has accustomed us to accept the development of modes of production as an almost autonomous process; as such, it can provide a basis from which to explain developments in other sectors. Clearly, the argument of *Madness and Civilisation* can be linked to a Marxist interpretation of the relation between the development of capitalism and the moral emphasis on work. But no such motor is apparent in the argument of *The Order of Things*: little account is given of how and why the transition from one episteme to another occurs. Foucault's enigmatic suggestion in *L'Ordre du discours* is that it is a matter of chance (*le hasard*), but in practice, in analysing de Sade's work as signalling the shift from Classical to nineteenth-century episteme, he offers another explanation: 'The obscure but stubborn spirit of a people who (actually) talk, the violence

176

and the endless effort of life, the hidden energy of needs, were all to escape from the mode of being of representation'—and in emancipating themselves from representation destroy the episteme grounded in representation.

Here, however, we are back in the world of Lacan. Lacan's theory distinguishes between 'desire' and need and demand. *Désir* is the 'hidden energy' of the Other (the unconscious), which becomes trapped in the labyrinth of the symbolic order, in institutionalized language, as soon as it tries to formulate itself as *need* : what emerges is only *a demand* that can be specifically satisfied but which merely leaves a residue of inarticulate unfulfilment. Desire can never, in fact, be met, for it is at root the desire of and for the Other that speaks in us. Lacan sees the genesis of this unutterable and unsatisfiable desire in the mirror-phase of childhood: that stage when, in order to struggle from animal birth to human life, we identify ourselves with an ideal-image of ourselves—as the motor-inco-ordinated child tries to become its apparently perfectly-formed mirror-reflection. We need the *Ich-Ideal*, the self-image, to achieve identity; but that image is given only in the cluster of roles that await us in the social world of signs, symbols and signifiers, and those signs (in the Father and the Law, Order and Death) deny the Other whose realm is the unconscious language.

That denial is, however, specific, is rooted initially in the role-assigning family into which the child is born, as Freud, Lacan and Foucault (in *Madness and Civilisation*) all recognize. And the family, too, is encoded, whether by the incest-regulations studied by Lévi-Strauss or by the patriarchal and exogamic kinship-structures of contemporary Western society, with their accompanying determinate ideological formations that govern the roles of paternity, maternity, conjugality and childhood.[14] And family-structures and familial ideology are interlocked into the specific economic

---

[14] See Louis Althusser, 'Freud et Lacan', *La Nouvelle Critique,* December, 1964/January, 1965.

structures and political ideologies of the societies that contain them.[15]

It is *perhaps* through this route that any analysis of the origins of episteme-ological transformations might proceed: the new episteme answering to new needs formulable within new familial and social codes arising out of changed economic contexts in ways that we can track within a Marxist frame. But 'Man', of course, remains radically de-centred still. Whether the emphasis lies on the development of economic formations, on the hidden energy of desire, or on the availability of a language to translate desire into different needs, the problem remains: mankind seems dominated by chance and/or by necessity. Can we now see a way of cracking this problem? We cannot. For the solution requires, at least, a new episteme in which to be thought. But we can perhaps push towards the limits of our present episteme.

Lessons from the Fate of Ought

When George Eliot considered 'the three words which have been used so often as the inspiring trumpet-calls of men, the words God, Immortality, Duty' and 'pronounced, with terrible earnestness, how inconceivable was the first, how unbelievable the second, and yet how peremptory and absolute the third',[16] she was acknowledging that, in the nineteenth-century episteme, 'God' was, strictly, in-conceivable: part of the definition of an episteme is what is *not* thinkable within it. But she was also pointing to an element of absolute necessity felt within that episteme, the necessity of Duty, 'the sovereignty of impersonal and unrecompensing Law', the demand of Ought.

We could perhaps trace the origins of this sense of Ought to George Eliot's own family and social origins; but

---

[15] See my article on the political theology of marriage in *New Blackfriars*, February, 1971.
[16] The original version of this famous incident is in *Century Magazine* 23 (November, 1881).

more clearly we can locate that particular intuition of Ought in the development of moral language generally. Alasdair MacIntyre's two recent essays provide a groundwork.[17] His historical-linguistic analysis distinguishes 'three stages in the use of *ought*: a first in which *ought* and *owe* are indistinguishable; a second in which *ought* has become an auxiliary verb, usable with an infinitive to give advice; and a third in which the use of *ought* has become unconditional'—the final moral appeal. MacIntyre places these different stages of meaning at different historical stages.

The equation of 'ought' with 'owe' occurs in a mediaeval society of feudal duties and obligations, whether in Britain (e.g. Wyntoun's 'Robert the Brus, Erie of Karagh, *aucht* to succeed to be Kynrike') or in the society of the Norse sagas ruled by vendetta obligations. We can clearly relate this stage to the kind of analysis Lévi-Strauss has performed on kinship-rules, with their various 'obligations' governing who 'ought' to marry whom, in a relationship of exchange and gifts given and owed.[18]

The second stage of 'ought' is in the form of a: 'You ought to do X *if*—', the conditional clause referring to some good aimed at. The necessary logic of this stage is an agreement, ultimately, that there is some final good, though different moral systems may define the 'good' in differing ways.

The third stage tends to arise when the question can be put: '*Which* moral system *ought* I to follow?', which is strictly unanswerable (indeed, a sophism) since the ground for an 'ought' of that kind can only arise *within* a moral system. That stage easily shades into a situation where 'ought' is increasingly emptied of its moral significance. One of the dilemmas facing Marxism, for example, is the question: 'Why ought I to be a Marxist?' One tendency, in present

---

[17] A. MacIntyre, *Against the Self-images of the Age,* Duckworth 1971, chs. 15 and 16.

[18] Consider the connections between Levi-Straus's work and that of Marcel Mauss.

'Communist' societies, is to answer that question with the totalitarian response: you ought to be a Marxist because that is the rule of the society. With this in mind, I now want to suggest a parallel problem for theology.

Bernard Lonergan has recently conceded that there is a discontinuity in *Insight* between his analyses of intellectual conversion and of religious or Christian conversion (the problem of why 'ought' I to believe).[19] This is, it seems to me, a symptom of a broader discontinuity in theology at present: a gap between the modes of argument, assumptions, evidence and vocabulary employed in theology 'within' the discourse of faith (the re-interpretation of beliefs) and the kind of language available for a theology concerned with the move 'into' the discourse of faith. Lonergan's recent emphasis on re-building theology from the experience of 'conversion' at least begins to acknowledge this discontinuity as central.[20]

But the discontinuity is, as Lonergan, also seems partially to realize, a discontinuity of cultures.[21] In other words (I would argue), theological discourse *within* faith has accommodated itself to some extent to the *present* episteme, while much theology of conversion still tends to have hidden roots in a *previous* episteme (proofs for the existence of God, etc). The bridge between the two tends to be unargued, either assumed, as in Lonergan's work,[22] or simply asserted, as, for example, in Terry Eagleton's recent argument *based* on the 'certainty' of the Christian.[23]

---

[19] 'I'd be quite ready to say: let's drop chapter XIX out of *Insight* and put it inside theology', interview in *Clergy Review*, June 1971, p. 426.

[20] See C. Curran, 'Christian conversion in the writings of Bernard Lonergan', in *Foundations of Theology: papers from the International Lonergan Congress* 1970, ed. P. McShane, Macmillan, 1971.

[21] Lonergan, 'Dimensions of Meaning', *Collection*, 1967, ch. 16.

[22] Cf. Charles Davis, 'Lonergan and the teaching church', in *Foundations of Theology*.

[23] Terry Eagleton, 'Faith and revolution', *New Blackfriars*, April, 1971.

Yet 'certainty' would seem to be at the same stage of its history as 'ought': the real epistemological question is not about certainty *within* systems of thought or ideologies, nor even about how I can be certain about *which* ideology is 'true', but, more deeply, *why should* I be 'certain' about anything? Foucault's attempted return to the Sophists acknowledges the new twist in an old question (Descartes' *How can* I be certain about anything?'). Christians, on the other hand, tend towards a somewhat Stalinist response: you can be certain because the rules of the society tell you you can be (revelation, magisterium, infallibility, etc.)[24]

Theological directions

At the moment, I feel that we cannot think an answer to the moral dilemma or to the ideological dilemma. But *if* we want to continue trying to do 'theology', then the direction might be an exploration of Foucault's suggestion that the philosophical space opened up in our present episteme points towards a fusion of formal ontology and 'logic' with a hermeneutics of history. There are some more or less preliminary steps we still need to take in that direction.

We need an adequate historical-linguistic analysis of the word 'God' itself in relation to changing epistemes, an archaeological not doxological inquiry. Paul van Buren tried unsuccessfully to begin this task, in his analyses of the 'logic' of Chalcedon; Lonergan and Dewart have approached the related problem of the 'dehellenizing of dogma' and Hugo Meynell has proposed a Lonergonian approach to the 'development of doctrine'.[25] But Foucault's argument, I think, undercuts these approaches.

---

[24] The problem of 'certainty', of course, was the final pre-occupation of Wittgenstein, cf. *On Certainty*, 1969.
[25] Van Buren, *The Secular Meaning of the Gospel*, 1963, ch. II. L. Dewart, *The Foundations of Belief*, 1969, Lonergan, 'The dehellenization of dogma', *Theological Studies*, June, 1967. Meynell, 'On dogmas and world-views', *New Blackfriars*, October, 1970.

Meynell, for example, argues that '*homoousios*' indicates the adoption not of a Hellenic concept but of a Hellenic *technique*, which consists primarily in 'wean[ing] thought away from the primitive level by making abstraction possible.' But Foucault (and Lévi-Strauss) would tend to reply that the Hellenic technique of abstraction is no more and no less valid than the 'science of the concrete' or the role of 'resemblance' or 'representation' in other epistemes, and may be less appropriate for resolving certain logical contradictions.[26] If we remember that Christology and Trinitarian doctrine are basically concerned with the peculiar logic of Same/Other distinctions, then Foucault's struggles with the notions of Same and Other may help us. If we also try to think within a Hebraic episteme in which both '*les mots*' and '*les choses*' (and '*les actes*') could be translated by the single word, *d'barim*, then perhaps we can begin to grasp what the *archaeological* level of an *épistémé* is.

The second step we might try to take would be a further exploration of the logic of that word spoken by Lacan's Other.[27] The logic of madness, at the verge of the late eighteenth-century epistemological break, gave us the theological insights of Christopher Smart and William Blake. The peculiar logic of music (akin, of course, in Lévi-Strauss, to the logic of myths) has already been brilliantly suggested, by Schoenberg's *Moses und Aron*, as the only—though (in Schoenberg's scheme) inappropriate—language of public revelation for the unutterably Other that 'lives out its life in me'. The deep *désir* of the Other in us may be, as Augustine recognized, a desire that can find no rest except in the divine. To explore this view of man may be the only way to begin to handle the Feuerbachian recognition that 'God' is a projection of Man's needs.

---

[26] The study of 'Comparative Religion' can, perhaps, contribute to *theology* (as distinct from sociology) only if it tackles the 'epistemic' differences?

[27] Some recent (unpublished) essays by Sebastian Moore are the only English theology I know to be influenced by Lacan.

But if the transformations of epistemes require accompanying economic, social, familial and political changes, then we must also agree with Marcel Xhaufflaire (the best recent interpreter of Feuerbach)[28] that 'theology' faces a period of praxis first. It is worth remembering that Regis Debray, like Michel Foucault, is a student of the Marxist Louis Althusser, and that Lacan's group of psycho-analysts played an active role in the May 1968 *événements*.

We have long suppressed that other, unwelcome, aspect of the news of a self-chosen death that reached us at Golgotha—the task of re-creating the world. Only after we have returned to that might we be able to recall the forgotten name of the author of the four last things—not Signor Signorelli, but—in Aquinas's cautious phrase—'that which we call God'.

But perhaps some things are best displaced and forgotten—for a time?

---

[28] See my review of Xhaufflaire, *Feuerbach et la théologie de la secularisation*, *New Blackfriars* November 1970.
[I returned to issues of 'conversion' in essays now re-published as *Literary Conversions*, 2015.]

LOOKING BACK ON SLANT

[The following 'e-mail interview' is partly based upon my replies to questions from Jay Corrin in February 2009 when he was researching his book on *Slant* mentioned in the Foreword. Since the first question plunges *in medias res*, for some of the general context see 'English Roman Catholicism in the 1960s' included above. This 'subjective' personal account is intended to complement, or contrast with, that more 'objective' account. I include it here partly because in trying to write that account of the 1960s it was surprisingly difficult to find relevant first-person reminiscences. Not that such reminiscences are always reliable, of course. I have not annotated contemporary references, leaving that to the resources of Google.]

Do you have any memories of Fr. Herbert McCabe's troubles regarding the decision of Charles Davis to leave the priesthood? McCabe was dismissed for a time as editor of New Blackfriars *for making reference to the Church as 'corrupt' and this was followed by various protests.*

From November 1965 until he left Cambridge, Herbert lived next door to me. The Dominican house Blackfriars even shared a garden gate with St Edmund's House, where I was based from October 1965, and we regularly drank together at an Irish pub called *The Prince of Wales* in the Histon Road, an ordinary local, not a student pub, which had the benign policy of letting anyone who got inside before 10.30 pm (the official closing time) continue to drink till dawn—so our conversations were lengthy if not always coherent. But I recall very little of Herbert's own reaction at the time of the dismissal, beyond his hilariously sharing the generally sarcastic view that Roman clerics hadn't a clue about the English language. He didn't actually say very much about it to me in directly personal terms, though the political-theological debate about staying in the church was exercising *Slant*, and our conversations, at the time.

I had been a guest at Charles Davis's wedding on 4th February, as was Herbert, a couple of days after the 'corruption' editorial had come out, but I don't recall anyone even mentioning the editorial at the occasion itself. It just didn't seem like an issue—until the *Sunday Telegraph* blatantly publicised it. I had been invited mainly because I had known Charles's wife, Florence, whom I had met through an old friend who (among other things) ran the *Slant* group in Bristol, John Wilkinson. The aftermath of the wedding included my being summoned to Liverpool to be interviewed by the Rector of Upholland (I was still technically a seminarian), who opened the proceedings by telling me that Archbishop Heenan was furious and wanted to know how I justifed attending the marriage of a 'heretic'. (I'm not sure Heenan himself would have used that incorrect term). It was clear from the detailed grilling that somebody had given Heenan a full list of all those invited, and I remember later idly speculating with Herbert as to who it might have been.

Later that same February the Cambridge Aquinas Society (a kind of catholic students club) which I think was being run then either by Francis McDonagh, or by myself and Michael Heffernan, had invited Archbishop Roberts S.J. to give a paper, and his talk was dramatically interrupted by the stand-in Catholic Chaplain (who was called Christie?) publicly accusing him of heresy (over contraception) and trying to stop the meeting. It made for some more headlines (the incident even got coverage in *Time* magazine, I remember), but Herbert had already left Cambridge, so wasn't involved.

By then the entire campaign for Herbert was well under way, largely organised by the Newman Society but using *Slant*'s subscription list among other sources, as well as, obviously, Sheed & Ward, which published the book by Clements and Lawlor in double-quick time.[1]

---

[1] *The McCabe Affair: Evidence and Comment,* edited by Simon Clements and Monica Lawlor, London, 1967

Later, two related half-memories. After Herbert had been re-installed as editor (his resumed editorial began: 'As I was saying. . ') he was amused by my wanting to entitle a *New Blackfriars* piece of mine 'Corruption Begins at Home? ' (it was about marriage) and as far as I can recall nobody by then jibbed at that continued use of the word 'corrupt'. And, secondly, a regret: in 1967 I asked Donald MacKinnon to write a review for *Slant* of Charles Davis's book *A Question of Conscience*—but being Mackinnon it never quite got delivered, though I think a version was finally broadcast on BBC Radio 3.

After the wedding itself, since Charles and Florence were living in Cambridge I kept in touch for a few years, until they went to Canada. There was an informal discussion group organised by an Anglican vicar, which had connections with a journal called *Theoria to Theory*—Dorothy Emmett, who had just retired from Manchester University, was the main figure in that grouping, I think. And Charles occasionally attended Donald MacKinnon's 'D Society', as I did, so we met there too. But there was not a great deal of contact. Others in St Edmund's House knew Charles much better, of course.

I vaguely recall that on some occasion a few years before his 'defection' Davis had appeared at a conference (at Spode house, or perhaps a Downside Symposium?) which was more normally attended by *Slant* and *New Blackfriars* people. Since Davis was then editor of the *Clergy Review*, we even wondered if he hadn't been sent as a spy for the hierarchy! Charlie was incapable of waking up in the mornings, so was a risky speaker for early morning conference sessions—and he couldn't stop nervously adding 'sort of' to whatever he said—including the memorable phrasing on one occasion: "Jesus-sort-of-Christ"!

As a writer for Slant *which particular Dominicans had an influence on your views? I'm thinking of the role of Herbert McCabe and Fr. Laurence Bright in this context.*

I was personally very much directly influenced by Herbert, since I seemed to spend quite a lot of time arguing with him (not just when drinking in *The Prince of Wales*), and his particular way of conducting an argument left traces: a firmly Wittgensteinian mode that wouldn't let you get away with loose talk. I once spent an entire afternoon with him in Henecky's Bar in the Strand arguing about in what senses the tube map was or was not a representation of London. . . We all tended to fall into a mimicking of Herbert's intonation and rather aggressive questioning style. Intellectually, Herbert alerted us to the genuine possibilities of thinking with Aquinas, and both his sermons and his editorial comments were pithy and provocative. But the couple of books he allowed to be published at that time (he's been far more productive posthumously!) were somewhat disappointing, since I think there was still the notion that a *major* work of theology *had* to emerge from *somewhere* in this turmoil of ideas—and these books of Herbert's weren't quite there yet. I even heard that Herbert himself went round bookshops trying to get pulped any copies of his *The New Creation*, since he had come to dislike it so much.

Politically, I tended to be rather turned off by Herbert's heavy Irish Republican mode: the pub singing of rebel songs left me stone cold and I would normally slide out when that started. But I *think* it was mainly through Herbert's influence that an Irish *Slant* (called *Grille*) began, and it was through Herbert rather than my own Liverpool-Irish connections that I occasionally had contacts with People's Democracy, the early Civil Rights-based political grouping in Belfast. I also have vague memories of being in Dublin at McDaid's pub and being introduced to Cathal Goulding and other Official IRA figures through a Herbert contact (possibly Seán Mac Réamoinn? who was then with the *Irish Times* and had reported on Vatican II— he died last year).

The main other intellectual impact on me from among the Dominicans was that of Fergus Kerr. Fergus was hard to entice into discussion but he was the main avenue for the influence of Heidegger and the post-Heideggerians. His characteristically incompleted articles for *New Blackfriars* were quite stunning. I once threatened to collect them into several volumes to be entitled 'To Be Continued'.[2] I can remember Fergus going on about Derrida and Lacan long before almost anybody else in the UK, around 1966-67? So I bought Lacan's *Ecrits* and tried to struggle with it, but finally lent it to Sebastian Moore (a wonderful Benedictine theologian, who was Nicholas Lash's uncle, who was then at St. Edmund's also), who was overwhelmed and promptly scribbled lots of Lacanian poems, which somebody showed to Lacan, who is reported to have said: "At last, somebody understands me— and he's *English*!!"— all thanks to Fergus. Fergus had been taught by Donald MacKinnon and one could see the continuity. Fergus's occasional forays into cultural criticism as well as theology were also memorable— his account in *New Blackfriars* of Scottish folk song made a lot of sense of some of Raymond Williams's more gnomic utterances on common culture.

And Cornelius Ernst was important, for me at least. An essay by Cornelius (there were too few) could leave you thinking, hard, for days.[3] I once invited him over to talk to the Aquinas Society on a topic of his choice—and he said he would talk about 'Ricoeur and Evil'. So I rounded up every postgraduate in Cambridge who was working on Ricoeur or anything remotely cognate, and managed to get a good

---

[2] For example, the following, all in *New Blackfriars* between 1965 and 1974: Heidegger among the Theologians, April 1965; Delusive Radicalism in Modern Theology, January 1966; Language and Community, November 1967; Eschatology as Politics, April 1968; Politics and Theology: Retrospect and Agenda, August 1968; Ataraxy and Utopia, March 1969; Liberation and Contemplativity, April 1969; Resolution and Community, June 1969; Liturgy and Impersonality, October 1971; Cultural Continuity and a Scottish Tradition, November 1972; Communes and Communities, September 1972; The Essence of Christianity: Notes after de Certeau, December 1973; Metaphysics after Heidegger, August 1974; Derrida's Wake, October 1974.

[3] See *The Theology of Grace*, 1974, as well as his contribution to the English *Summa Theologiae*, Volume 30, *The Gospel of Grace, 1a2ae. 106-114*, and the posthumous collection, *Multiple Echo: Explorations in Theology*, edited by Fergus Kerr and Timothy Radcliffe, 1979

solidly well-informed audience—only for Cornelius to arrive without his paper: he'd left it on the train. So, very apologetically, he simply improvised. After an hour, he stopped. From the chair, I implored questions. There was a dazed silence. Utter awe. After five minutes we adjourned to the pub and I asked Cornelius to say it all again, slowly, in words of one syllable. He wouldn't, of course. I recall a single short footnote in Cornelius's introduction to his translation of volume I of Karl Rahner's *Theological Investigations* which more or less sketches an entire Wittgenstein-Heidegger theological *rapprochement*. Needless to say, he was sometimes temperamentally almost incompatible with his *confrères* in Oxford Blackfriars!

Laurence Bright, by contrast, I never really thought of as a thinker (which may be deeply unfair: I hadn't then read his earlier work on the philosophy of science),[4] but he was endlessly in touch with people. My titular role as reviews editor on *Slant* was a joke (and semi-protection, as I was still a seminarian), since Laurence was almost invariably the one who knew someone who would know enough to review whatever came along. And Laurence seemed to be the great inter-connector, between the Newman Society or *New Christian*, or The Renewal Movement or the Student Christian Movement, and so on, though I think only in terms of the specifically christian left scene. There was an occasion when Laurence lost his address book and his appointments book and it looked as if most catholic left activities would just have to pause until he found them again. He always seemed to be giving a talk somewhere or editing yet another series or a journal. He was also very persuasive: he managed to get pieces for *The Newman* out of me which I would never have dreamt of trying to write at the kind of short notice he constantly took for granted. But I don't myself feel that I ever really got to know him, and I think of him more as a somehow languidly energetic organiser than as an intellectual or political influence on me.

---

[4] *Whitehead's Philosophy of Physics*, 1958.

It's important to note that there was a generation of younger Dominicans, more our own age range, who wrote little at the time but who were often part of the ongoing debates at the December Group or at Blackfriars Oxford into the small hours. Alban Weston I remember—whose brother, Gerry, I had known at Upholland and who was to be the first person killed by the Provisional IRA in England: they blew up the officers' mess at Aldershot in 1972 in retaliation for Bloody Sunday, and Gerry, as an RC army chaplain, was having lunch there. I'm not sure what the conversation between Herbert and Alban might have been the following morning. There was also Geoffrey Preston, Timothy Radcliffe, Guy Braithwaite, etc.

And then there were older Dominicans who also had a different kind of influence. Kenelm Foster's expertise in Dante and Aquinas was always around for me at least (he was a regular visitor to St Edmund's where he had a Fellowship—though Kenelm was sometimes horrified at what his leftist colleagues were up to), and Gervase Mathew's polymathic erudition opened up historical perspectives, while the presence of Conrad Pepler at Spode House, Hawkesyard, (where Slant conferences tended to happen) was always a reminder of a longer Dominican tradition and the connections with Eric Gill and Ditchling etc. And Adrian Cunningham would be encouraging us to reconsider Victor White, and Angela Cunningham had known David Jones (who ended as a Tertiary brother or something, yes?). So the sense of a complex Dominican tradition was very present, over and above the direct impact of Herbert and Fergus and Cornelius.

It's perhaps worth saying that Herbert was very successful at re-articulating catholic doctrine, in a way that very persuasively combined Aquinas with Wittgenstein and Marx, but only from *within* a position of faith. He was pretty unhappy, and often dismissive, when faced with the question of why one might believe the christian faith in the first place. I once remarked to him that of the first four words of the creed "I believe in God" there were three I didn't understand and the fourth ('in') was opaque. Herbert just shrugged and suggested I get another round of drinks. (I was echoing a wonderful anecdote about Donald MacKinnon's booming voice being reduced to sudden intermittent silences as he agonised over saying the creed, uncertain which phrases he could actually endorse!)

It should also be said that there were lots of other theological influences around, apart from the local Dominicans—not least because Sheed & Ward was publishing and translating many continental theologians. Donald MacKinnon was personally important to me, as were Nicholas Lash and Sebastian Moore, and— only in his writings—Bernard Lonergan. I had also imbibed a fair amount of theological thinking from Tom Worden, a neglected figure, who taught at Upholland, edited *Scripture* or the *Catholic Bible Bulletin* or something but published little, and from Alex Jones, also at Upholland, who had more or less single-handed translated the *Jerusalem Bible*. Both were superb teachers.

Did you see any merit at the time in drawing on Marx and the European and American sociologists in shaping your own views on what was needed to advance a more progressive Catholic social agenda? Of course, I'm interested in your own views on the matter of linking up with the secular New Left during these years.

I'm not sure I can get this question properly into focus, or can offer a coherent alternative way of putting the point. For a start, Marx was such an obvious and massive presence that it would be difficult for us not to try to reconcile 'catholic thinking' with Marx, rather than *vice versa*. I don't think it was at all a matter of looking to Marx from the outside, as it were, and seeking 'merit' in his work for catholic purposes. We were trying both to make sense of and to change the world, and Marx was simply unavoidable. So I'm also not persuaded that what we were trying to do is best described as 'to advance a more progressive Catholic social agenda.' We were, along with millions of others, trying to change the global capitalist system and we happened to find ourselves also positioned as—among several other identifications—'catholics', i.e. within one of the more reactionary support structures of capitalism. And so one of the many places in which to try to make a difference was this weird catholic apparatus, which was a peculiar combination of potentially progressive mass membership and reactionary hierarchical absolutism.

Because the global links that were in several ways open to somebody who was a catholic were themselves potentially important, it made basic political sense to work for some of the time within that apparatus. After all, even the Fourth International might find it pretty difficult to have such immediate links to events and people as scattered and accessible as the catholic church did! Internationalism, if you like, came naturally to catholics. I remember thinking that within the fairly small clerical community at St. Edmund's there were people who between them had close experience of almost every place on the planet. But of course, beyond any simple instrumentalism, trying to construct some form of syncretism between our left commitments and our received catholic upbringing and intellectual formation was also a problem to be solved for ourselves, and therefore perhaps on behalf of others too. And one of the obvious advantages of a catholic upbringing within Britain was that at least we were attuned to some aspects of the wider European theoretical traditions, in a way that much of the English left wasn't at that time, given the insular and anti-theoretical education always prevalent in England.

When Perry Anderson gave a draft version of his highly influential 'Components of the National Culture' article (*New Left Review*, 1968) to the Tawney Group in Cambridge (which included such venerable 1930s left figures as J. D. Bernal, Joan Robinson, and Joseph Needham) he concluded by arguing that what was needed was a publishing house prepared to publish translations of major continental theorists—and the one example he said he could think of was a little known catholic publishing house called Sheed & Ward! S&W at one point, if I remember right, got the contract to publish the whole of Adorno, for example, but couldn't fulfil it. And the very first 'New Left Books' book (the implementation of Perry Anderson's programme, later to be called Verso) was actually a joint publication by S&W and NLR: Nicos Poulantzas, *Political Power and Social Classes*.

So it wasn't so much a matter of 'linking up' with the 'secular left'—we were ourselves already part of that left, but also happened to be catholics, so had some responsibility to work (as well) in that area—just as someone who was an academic historian or a trade union organiser or a hospital orderly would seek to 'link' their various roles and responsibilities within a left perspective. Though one aspect of theoretical work, that of intersecting with a theological tradition of thinking, was obviously specific.

Remember that 'the secular left' at that time in Britain (let alone elsewhere) was a pretty rich brew, with several dozen options on offer, from the International Marxist Group to International Socialists, from the Communist Party to the various fragmentary residues of the left still lingering within the Labour Party or in the remnants of the Independent Labour Party, from the various emerging 'new social movements' to all that flower power effervescence. David Widgery's *The Left in Britain, 1956-1968* captures the flavour pretty well, I think.

Being part of the 'catholic left' was always an oddity, and not normally one's main identifcation. I'm not sure how I can best put this. Maybe this way: if I think back to, say, the summer of 1967, what I remember was not so much the continuing backwash from 'the McCabe affair', but— simultaneously, it felt like—working shifts in a steel factory (Delta Metal) just by the Blackwall Tunnel in East London, serving early morning breakfasts in a nearby transport café, attending meetings of a Shop Stewards Liaison Defence Committee some evenings, and travelling across London most nights to late sessions of the Dialectics of Liberation Congress at the Roundhouse, listening to R. D. Laing or Allen Ginsberg or Stokely Carmichael or Herbert Marcuse or whoever till the early hours of the morning and then crawling back across London in the dawn to do my café and factory shifts.

As it happens, some of this was indeed possible through christian connections, because I was staying that summer with an Anglican vicar in Greenwich who ran an outfit called SLIM—the South London Industrial Mission, a kind of Anglican worker priest operation modelled on French Catholic efforts, whose local bishop-boss was, as it happened, John Robinson, Bishop of Woolwich, whose *Honest to God* Herbert had justly trounced back in 1963. But my only memory of a specifically 'catholic left' moment that comes to mind from that summer is that at one session of the Dialectics of Liberation Congress three tall Dominicans swayed into the crowded Round-house in full black-and-white robes, to delighted   ironic applause, and I actually knew who they were (though I've now forgotten)—and the other moment (though it may have been the following summer) was trying to persuade Neil Middleton that Sheed & Ward should translate and publish a brilliant new book-length polemic entitled *Société du spectacle*, which had just come out in Paris and which the author Guy Debord had declared to be copyright free, so S&W could actually afford it!—though when Debord learned that it was a 'Catholic' publishing house he apparently went ballistic and S&W never did it. A pity.

Any rate, the overall point is that—most of the time—we were all involved individually in a variety of efforts and we sometimes came together as Slant or as the December Group or whatever. Neil Middleton, for example, was involved (exactly how I can't recall) with the newspaper *Black Dwarf*, Chris Holmes with the Notting Hill Housing Community Trust (which later was to develop into the very important Shelter organisation, which he later headed), Peter Grant was involved with the   early gay movement, somebody else (maybe Peter Mahoney??) with the squatters movement, and so on, just as most of us 'after Slant' continued with other 'secular' commitments.

Your question about Marx, for example, reminds me that—as I recall the story—more or less the first thing Neil Middleton did after he left Sheed & Ward and later became commissioning editor at Penguin was to get on a plane to

Moscow and Berlin and negotiate the rights to what became the Penguin Marx (co-published with *New Left Review*, of course). He didn't do that 'as a catholic'—though it's perhaps ironic that the most prolific home-grown academic 'Marxologist' in the UK at the time was probably David McLellan who was indeed a catholic. (And whom I still see regularly, and who was a friend of Ian Gregor and other 'liberal' catholics.)

The *May Day Manifesto* attempt was perhaps the closest, in my view, to a political stance broadly shared by most of *Slant*, but even that provoked fierce critique in *Slant* itself (by Martin Shaw, in particular), but for example when Terry and I were supposed to organise an MDM conference on the communications industry it was simply as leftists that we were doing it—not that I did much on that occasion: by the time I called round on the morning after to get the thing going, Terry had, quite characteristically, already written all the necesssary organising letters and we went off for a drink instead. I remained involved with the Free Communications Group for a while after that, but nobody else on *Slant* was specifically interested in that territory. And even when Terry's work segued into 'marxist literary criticism' I think I was the only other 'Slant' figure who was also working in that area: the series of 'Essex conferences' on literature and politics were a gathering place for the 'secular left' and Terry and I would usually meet up there, but not primarily because we had been on *Slant* together.

There were, I suppose, specific aspects of the 'catholic left' combination that enabled things that might not have happened otherwise. That Leo Pyle was a '*Catholic* Marxist' probably made a difference when he went to work for Salvador Allende in Chile,[5] and that perhaps also enabled us to invite various of Allende's ministers to a meeting of the December Group at Spode just after the coup. Or my own encounter with Znak in Krakow during the Solidarity

---

[5] See Leo Pyle, 'Chile 1970-73', *New Blackfriars*, December 1973.

period,[6] or a brief visit I paid to Guatemala in the 1970s, might not have happened without those connections (though it was primarily to join up with Xavier Gorostiaga that I went on that occasion).

As for drawing on 'the European and American sociologists', I'm not quite sure what you mean. We had obviously read the classics, Weber, Durkheim, Pareto, etc., and I had a particular interest in Dilthey because of my research topic, and Lévi-Strauss was beginning to be influential, but I remember I found Terry's passing interest in Talcott Parsons more or less baffling. I couldn't see that the usual American sociologists had much to offer. The Frankfurt School were very 'present' for me—not least because Paul Connerton (who did an excellent Frankfurt School anthology for Penguin)[7] was a good friend I constantly argued with, since he too lived in St Edmund's House. In general, I would certainly have gone along with Anderson's critical account of Anglo-American and emigré sociology in the 'Components' piece, though I was more directly influenced by Georg Lukacs, and by Lucien Goldman, than was normal among NLR theorists. My doctoral thesis was a a weird conflation of Lukacs with elements of Jacques Lacan as well as of E. P. Thompson and Raymond Williams,

I did get involved with some more or less positivist sociological work just once—Bob Towler did a survey of Cambridge theology students for me, and people like Monica Lawlor and A.E.C.W. Spencer were doing

---

6 I was in Krakow, on a freezing cold night when Solidarity was declared illegal. A man in an ominous black overcoat called at my lodgings and interrogated me, in apparently hostile fashion: "If you are Sharratt, tell me: what are the names of the daughters of Martin Redfern?" ! —this as a way of establishing my identity, since Martin ran Sheed & Ward, before I was bundled into a closed black car —luckily only to be taken to a clandestine meeting of the Catholic group Znak!

7 See Paul Connerton, *Critical Sociology*, 1976; *The Tragedy of Enlightenment: An Essay on the Frankfurt School*, 1980; *How Societies Remember*, 1989; *How Modernity Forgets*, 2009.

interesting inquiries into British catholic culture, which we wanted to follow up in the abortive proposal for a *Slant Register* annual. But we couldn't commission full-scale research and most of the sociological work which the UK hierarchy did commission got firmly locked away! As it happens, Tony Giddens was an early participant in some of the St. Edmund's inter-disciplinary seminars, as were Edmund Leach and various other local social theorists,[8] and since 'Social Sciences' were only just getting recognised at Cambridge in 1968 I was nearly pushed into the nascent faculty for my PhD — but in general 'the European and American sociologists' apart from the 'western marxists' were not, I think, part of our intellectual make-up.

Could you tell me about your own upbringing within Catholicism and being part of that post-WWII generation that came to question the old ways of looking at things politically and religiously?

I was born in Liverpool, October 1944, a working class family, partly Irish Catholic background. My maternal grandmother had 'come over' from Ireland, from Meath Street, Dublin. My dad, born in Liverpool, had begun his working life with only the prospect of following his father and all his male relatives onto the Liverpool docks, but the war jolted him (through being a despatch rider and a signals technician) into working after the war as a telephone engineer. He then followed an instructive (for me) path: after the telephone exchanges became automated, he moved into working as a dole clerk at the Liverpool Labour Exchange, then became an industrial rehabilitation liaison officer (trying to get industrial accident victims back into work), then realising that the sensible thing was to stop industrial accidents in the first place, became a Health and Safety Factory Inspector. He retired early when the Inspectorate became reorganised to accommodate a 'scientific' specialist graduate intake who had never actually

---

[8] See 'Proof and evidence at Cambridge', *Herder Correspondence*, VI, 5, May 1971.

worked on the shop floor—he was not impressed! The lesson I took from this trajectory was that you had to follow the faults of the system further, to their root: why 'industrial accidents' happened wasn't just a matter of health and safety 'accidents' but of the entire organisation of industrial work. Hence, eventually, my own marxism. I was also influenced towards a later academic involvement in 'communications' by my Dad's various telephone jobs.[9]

My mother's father had risen from merchant seaman to being a captain of a tramp steamer plying the Med, but when he died in the 1930s my grandmother had no pension or help from the shipping company and seven kids to bring up. The lesson I took from that was not to believe that the company was in it for you! My Mum worked part-time in various shops and offices and my Dad continued to do extra night shifts as a telephone operator. All this left little time

---

[9] Allow me an anecdote: When I was in Hyderabad in the 1980s, I was suddenly landed with speaking one night to the Telegu Revolutionary Writers Association and since I hadn't had advance notice, I just improvised a personal account of how I got into marxism—including a reference to my Dad's trajectory from telephone engineer, and to Raymond Williams' work on communications, etc. So after the talk I was asked by some local telecoms trade union people if I would meet them the following day. They were in a dispute with the Andhra Pradesh government which, as with most of India, was then rapidly privatising the state telecoms service. Since I didn't think they had a chance of actually staving off privatisation, I suggested that they at least put forward various un-traditional demands which I thought the government would be prepared to concede, knowing that soon the private companies would be paying for them anyway. One of the demands I suggested was a free telephone for every telecoms worker. At the very most I thought they might succeed in getting free telephones for union branch offices and officials, which would at least enable them to organise more effectively. A few months later I heard from a Hyderabad friend, Venkat Rao: 'Today the government has announced the acceptance of this specific demand and is providing rent-free telephone facility to all 320,000 telephone workers in India. Incredible news.' My Dad would have been, as we say in Liverpool, 'chuffed'!

for any interest on their part in 'politics', and they would probably both have voted Tory, though my older sister got involved with the YCW (Young Christian Workers) and I remember myself getting agitated about a local campaign over high council rents. I grew up a cradle catholic in a family that had Pius XII on the wall and a maternal grandmother who as a girl in Dublin had been told to genuflect whenever a priest walked past.

When I was about ten I thought I had a 'vocation' for the priesthood, so ended up at St. Joseph's seminary for the Liverpool archdiocese at Upholland, near Wigan in Lancashire. There I (and every other kid, whatever their apparent intellectual inclinations or alleged prior abilities) got a pretty rigorous course in Latin, Greek, Hebrew, ancient history, maths, etc., etc., —all of which convinced me later that class-biased educational apartheid is profoundly wrong-headed. You can teach anyone anything. I stayed through the lower school and then did two years of Philosophy: Aristotle and Plato in Greek, Aquinas and Duns Scotus in Latin, Descartes and Sartre in French, some Kant and Hegel in translation since we didn't have a German teacher—this was post-war Liverpool still! Teachers included Tom Worden and Alex Jones (editor of the English *Jerusalem Bible* and uncle of Anthony Kenny who had passed through Upholland a few years before)—until I was suddenly summoned one day and told I was going to Cambridge to read Classics. The policy had previously been to send 'bright prospects' to pick up a degree after ordination, but they (foolishly?) experimented with me and sent me before completing the usual four years of Theology.

So I ended up as an undergraduate resident of the Cambridge Catholic House of Studies, St. Edmund's, which had been founded by Anatole Von Hügel in the 1890s.[10] I actually read English Literature, not Classics, and split my time between St. Ed's—which we were gradually changing

[10] See the account by Garrett Sweeney, 'St. Edmund's House: an embodiment', in *Bishops & Writers*, edited by Adrian Hastings, Anthony Clarke, 1977.

into one of the first Cambridge graduate colleges—and Fitzwilliam College, which had just become an undergraduate college. Apart from politics, I was mainly involved at Fitzwilliam with an excellent theatre—we did an annual African play when it wasn't fashionable, for example, and I got to meet people like N'gugi through a catholic left academic who had been expelled from every dictatorship in West Africa—but that's another story.

The Catholic milieu of St Edmund's was important to me, and perhaps relevant to some of your other questions, about the distinctions between radical and liberal catholics. During my time there (I stayed till 1971, having graduated in 1968 and then started a PhD on 19th century working class autobiographies, and was offered a Bye Fellowship), it was only about 100-strong membership, but that included—for longer or shorter periods—international catholic scholars like Ernan McMullin of Notre Dame, Olaf Pedersen from Denmark, Charlie Curran, Gerry O'Collins, Leonard Boyle, Walter Ong, and such local regulars as Walter Ullmann, Mary Hesse, David Knowles, together of course with a wide range of non-catholic visitors.

Part of what was exceptional about it was that—precisely because it was a 'catholic' institution—we were effectively the first place in Cambridge to abolish social distinctions between Fellows and other members, and we were actually the first to become a co-ed college. So even as an undergraduate I was on completely easy terms with anyone passing through, however eminent. It was a hell of an education! The main intellectual cast of the place wasn't theology (though there was a fair amount of that in the small hours arguments) but the history and philosophy of science, which was more or less just emerging properly at Cambridge then, and St. Edmund's had some of its main local practitioners associated with it. We even had the only man I know to have had a planet named after him, Michael

Hoskin,[11] and in Bruce Elsmore one of the designers of the Cambridge array which disovered pulsars.

It was not unusual for the evening dinner table (there was no 'High Table') to have, say, Ernan McMullin, Gerd Buchdahl, Alan Shapiro, Mary Hesse, Olaf Pedersen, Mike Hoskin, arguing intrinsic versus extrinsic causality in science while Nick Lash, Sebastian Moore, Peter Harris and, say, Gerry O'Collins or Leonard Boyle argued about Newman's development of doctrine alongside them. I enjoyed joining in—and my seminary education gave me the confidence, so I'm deeply grateful for both phases of my 'catholic' education.

In addition, within St. Edmund's, there was a group of Jesuits centred on Xavier Gorostiaga (and another Xavier, Beltran) who had spent time in Central America but their group of about twenty Jesuits had then scattered over several countries and several universities, to pick up specialist advanced degrees in various disciplines like economics, development studies, engineering, transport etc., etc.—with the plan of re-convening, now more adequately equipped, to work for radical social change in Latin America. This eventually became, of course, the Jesuit branch of the Nicaraguan Sandinista government! (I went out to Guatemala to consider joining Xavier's group in the 1970s, but realised that with my poor eyesight—no driving licence—and hopeless incapacity at learning Quiché, the language of the campesinos, I'd be less useless in the UK.)[12]

And Xavier's group was not the only Third World presence —St Edmund's always had a fair scattering of old lags who had done time in far flung mission fields and were enjoying a sabbatical term or year, so the place was full of

---

[11] In 2001 the International Astronomical Union gave the name Hoskin to Minor Planet 12223.

[12] I was amused recently to see the rabid right-wing website Vaticanassassins.org claim that: 'It was the Jesuit priest Xabier Gorostiaga who took away the Panama Canal from the Americans, and who created the first economical program of the Sandinist Nicaragua.' Absolutely correct! Xavier did both.

people who actually knew their way around the globe—another education for a Liverpudlian whose family had scattered over five continents (most were sea-going) but who in 1965 hadn't yet crossed the English Channel—it's a long way from Liverpool.

All this was fine. Except that I had actually argued myself more or less into a personal atheism even before leaving the seminary, so there were some intellectual tensions! What therefore the *Slant* group partly represented for me was actually a second chance at seeing if this catholic faith business might make sense after all—and that gave an edge to my whole involvement. For about five years it seemed to hold open that possibility, and St Edmund's and Blackfriars next door were good places to rediscover the best of catholic tradition, not least the point of a liturgical celebration among a community whom you actually knew and worked with.

There was also of course a wider group of catholic students in Cambridge at the time, a few of whom I remember: Mike Heffernan (who became a BBC drama producer in Northern Ireland and died young), Eamon Duffy (still there!), Nicholas Boyle (still there, biographer of Goethe). It was clear that many of us were utterly disillusioned with the hypocrisies and evasions of the local and global hierarchy, especially over contraception and over social justice, but on the whole most catholic students at Cambridge shrugged and seemed simply to ignore the official church—though there was also a small deeply conservative group, and ironically one of them was also at St Edmund's, David Watkins (still at Cambridge, a historian of architecture).

Which helps make the wider point: under the same roof were Nick Lash, Xavier Gorostiaga, David Watkin, myself, Jim Burtchaell, Larry Barmann (American 'liberal' Jesuit, studying the English Modernists) and the then-80 year old

Mr, Fitzgerald, who had known Friedrich Von Hügel at the height of the Modernist crisis.[13]

I know that the Slant writers took serious issue with Catholic liberals, many of whom dismissed their radical views as too extreme and irrelevant. Do you have any memories of this?

As perhaps is now clear, my memory is actually of daily encounters with a range of catholics, from liberal to somewhere near Pius X, let alone Pius XII. Though I should also make it clear that there was very little overlap between my contacts at St. Edmund's and the core Slant group— Xavier Gorostiaga met Herbert McCabe, for example, but not Terry or even Leo Pyle. Most of those who were members of or passed through St Edmund's (and the House was one main conduit for catholic academics around the world who wanted time in Cambridge then—we offered cheap rates and reasonable food!) were 'liberal' and had no interest in Slant's activities, but there were simply no easy categories.

One example would be Adrian Hastings, who regularly spent periods in the House from 1966, brought up in profoundly traditional Roman Catholic and English ways and (in my sense of him) not at all 'progressive' in strictly theological terms, but both in matters of church discipline (his opposition to imposed celibacy) and in his repeated commitment to exposing atrocities in wars (from Mozambique in the 1970s to Kosovo in the 1990s) he was politically exemplary. It's worth remarking that Adrian's highly effective campaign in 1972-3 over the 'Wiriyamu

---

13   See Lawrence F. Barmann, *Baron Friedrich von Hügel and the Modernist Crisis in England*, Cambridge, 1972. Reading von Hügel's diary for the day the Modernists were condemned, Larry suddenly realised that 'young Mr Fitz' had been to tea that very day with von Hügel—but when promptly asked, Mr Fitzgerald said, with some disdain, that of course he didn't discuss *theology* with the Baron...!

massacre'[14] probably would not have taken off without the old catholic connection with William Rees-Mogg at *The Times* and that Adrian also had an outlet in *The Tablet* for nearly 50 years. But Adrian had no interest in *Slant*, as I recall—and I think he (perhaps quite rightly) ignores the whole 'catholic left' movement in his various published histories of 20th century UK religion.

Incidentally, it may also be worth remarking that John Cumming, once a *Slant* editor, was on the *Tablet* editorial team by the mid-1970s—and recruited some old lefties, including me as poetry reviewer—and that both Angela Cunningham and Julian Filokowski, who went to Central America for CAFOD partly as a result of being introduced to Xavier Gorostiaga at St Edmund's, are currently on the editorial masthead—though for how much longer?

Of course, most *Slant* editors spent time on the road, going to give talks at various places up and down the country, local Slant groups, catholic student organisations, chaplaincies, conferences, study days, parish meetings, Newman groups, etc., etc.—there always seemed to be a steady demand for 'a speaker from Slant' and though I think Laurence Bright took the bulk of the load, most of us did our bit. I once came across a battered old folder of mine with 'current talk' scribbled on the outside and a series of dates and places crossed out all over the cover, about thirty in a matter of weeks—I was pretty appalled at the thought of how much sheer travel we got through. And it wasn't just catholics who invited us—I grew wary of keen Methodist ministers who would finally say, about 11 p.m. at the end of some awful evening of crossed wires: "Now I'm sure you'd like a drink before I show you your room"—and then offer me a cup of hot chocolate.

So, encounters with liberals and every other shade weren't only a matter of set-piece confrontations in print, or

---

[14] The *Telegraph* obituary for Adrian Hastings noted: 'Portugal's growing isolation following Hastings's claims has often been cited as a factor that helped to bring about the "carnation revolution" which deposed the Caetano regime in 1974.'

of thunderous denunciations from the episcopacy (John Charles McQuaid, most eminent Archbishop of Dublin, in particular seemed to think he had the right to ban us physically from 'his' archdiocese), but pretty well part of the job. And most 'liberals' were on perfectly good terms with us—e.g. Ian Gregor, who adopted a tone of almost Pickwickian fatherly concern over myself and Terry. More difficult, in my intermittent experience of them, were that extraordinary married duo, Elizabeth Anscombe and Peter Geach—I remember being absolutely baffled on one occasion (a catholic philosophers conference of some kind) at an exchange between Anscombe and Geach, which had begun as a two-headed critical onslaught on (I suppose) Kenny or Herbert, but ended up in a total philosophical entanglement between the two of them, with both of them swapping their own position for the other's—without realising it! I could never really grasp the connection between their versions of Wittgenstein and their adherence to a very 'traditional' view of 'the Faith'.

Anthony Kenny I never knew personally, though he had been at Upholland a few years before me, but he was, I assume, an Oxford sparring partner for Herbert and, I think, Terry—but Kenny had an honourable reputation at the time (partly based on mere rumour, as I realised later) of having in effect sacrificed his priesthood by defying a ban by Archbishop Heenan (then at Liverpool) on his contributing to a symposium (edited by Walter Stein—another friendly liberal-radical) on nuclear weapons.[15]

And then of course there were the Anglican 'liberals', not least those in Cambridge, like Alec Vidler at King's, Hugh Montefiore at Great St. Mary's, or Peter Baelz at Jesus (Terry's college). There was a degree of 'dialogue' there too. Vidler was friendly with Adrian Cunningham, and later even lent me his very scarce copies of the unpublished 'Moot' papers, from the 'christian conspiracy' of the 1930s and 1940s to which T. S. Eliot (a core member) indirectly refers

---

[15] The story was actually more complicated; see Kenny's own memoir *A Path From Rome*, 1985.

in *The Cocktail Party*—Vidler had acted as secretary to the Moot. I was also myself fairly active in what I think was called the Cambridge Theological Colleges Union—a sort of student federation with members from the five or so Anglican, Presbyterian, Lutheran, and Methodist clerical training colleges based in Cambridge, plus honorary status for St Edmund's. I co-organised a conference on theological education involving all those colleges, and got money to commission a socio-psychological profile of all Cambridge theological students (done by a very young Robert Towler).[16] I seem to recall that the results were so utterly depressing (politically) that I became a lot less critical of our own catholic reactionaries, let alone liberals!

The Student Christian Movement was also important—both the press and the membership, which often had a real political edge to it. One of the better conferences Slant got involved with was a major one organised by SCM at Manchester on 'Race and Poverty', with maybe 2,000 delegates and a host of global speakers. At some point I remember we occupied the South African Airways office, with a slightly bemused Archbishop Helder Camara in attendance.

How much of the Catholic New Left was a product of generational conflict, especially based on the new consciousness inspired by access to university education after WWII? Was there a desire to escape from the earlier working-class culture that was dominated by clerical authoritarianism? My reading of Slant is that it wanted to target the Catholic middle class as a way of moving the Church to more progressive positions and in fact pretty much ignored the working class (lacking the imperative class consciousness for the job). Do you have any thoughts on this?

Not much, I'm afraid. In general, I sort of took it for granted that I was working class, that Terry was also, that Angela and Adrian had been some kind of London

---

[16] See his *Homo Religiosus: Sociological Problems in the Study of Religion*, 1974 and *Fate of the Anglican Clergy*, 1979.

anarchists (which sort of un-classified them—Londoners were not real working class to us Northerners!), that Laurence was probably a toff in secret, that Herbert was Irish, Neil had been in the Communist Party so was probably middle class, and Martin was a businessman. . . In other words, the personal categories of 'class' were a bit fluid!

As for any clear 'class strategy' within the church, I'm not sure we actually thought in those terms—Adrian was always articulate on the subject of the quasi-class cultural composition of an English catholicism uneasily yoking together ancient aristocratic recusants, Anglican middle class converts, and an immigrant Irish working class, but though in practice Britain in the 1960s was clearly the site of fierce class struggle crossed with generational conflicts of several kinds, nobody—let alone Slant—had (in my view) anything like a coherent revolutionary strategy for the society as a whole, so any 'applied' such strategy within the church was even less thinkable. We merely tried to influence or even take over most of the 'catholic' organs and institutions available to us, including local parishes where we lived or had come from. But of course we were at that stage mainly students, so our immediate territory tended to be student shaped.

So I don't think we were trying 'to escape from the earlier working-class culture that was dominated by clerical authoritarianism'—since we weren't trying to escape from that culture in the first place, only to get rid of the clerical authoritarianism, and I don't think we 'in fact pretty much ignored the working class' since we spent a fair amount of energy, along with the rest of the left, trying to work with and within various working class organisations and institutions, from various Trades Unions to the Workers Educational Association, and if working class catholics were around that was a sort of bonus. The CP leadership at one point, I think, were under some sort of vague illusion that if we could only be recruited to the CP we might eventually bring along a few million working class British catholics to the CP, but *we* didn't believe that!

The generational aspect was obviously important—without the 1944 Education Act and student grants certainly few of the Slant group would have been at Cambridge at all, and of course one facet of that entry of a working class generation into Oxbridge was that we tended to be more intellectually attuned and committed than the usual public school lot, so ended up getting a more than average share of the Firsts and the Fellowships for a while.

I'd add that in a strange sort of way it wasn't 'the (European) working class' which was the strategic focus of our, or at least my, primary political perspective: remember that, despite the importance of the Paris *événements* and the Prague Spring, this was the high point of support for 'Third World' movements. It may be worth remarking that when I once asked Herbert how he first became involved in politics, it wasn't Ireland he talked about, but he recalled being at Manchester University 'with Jomo (Kenyetta) in one corner of the students union bar and Kwame (Nkrumah) [or was it Kambarage Nyerere?] in the other'—since many of the future leaders of the anti-colonial struggle were in Manchester for the 5th Pan-African Congress in 1945, when Herbert was a student. Africa, especially apartheid, was almost as big an issue as Vietnam, and there was a project (SCM financed?) that brought ex-guerillas from Zimbabwe and Mozambique into the UK—one of them unfortunately is now something very nasty indeed in Mugabe's government.

How many of the 'Slant' group remained Catholic? For those who left, what may have been the reasons?

I've no idea, I'm afraid. On both counts. My own reversion to atheism was in the early 1970s—my piece on Foucalt for *New Blackfriars* was a sort of signing-off, and it was basically because (whatever the virtues of apophatic theology) I found I simply couldn't say I believed in something (the notion of 'God') that made no coherent sense. I had the other usual objections and general disgust as to how the church hierarchy treated people, but my main disaffiliation was theological. I had very little to do with old Slant comrades, as 'Slant', after I moved to Kent in 1971 though I would see some of them in other contexts.

Other than Adrian Cunningham, did many other Catholics on the Left recognize any affinity with the more radical political and cultural critique of Chesterton, Belloc, and the Distributists, and their complicated positions regarding modernity, some especially before WWI being very radical and on the Left?

I think I had always rather warmed to Chesterton but found Belloc boring, with Distributism not really of interest. I think Terry was ambivalent about GKC on stylistic grounds! Adrian kept us alert to various 1930s strands, and Ezra Pound's peculiar 1920s affiliations were also of interest. I got to know Joseph Needham for a while and he used to enthuse about Conrad Noel and the Christian Socialists of that period, and I had a research interest in various 19th century socialist tendencies including the commune movement, F. D. Maurice, William Morris, the Fraternal Democrats, and so on, and was therefore aware in reasonable detail of the several dispersed continuities into the 1920s, but looking back at the specifically Catholic element in the pre-war Left was a relatively minor interest compared with the immediate and dominant preoccupations at the time with various 'Third World' currents and liberation struggles, including the involvement of catholics (on both sides!)—though I do remember being interested in *Esprit* and the Mounier group in organisational terms (I liked the story of Eugene Ionesco being employed to order, but not collect, a copy of the first issue of *Esprit* in every bookshop in Europe!), and the connections between Personalism and the Worker Priests or Dorothy Day's Catholic Worker movement in the States were vaguely important as a model. But not the Distributists, no.

Did the writings of Teilhard de Chardin have any appeal to those on the Catholic Left? I know Eagleton and Bright had little time for his ideas and Wicker says as well that he was essentially poison to the

209

English Left Catholics. The French Left admired him as did Garaudy on the Marxist side.

There was a Catholic Teilhardian (I can't recall his name) in St. Edmund's at the time, who wanted to bring Teilhard and Marx together, so I had read him quite a lot—but I thought the comment that every scientific specialist thought Teilhard was simply wrong on their own specialism but quite impressive in all the others, was about right. The philosphers of science in St. Edmund's were pretty unimpressed, though I think Ernan McMullin did the odd critical paper for the London Teilhard Society. I do remember some discussion, not with Slant people, on possible affinities between Teilhard and Marshall McLuhan, in terms of shared catholic tendencies towards global noosphere thinking, etc., and I was certainly interested in McLuhan. Garaudy was pretty thin anyway—I reviewed one of Garaudy's books in *Slant*, very negatively.

How involved was the Catholic New Left in the Campaign for Nuclear Disarmament? Brian Wicker told me that it was a crucial element in his own support of the Catholic Left.

Various kinds of involvement by various people, too numerous to summarise. For example, Walter Stein was a good friendly critic of Slant and he had been heavily involved in the nuclear weapons issue for years. Adrian and Anglea Cunningham had been active in Christian CND. Certainly Brian Wicker was. Some Dominicans had been active in the early days of CND—there was a good story that one Dominican (Sebastian Bullough?) organised a performance of be-robed O.P.s dancing to 'Here we go round the mulberry bush' outside Aldermaston on one march, which was filmed by a baffled US TV crew, and Teddy Kennedy saw the footage, equally baffled, so—the Catholic connection—invited the Dominican over to clarify the point of the chant and he ended up testifying to a Congressional Committee on nuclear disarmament. (The quasi-nursery rhyme 'Mulberry bush' is supposedly a plague song - ' 'tishoo all fall down! '—though my local Canterbury friends now tell me it's actually a reference to the knights who came to murder Becket and left their weapons under the mulberry tree in the cathedral precincts!)

But most of the time I think we were just part of the general CND membership—I vaguely remember some friends in Liverpool persuading their parents to allow them to go on an early CND march because a local well-heeled supporter turned up in a Rolls Royce to fetch them!

Far more important was the Vietnam Solidarity Campaign, where Slant was directly involved, including having contingents and the odd banner on the various large marches and using the flat above the Sheed & Ward offices in Maiden Lane as a bolt-hole for medical or emergency situations on some of the marches. There were overlaps with people like Cecily Hastings, who after long involvement in various christian peace organisations had (if I remember right) walked in protest from South to North Vietnam, across the DMZ, under the aegis of Pax Christi. By the late 1960s CND was fading, along with the early New Left focus on it and the sense that single issue campaigns were limited and had to be replaced by the various Trotskyist groupuscules and by the totalising attempt of May Day Manifesto. Stuart Hall, one of the original major influences within CND, was of course a major influence on all the British left well into the period and Edward Thompson's role in END was to be important later.

Did you or your associates see any efficacy in the Christian-Marxist dialogue during these years?

Well, there were some more or less Vatican-approved formal 'dialogues' with European CPs which happened occasionally. But we were, after all, ourselves both Christians and Marxists, so we were not just dialoguing in that sense! You might look at George Vass's *Slant* articles on the Marienbad conferences. Slant's own dialogues with the British CP, at James Klugman's invitation, were pretty pointless, I remember—Klugman wasn't at all on the kind of wavelength that would have made even intellectual

211

dialogue fruitful. It's worth pointing out, though, that S&W in Maiden Lane were, after all, only one street away from the CP headquarters in King Street, and that the Africa Centre was right opposite the CP, so there was a fair amount of casual as well as formal 'dialogue' going on—we drank in some of the same Covent Garden pubs after all. Just as the *New Left Review* offices were more or less next door to the Newman Society premisses for a while, and in the late 1950s the Partisan Club was just off Soho Square, next to both (though only the New Left could make a financial loss on a central London coffee house!). Geographical proximity was important in such a tiny town as London! One regular protest target, South Africa House, was on the next corner, for a start. So there was a lot of 'dialogue' going on all over the place! And of course various personal syncretisms.

In what ways might Marxism have shaped the christian left's social, political and economic critique? I see a certain resonance in Slant's condemnation of what it called Thomistic 'dualism' (a focus of Neil Middleton's writings) and the programs taken up by Liberation Theology in Latin America.

Well, how long have you got? Apart from re-stating the obvious—that marxism, or rather actually reading and re-thinking Marx's own writings, was integral to our overall shared positions—I will only offer one specific anecdote on the issue of 'dualism', to illustrate the real complexity at the time. One Latin American Jesuit I remember with affection was Romeo Luna Victoria who at one stage taught philosophy at the Military Academy in Lima, Peru.[17] I remember arguing with him at length about the role of Cartesian dualism. His position was that he insisted on teaching Cartesianism in the Lima Military Academy— because the military had first to go through a bourgeois enlightenment and rationalist phase before you could broach marxism with them. Since Romeo's teaching influenced a generation of leftist colonels (almost a contradiction in

---

[17] See his *Ciencia y práctica de la revolución, manual para dirigentes políticos*,1965, and *Por una democracia socialista en el Perú*, 1978.

terms) and one of his pupils was Juan Velasco Alvarado, who after the coup in October 1968 initiated perhaps the most far reaching agrarian reform in Latin America, who was I to disagree with Romeo! (But I still did.)

Or take Ivan Illich, whose books S&W were publishing (before Neil took them to Penguin) and whose work at Cuernavaca and elsewhere (Herbert McCabe was I think a visiting lecturer there) was crucial in some of the developments of liberation theology. Illich was hardly a marxist but important to the mix that was 'the christian left'. It would take too long to discriminate between the various strands in 'Liberation Theology' but there were considerable differences between, say, Gustavo Gutiérrez, Camilo Torres, and Xavier Gorostiaga.

In your view, what was the relationship between the CNL and the secular New Left? Did the CNL have any input drafting the programs put forth in the May Day Manifesto?

As individuals a few of us were quite involved with May Day Manifesto. Charles Swann who was a friend of us all, was at Jesus College and close, like Terry Egleton, to Raymond Williams, and he acted as the secretary for the Penguin version of the manifesto itself—but I remember Terry once joked that he himself contributed just one sentence, which was then cut to a parenthesis (it was about French foreign policy I think!). There's a fairly detailed, if somewhat jaundiced, account in Fred Inglis's book on Raymond Williams of the mildly surreal process of putting together the two versions of MDM.[18]

Terry and I certainly stayed involved for a couple of years, though Neil Middleton and Martin Shaw were critical of the whole project (though perhaps it was Neil who had published the 1968 version at Penguin?—my memory of dates is fluid these days, I'm afraid), and I remember endless meetings of what was, I think, partly a spin-off from May

---

18 Fred Inglis, *Raymond Williams*, 1995, p.198ff.

Day, the Free Communications Group, which included an impressive range of UK leftist journalists (Paul Foot was characteristically energetic), published a journal (*Open Secret*), prepared a bid for the Channel 4 TV franchise, tried to set up a London Left Radio, etc., etc. But there were a lot of other spin-offs, including some of the 'alternative strategy' economists' programmes, and it would be rather difficult to assess the longer term influence of May Day Manifesto. It was partly scuppered in the short term by the usual left-sectarian divides—I suspect getting large unions notionally signed up was actually easier than getting tiny left groupuscules to cooperate with each other!

What is your estimate of the significance and influence of the CNL? Could you place them into any broader context of post-WWII British Catholicism?

I suppose it could be claimed that the bunch of us who came together briefly as 'Slant' went on to have some minor influences in various spheres which wouldn't have happened in quite the same way without that involvement in the christian new left. My own personal choice (after deciding I would be useless in Guatemala) was to work to change educational institutions, rather than produce cultural criticism or theory, still less theology. So I got involved in setting up various new degree programmes at Kent University and elsewhere—the first Film Studies program in the UK, the first Psychoanalytical Studies MA, and the first to explore 'multimedia' computing within a humanities program, so by the 1980s I was mainly involved in what was just then becoming the interface between television, film, communications, and computing, with work both here and in India. My main outlet for writing for several years was the *New York Times* review section rather than academic publications.

The most usefully influential of us was, in my view, Chris Holmes who helped found and then ran Shelter, the organisation for the homeless, or Neil in his days at Penguin, but Terry's is now the most high profile among academics

214

and generally within the culture world. But as with Raymond Williams's once very influential body of work, one wonders how long such influences last?

Raymond once made a ruefully useful (or at least consoling) distinction: that the left often thinks it has 'failed' when all that's happened is that—as might have been expected in the first place—it's been *defeated*. And, as he also once remarked, reviewing a book on the Romantics, 'the history of ideas is a kind of middle age'— in other words, it's hard to revive, even in one's own memory, the excitement and passions of a past period. I know what he meant.

*

6171644R00132

Printed in Germany
by Amazon Distribution
GmbH, Leipzig